Icelandic National
League of North America.
83rd Annual Convention.
April, 2002
Minneapolis.

The Culinary Saga of New Iceland

Kristin.

The Culinary Saga of New Iceland
Recipes from the Shores of Lake Winnipeg

Kristin Olafson-Jenkyns

coastline

Copyright © 2001 by Kristin Olafson-Jenkyns.
All Rights Reserved. First Printing 2001.

Cover painting by Kristin. All other photographic credits are printed on page 235, which constitutes a continuation of this copyright page.

Canadian Cataloguing-In-Publication Data

Olafson-Jenkyns, Kristin, 1952-
The Culinary saga of New Iceland: recipes from the shores of Lake Winnipeg
ISBN 0-9689119-0-0

English with Icelandic recipe titles.

1. Cookery, Icelandic. I. Title.

TX723.5.I2O43 2001   641.594912   C2001-901657-3

Printed in Canada.

Designed by mackenzie kristjón.
All translations by Elva Jónasson.

If you would like to know more about either Kristin or the recipes in this book, please e-mail: postmaster@coastline-publishing.com

or write:
COASTLINE PUBLISHING
Suite 511
3-304 Stone Rd. W.
Guelph, ON N1G 4W4
Canada

www.coastline-publishing.com

Dedication

Clockwise from top left:

Sesselja (Sella) Sigridur (Johannesson) Thorvardson (1898-1981)

Kristrun Helga Grace (Marteinsson) Sigurdson (1896-1981)

Sigurdur Victor Sigurdson (1895-1970)

Sigurbjorg (Sigga) Steinunn (Olson) Eyolfson (1907-1990)

Asbjorg (Asa) Halldora (Olson) Olafson (1912-1964)

Lois Lillian (Sigurdson) Olafson (B. 1931)

Dear fellow Icelandic descendant,

    Currently I am in the midst of compiling a collection of traditional Icelandic recipes as they were prepared by the first Icelandic settlers in New Iceland (Manitoba's Interlake region) -the largest Icelandic settlement in America- and following through to us, their descendants today.

    The sources for these recipes have been various cookbooks published in the Interlake area as well as from my family. As the women had to adapt their cooking to the indigenous ingredients of their new land, the recipes had to change (e.g. Icelanders did not eat whitefish before they emigrated). Icelanders who emigrated to the many other settlement areas across Canada and the US would have been subject to their varying environments as well. However, overall I think their descendants will find similarities in the recipes that developed in our area.

    Surprisingly, when food preservation was no longer the main concern as cooking facilities improved (i.e. stoves and refrigerators became commonplace), women continued to prepare these same foods with a love and respect for their tradition. Hopefully the retention of these recipes will serve to foster the spirit of hospitality and the love of social entertainment that has always characterized the Icelanders.

    I am enclosing a recipe for you to test. I would appreciate your contribution as I believe the feedback received will be of great benefit for producing an interesting and comprehensive cookbook to pass down with pride to our daughters and sons. It is my intention to include with as many recipes as possible the name of a tester as well as their city of residence along with a brief comment. Please try out your recipe and return it to me with your name, address, phone number and any suggestions or comments -I want to know if you enjoyed the results or not and if the recipe itself was understandable. If you have recipes that you think should be considered for inclusion please send also. For these additional recipes I receive I will compare them to the ones I have and decide on the best one. (Hope you trust me to do this!)

Thank you and good luck with your recipe!

Kristin

Kristin

P.S. No one is being asked to prepare Svið -singed and severed sheep's head- a delicacy unlikely to have mass appeal.

Contents

Introduction 13
New World Settlements and the Founding of New Iceland 19
New Icelanders and the Lake Winnipeg Fisheries 33

Fiskimatur (Lake Winnipeg Fish) 41
Kjötmatur og Súpur (Meat and Soups) 77
Grænmeti, Pækill og Niðursoðnir Ávextir (Side Dishes, Pickles and Preserves) 109
Búðingur(súpa) og Deserar (Puddings and Desserts) 123
Brauð (Bread) 139
Kaffibrauð (Sweetbreads, and Fried Cakes) 161
Kökur og Smákökur (Cakes and Cookies) 181
Hressandi Drykkur (Refreshing Drinks) 209

Viðbætir (Appendix) 214
Notes on Ingredients 215
Icelandic Food and Drink 223
Icelandic National Costume 227
Phonetics 231
Endnotes and Bókfræði (Bibliography) 233

Index of Recipes

FISKIMATUR (LAKE WINNIPEG FISH)

Lois Olafson's Baked Lake Winnipeg Whitefish	44
Mrs. G. F. Jonasson's Fish Fillets with Dressing on Top	
Fiskur á Fati (Fish on a Platter)	45
Pan-Fried Pickerel Fillets	
Steiktur Fiskur (Fried Fish)	46
Ingibjorg Sigurgeirson McKillop's Boiled Whitefish, Sunfish and Goldeye	47
Oven Steamed Smoked Fish	
Mrs. J.G. Johannson's Fiski Hveitbollur (Fish Dumplings)	48
Laurie (Olafson) Jervis's Djúpsteiktur Fiskur (Deep-Fried Fish in Batter)	
Plokkfiskur (Fish Stew)	49
Plokkfiskur (Fish Stew)	
Helga Gerrard's Stappa (Hashed Fish and Potatoes)	50
Mrs. Helga Jonsson's Novel Way of Serving Fish	
Mrs. L. Stevens's Fish Scallops	51
Fiskgratin í Skeljum (Fish au gratin in Shells)	
Áð Búa til Fisksúpa (To Prepare Fish Soup)	52
Mrs. Petrina Eggertson's 'Grandma's Fish Soup'	
Fiskisúpa (Fish Soup)	53
Mrs. J. G. Christie's Fiskibollur (Fish Balls)	54
Fiskfriggadellur	55
Fiskibollur	
Joyce Benedictson's Fiskibollur	56
Fiskkökur (Fishcakes)	
Ingibjorg Sigurgeirson McKillop's Canned Fillets	57
Ingibjorg Sigurgeirson McKillop's Canned Fish	58
Al Dryden's Harðfiskur (Hardfish)	
Ingibjorg Sigurgeirson McKillop's Harðfiskur	59
Ingibjorg Sigurgeirson McKillop's Platfiskur (Flattened Fish)	60
Ingibjorg Sigurgeirson McKillop's Fish Liver Sausage	
Ingibjorg Sigurgeirson McKillop's Soured Catfish Heads	

Forréttir (Hors d'oeuvre)

Smoked Goldeye Pâté	61
Smoked Fish Appetizers	61
Tomato Butter, Dilled Cream Cheese, Mustard Dill Sauce, Horseradish Sauce	
Pickerel in Orange-Tarragon Marinade	63
Fish Seviche	64
Profiteroles with Wild Rice and Fish Salad	
Pönnukökur with Tomato-Artichoke Heart and Fish Salad	65
Golden Whitefish Caviar on Rosettes	66

Fiskréttir (Fish Entrées)

Garden Medley Pickerel	
Dill Pönnukökur (Thin Pancakes)	67
Cucumber Sauce	
Pickerel Amandine	
Tomato-Mushroom Stuffed Whitefish	68
Hollandaise Sauce	69
Provençal Sauce for Fish	70
Pickerel Chowder	

Fish on the Grill

Blackened Fish with Creole Sauce	72
Fish Fillets Barbecued in Foil	74
White Wine and Herbs	
Greek Fillets	
Marinades for Grilling Fillets and Steaks	75
Hoisin, Mustard Dill, Lime and Ginger	

Kjötmatur og Súpur (Meats and Soups)

Sunnudagssteikin – Ofnbakað Lambalæri (Roast Leg of Lamb)	78
Ofnbakaður Lambahryggur (Roast Saddle of Lamb)	
Mrs. M. Brynjolfson's Roast Stuffed Shoulder of Lamb with Brown Potatoes	80
Að Salta Kjöt til Reykingar (To Salt Meat for Smoking)	
Soðið Hangikjöt (Boiled Smoked Lamb)	81
Beef Pot Roast with Prunes	82
Kálfsragout með Sveskjum (Veal Stew with Prunes)	
Saddle of Venison	83
Venison Pot Roast	
Ingibjorg Sigurgeirson McKillop's Roasted Wild Goose	
Savoury Stuffing for Goose	84
Mrs. S. W. Sigurgeirson's Roast Turkey	
Baked Grouse or Pheasent	
Mrs. O. Bjornson's Baked Chicken	85
Mrs. J. P. Markuson's Prairie Chicken "Icelandic Style"	
Steiktar Rjúpur (Roast Ptarmigan)	86
Guðrun Ágústsdóttir's Steiktar Rjúpur (Roast Ptarmigan) –A Modern Version	87
Roasted Prairie Chicken or Wild Duck	
Ingibjorg Sigurgeirson McKillop's Braised Duck (Wild or Domestic)	88
Mrs. Halldora Bardal's Fars (Cabbage and Ground Steak)	
Beef Stew with Dumplings	89
Mrs. S. Johnson's Kjötsúpa (Meat Soup)	
Kjötsúpa (Meat Soup)	90
Loa Johannson's Baunir Súpa (Bean Soup)	91
Baunir (Beans)	92
Mrs. J. Dalman's Split Pea Soup	
Ingibjorg Sigurgeirson McKillop's Hangikjöt og Baunir (Smoked Lamb and Beans)	93
Súr (Pickled) Pork Hocks	94
Rose Helgason's Kjæfa (Headcheese)	94
Kjæfa (Headcheese)	95
Shirley Sigurdson's Kjæfa (Headcheese)	96
Kæfa (Headcheese)	97
Steindor Jakobson's Rúllupylsa (Rolled Spiced Lamb)	98
Anna Skaptason's Rúllupylsa (Rolled Spiced Lamb)	99
Mrs. Lydur Lindal's Lifrarpylsa (Liver Sausage)	100
Rose Helgason's Lifrarpylsa (Liver Sausage)	101
Sigrun Stefanson's Lifrarpylsa (Baked Liver Sausage Pâté)	102
Leverpostej (Liver Pâté)	103
Blóðmör (Blood Sausage)	104
Steiktur Blóðmör (Fried Blood Sausage)	106
Hulda Johnson's Slátur	
Ingibjorg Sigurgeirson McKillop's Súr Slátur (Soured Blood Sausage)	107
Svið (Sheephead)	

Grænmeti, Pækill og Niðursoðnir Ávextir
Vegetables, Pickles and Preserves

Brúnaðar Kartöflur (Sugar Browned Potatoes)	109
Kartöplu-Kökur (Potato Cakes)	
Susie Erickson-Jakobson's Rauðkál (Red Cabbage)	110
Elva Jonasson's Brún Grænkál (Browned Cabbage)	
Kartöflur og Groengresi Hvítsósu (Potatoes and Green Peas in White Sauce)	111
Mrs. Gustaf Anderson's Creamed Peas, Boiled Beets, Rutabaga	
Judith Sigurdson's Sósu (Salad Dressing)	112
Kristin Thorvaldson's Sósu (Salad Dressing)	
Kál og Epli Salat (Cabbage and Apple Slaw)	113
Sylvia Sigurdson's Súr Sykurrófu (Pickled Beets)	
Susie Erickson-Jakobson's Súr Sykurrófu (Pickled Beets)	114
Röðbeder (Red Beets)	

Helen Kristjanson's Sweet Green Tomato Pickles	115
Mrs. F. A. Finson's Million Dollar Pickles	116
Nola Anderson's Dill Pickles	
Sigurros Palsson's Celery Sauce	117
Claire Stefanson's Chili Sauce	118
Mrs. G. O. Bergman's Rabarbarsúpa (Rhubarb Compote)	
Helen Kristjanson's Rabarbar og Fíkjusúpa (Rhubarb and Fig Compote)	119
Gudrun Erickson's Kryddaður Rabarbarsúpa (Spiced Rhubarb Compote)	
Mrs. R. Marteinsson's Canned Crabapples	
Mrs. B.W. Benson's Crabapple Jelly	120
Helen Kristjanson's Cranberry Jelly	
Ingibjorg Sigurgeirson McKillop's Choke Cherry Jelly	
Ingibjorg Sigurgeirson McKillop's Raspberry Jam	121
Freezer Raspberry Jam	

Búðingur(súpa) og Deserar (Puddings and Desserts)

Mrs. J. K. Johnson's Skyr	123
Lyla Thorarinson's Skyr (An Alternative Method)	124
Fresh Fruit with Cardamom Skyr Dip	
Ron Eyolfson's Skyr	125
Hræringur (Skyr and Porridge)	
Skyr Cheesecake	126
Mrs. B. Pell's Mysuostur (Whey Cheese)	127
Doreen Guttormson's Mysuostur (Whey Cheese)	
Leslie Gislason's Mysuostur (Whey Cheese)	128
Sætsúpa (Sweet Soup)	
Sætsúpa (Sweet Soup)	129
Sætsúpa (Sweet Soup)	
Judith Sigurdson's Hrísgrjónagrautur (Rice Pudding)	130
Lillian Eyolfson's Hrísgrjónagrautur (Creamy Rice Pudding)	131
Jólahrísgrjónagrautur (Christmas Rice Pudding)	131
Hrísgrjónagrautur (Rice Pudding/Porridge)	
Kristin Thorvaldson's Cornstarch Pudding	132
Miss Emma Hannesson's Prune Whip and Boiled Custard	
Flauelsgrautur (Velvet Pudding)	133
Mrs. T. Scambler's Citronsúpa (Lemon Pudding)	134
Brauðbúdingur (Bread Pudding)	
Kristrun Sigurdson's Blueberry Crunch	135
Bogga Dalmann's Epla Kaka (Apple Cake-Pudding)	
Apple or Rhubarb Crisp	136
Raspberry Supreme, Raspberry Strawberry Sauce	
Pineapple Rice Cream	137

Brauð (Bread)

Brauðgjörd (On Baking Bread)	140
Sella Thorvardson's Brúnt Brauð (Brown Bread)	142
Sylvia Sigurdson's Brúnt Brauð	143
Gudny Stefanson's Brúnt Brauð	144
Johanna Wilson's Brúnt Brauð	145
Laura Thorkelson's Brúnt Brauð -Adaptation for Bread Making Machines by Shirley Sigurdson	146
Mrs. B. Guttormson's Raisin Brown Bread	148
Mrs. J. J. Vopni's Bran Bread	149
Mrs. K. Thorsteinson's Anadama Bread	150
Ingibjorg Olafson's Baking Powder Biscuits	151
Elva and Steini Jonasson's Biscuit Adaptations	
Kristrun Sigurdson's Air Buns	153
Betty Jane Wylie's Laufabrauð (Leaf Bread)	155
Katrin Brynjolfsson's Flatbrauð (Flat Bread)	156
Runa Gislason's Flatbrauð	
Thura Thorsteinson's Flatbrauð	157
Ingibjorg Sigurgeirson McKillop's Flatkökur	158

Flatkökur	158
Mrs. S. W. Reid's Oat Cakes	159

KAFFIBRAUÐ (SWEET BREADS AND FRIED CAKES)

Sylvia Sigurdson's Pönnukökur (Thin Pancakes; Crêpes)	161
Kathy Arnason's Pönnukökur	162
Pönnukökur	163
Johanna Wilson's Pönnukökur	164
Pönnukökur with Mandarin Oranges	165
Ingibjorg Olafson's Lummur (Pancakes)	
Hrísgrjónalummur (Rice Pancakes)	166
Hrísgrjónalummur (Rice Pancakes)	167
Runa Gislason's Kleinur	168
Ingibjorg Olafson's Kleinur	169
Bergthora Einarson Morrison's Kleinur	
Dee Dee Westdal's Kleinur	170
Kleinur	171
Thorunn Johnson's Sour Cream Doughnuts	172
Sella Thorvardson's Ástrabollur (Drop Doughnuts)	
Elva Jonasson's Steiktir Partar (Fried Parts or Boats)	173
Rosettes	174
Mrs. Finnur Johnson's Vatnsdeigsbollur (Cream Puffs)	175
Smjörkringla (Butter Kringle)	176
Jólabrauð (Christmas Bread)	177
Helga Einarson Almquist's Jólabrauð	179

KÖKUR OG SMÁKÖKUR (CAKES AND COOKIES)

Lois Olafson's Vínarterta	183
Ingibjorg Olafson's Vínarterta (adapted by Elva Jonasson)	185
Thora Orr's Vínarterta	186
Vínerterta Nos. 1 & 2	188
Fillings for Vínerterta, Rabarbarmauk (Rhubarb Purée), Sveskjumauk or Aprikósumauk (Prune or Apricot Purée)	189
Joyce Benedictson's Vínarterta	190
Mrs. M. J. Matthiasson's Kanelterta (Cinnamon Torte)	191
Gunnþóra Gisladóttir's Kanelterta	192
Jólakaka (Christmas Cake)	193
Jólakaka	194
Ingibjorg Olafson's Rúlluterta (Jelly Roll)	195
Rúlluterta (Jelly Roll)	196
Kúrenu Smákökur (Currant Cookies/Bar)	
Featherweight Cake, Hurry-Up Cake and Lazy Daisy Topping	197
Judith Sigurdson's Matrimonial Cake	198
Sigga Eyolfson's Calla Lilies	199
Mrs. F. S. Frederickson's Calla Lily Sponge Cake	200
Elva Jonasson's Almond Cookies	
Kransar (Wreaths)	201
Vanillekransar (Vanilla Wreaths)	202
Gyðingakökur (Jewish Cookies)	203
Ingibjorg Sigurgeirson McKillop's Gyðingakökur (Jewish Cookies)	
Gyðingakökur (Jewish Cookies)	204
Hálfmánar (Half-moons)	
Sykur Smákökur (Sugar Cookies)	206
Johanna Wilson's Date-Filled Oatmeal Cookies	
Elva Jonasson's Engifer Smákökur (Ginger Cookies)	207

HRESSANDI DRYKKUR (REFRESHING DRINKS)

Augusta Jonasson's Lemonade	209
Lemon Syrup	
Cranberry Juice Cocktail	210
Ingibjorg Sigurgeirson McKillop's Raspberry Vinegar	
Diane Kortesluoma's Raspberry Vinegar	211
Sukkulaði (Creamy Hot Chocolate)	
Kaffi (Coffee) Traditions	212

The New Land and Waters

Hay meadows are best along the Icelandic River, but we assume adequate hayland can be found throughout the colony. A settler can therefore have as many cows as he wants. We have no doubt that the land is excellent for grain growing, and better than the very best that we have seen in Ontario. Granted, we did not have a chance to see what the land is capable of producing but to the best of our knowledge the soil is as good as in the better areas of Manitoba, and it is therefore obvious that the same products can be grown since there is no appreciable difference in the climate. We also saw good potatoes, which the Indians had planted in June. Also we saw Red River corn. Both grew along the Icelandic River. At the south end of Lake Winnipeg men raise good wheat, potatoes, barley, oats and Red River corn. All these crops grow well since no grasshoppers have ventured this far north...

With regard to fishing in Lake Winnipeg, we can speak from experience. There is a great variety of fish, and the Indians have nets in the lake the year round.

Settlers will also be able to hunt in the forest. There is considerable game, especially deer and in the fall there are many wild birds such as ducks and geese, some of which we shot while we were there.

There are many berries in the bush as well, such as strawberries, raspberries, pinchberries, blueberries and so on.

Translated from **Nýja Island Í Kanada (New Iceland in Canada)**. Ottawa: 1875. Reprinted in Nelson Gerrard's **Icelandic River Saga**. Arborg: Saga Publications. 1985. P.23.

The Tradition of Hospitality

Hospitality was an unquestioned custom. 'Geirrid... came out to Iceland. She had her hall built across the common travelled way, and all were [invited] to ride through it. There was always a table there with food on it, which was given to all who wished to eat.' The generous welcome of the saga days continued through the poorer centuries. Anyone who came by a farm hungry or tired was expected to stop. His horse was fed and watered and he was invited into the house, where he shook hands all around. Then he was asked to sit down, to talk and eat and drink, but his business was not discussed unless he volunteered it. When he left he was given something to take on his way, food or a gift.

Scherman, Katherine. **Daughter of Fire: A Portrait of Iceland**. Toronto: Little, Brown, and Company. 1976. Internal quote taken from Eyrbyggja Saga. P. 283-284.

Introduction

Vínarterta, Pönnukökur, Rúllupylsa, Fiskibollur

As a child, I found even the names of these Icelandic specialties fanciful and fun to say aloud. I was intrigued by my vision of Iceland as an enchanted place with a fantastical landscape comprised of fjords, waterfalls, geysers and volcanoes, and inhabited by little people and even trolls. This fascination extended also to the foods my mother, aunties and ammas prepared, making them all the more enticing.

My initial motivation for creating this book was to compile a small collection of favourite traditional recipes for my children and nieces. The collection grew incrementally over a number of years as other Icelandic descendants offered recipes and encouragement. Their sentiments are well summarized by my Aunty Sylvia Sigurdson, who grew up on Hecla Island: "I think you are doing a worthwhile project here. It's true that Icelandic women have always used food for hospitality and caring and on the whole are excellent cooks. These foods are well worth preserving and I think that many will appreciate having the recipes compiled. In any case, I think our heritage plays a big part in who we really are, and I think in our particular case –being Icelandic- we have no reason not to honour it."

The foods we choose to eat provide more than physical sustenance. The cooking of food, like fine art or music, is emblematic of cultural tradition and as such serves to foster our identities. As I immersed myself in these recipes, I was reminded of the warm sense of hospitality that I have always felt as a member of the New Icelandic community. While testing recipes, the aromas and tastes evoked memories of celebrations and everyday life... a summer morning, sitting with Amma Kristrun at her kitchen table, enjoying skyr with raspberries from the garden, little birds on the windowsill... the aroma of brown bread baking, anticipating Aunty Sella giving me the first warm slice, spread with butter... a tray of calla lilies filled with whipped cream at Aunty Sigga's home, so tempting, one tastes like more... memories of three of the special women to whom this book is dedicated... My Amma (Grandmother) Ása who, while an amazingly innovative cook, was also a talented painter and seamstress. It was her creative artistry that most endeared her to me.

These four women all had many and diverse gifts to share and exemplified for me the longstanding Icelandic tradition of hospitality, of the generous giving of whatever you have to give.

When the Icelanders immigrated to New Iceland (Manitoba's Interlake region) in 1875, it was with a great make-do spirit that the women adapted their recipes and cooking methods to the indigenous ingredients of their new environment. As a natural progression due to the improvement of cooking facilities, the increasing availability of an ever-widening variety of ingredients, and interaction with other ethnic groups, new recipes gradually evolved into new traditions. Today there is renewed respect for the raw ingredients available in the region, increased sophistication of cooking methods and recipes, and yet the influence of the traditional recipes is still very evident.

In compiling this book, I selected recipes that would represent current New Icelandic cooking as well as illustrate changes that have taken place since the early settlement days. Sources for these recipes were local cookbooks (the earliest dating from the 1930's), the New Icelandic settlement newspaper **Framfari** (1877-79), **Matreiðslubók (Recipe Book)** circa 1915, and recipes contributed by friends and relatives in addition to recipes of my own. My own recipes divide into traditional recipes acquired from my mother, aunties and ammas and later innovations influenced by traditional recipes. As you read this book, you will notice that the types of recipes are identified by various backdrops: articles from the **Framfari** are set on their Icelandic newspaper source, recipes from **Matreiðslubók (Recipe Book)** are set on handwritten pages from the original Icelandic book, and my later innovations are set on beach pebbles. You will also notice that there are two editions of **Cook Book** to which I refer throughout the book, one designated as 1930 and the other 1950. Although the second edition (published by the Dorcas Society of the First Lutheran Church) very definitely is from 1950, the first edition (published by the Ladies Aid of the First Lutheran Church) has no printed publication date and so the 1930 date is unconfirmed.

Wherever possible, the contributors of the recipes have been named (whether from a published source or personally contributed) and the recipes have been recorded as per their original source except where minor changes were deemed necessary for clarity. Most method sections have been divided into numbered steps for ease of following and uniformity. Some recipes were not previously set down in a written format and had to be translated into exact amounts from such inexact measures as a scoop, a handful, or a pinch. I learned to bake my Aunty Sella's brown bread by watching her bake it; she never had need of a written recipe. Nevertheless, this demonstrative teaching style was the preferred manner of passing on recipes. Regarding the popular traditional recipes (e.g. vínarterta), I endeavoured to include the most prevalent variations. I have learned in the process of collecting these recipes that there are as many subtle variations for pönnukökur as there are New Icelandic women!

Icelandic descendants (and sometimes their non-Icelandic spouses!) were enlisted to test many of these recipes. Their comments, names and locations of residence are included following each recipe. As well as being fun to read, the comments are full of helpful tips, suggestions and information which I hope will encourage the use of these recipes.

This book is meant for not only Icelandic descendants but anyone with an appreciation for cuisine, history and cultural diversity.

Acknowledgements

This book would not have been possible without the support of a great many people and if you notice that your name is not included here, I hope that you will forgive me.

I would like to thank everyone who contributed and tested recipes -the comments are invaluable, ranging from humorous to highly informative- and the many who so willingly provided information, advice and encouragement; **Elva Jónasson** for providing all of the Icelandic translations, for always knowing the answers to my endless questions, and for unrelenting patience throughout the duration; **Guðrún Ágústsdóttir** for recognizing the additive value that her amma's Recipe Book would provide and for graciously offering her expertise to confirm the translations and to explain the ingredients and the cooking methods; **Nelson Gerrard** for advice along the way -his books The Icelandic River Saga and The Icelandic Heritage were valuable historical resources (and a special thank you for generously allowing the reprinting of his 'Icelandic Food and Drink' article -located in the Appendix); **Betty Jane Wylie** for permission to excerpt the letter to her amma, including her Laufabrauð recipe from her enjoyable and enlightening book Letters to Icelanders -Exploring the Northern Soul; **Laurie Olafson Jervis, Judy Lehn, and Pat O'Hara** for being great friends -all of the listening, morale boosting and confidence building were greatly appreciated; **Jenny Kitson** for such warm and wonderful hospitality and for the unlimited and completely essential use of the fax machine; **Jenivieve de Vries** for outstanding patience and support especially during the last few weeks of production; **Lois and Irvin Olafson** whose interest in and dedication to their Icelandic heritage provided inspiration and motivation; **Mark, Reyna and Spencer Jenkyns** -for putting up with my obsession (always with the hope that after this project, the dining room table might become free for actual food instead of descriptions of food); and **mackenzie kristjón** for realizing and enhancing my vision of the book's design.

Others who have helped along the way include Kathy Arnason, Susie Erickson-Jakobson, Brian Jakobson, Helen Kristjanson, Eric, Marno and Steven Olafson, Ingrid and Judy Sigurdson, Shirley Sigurdson, Sylvia Sigurdson, Kris Stefanson, Lorna Tergesen, and Johanna Wilson. A special mention goes out to Steini and Kendra Jónasson for their steadfast good cheer.

Notes on Matreiðslubók (Recipe Book)

Guðrúnar Jónsdóttir
Fri (from) Seljamýri, Iceland

The opportunity to examine **Matreiðslubók (Recipe Book)** by Guðrún Jónsdóttir was presented to me by her granddaughter, Guðrún Ágústsdóttir (wife of Svavar Gestsson, former Consul–General for Iceland in Winnipeg, Manitoba). The aged, sepia-coloured journal was written circa 1915 while she attended the Women's School in Reykjavík and provides treasures beyond its contents. The pages are enscribed with beautiful and uniformly handwritten recipes, well organized under the following heads: Grautar og Súpur (Porridge and Soups), Fiskmatar (Fish Recipes), Marmelade, Kjötmatar (Meat Recipes), Deserar (Desserts), Salöt (Salads), Kökur og Fleira (Cookies and Other). Each recipe title is numbered and underlined with a neat calligraphic wave, and the ingredients and method are presented in a consistent format. The integrity of the writer and the school is evident in this endeavor demonstrated through the meticulous care taken in the recording of these recipes.

This book provides insights regarding cooking in Iceland not long after the major tide of immigration to North America and allows for useful comparisons between the recipes as they came to be established in New Iceland and how they continued to be prepared in Iceland. Although the comparisons are by no means definitive, they do provide historical flavour.

Comparisons made throughout this book to New Iceland recipes afford an informative basis for considering the retention of traditional recipes and its importance for the emigrants given the indigenous ingredients of the land to which they came. Beyond basic survival, that they prepared available foods in as close a manner as possible to what they were accustomed to was important for their cultural well-being. It preserved ties with their homeland and their identity. Following an overall review recipes were selected for their comparative value on the basis of being considered the most 'traditional' by New Icelanders.

Guðrún Jónsdóttir
By Guðrún Ágústsdóttir

My amma Guðrún Jónsdóttir was born April 29th 1894 on Gilsárteigur, a farm in east Iceland (near Egilsstaðir). Her family moved to Seljamýri in Loðmundarfjörður, a fjord that is between Borgarfjörður eystri and Seyðisfjörður where she grew up.

As a young women she had saved enough money to go to Kvennaskólinn í Reykjavík, (The Women's School) where she spent one year and at the same time she took organ lessons. Her recipe book was written that year. She had three children, Kristine (1922) my mother Ragnheiður (1924) and a boy that died young. She passed away in 1941, 47 years old.

Kvennaskólinn í Reykjavík was founded in 1874 to give girls/women a good education in both theoretical and practical knowledge. In 1946 it became a grammar school for girls and in 1979 a secondary grammar school (junior high) for both girls and boys.

Kvennaskólinn í Reykjavík

The following is an excerpt from the column 'News from Iceland' in **Framfari** (July 31, 1878):

The school for girls in Reykjavík. The construction of a new schoolhouse is planned for this summer so the girls can be divided into two classes according to the knowledge they possess; those who are well advanced in book learning can then attend the class devoted exclusively to needle work, while at the same time the girls desiring it can obtain board and lodging in the schoolhouse itself. In one class only book knowledge will be taught, in the other only needle work. Girls who do not live at the school will be permitted to attend needle work classes at specified times. Only girls who have been confirmed and are well-mannered will be admitted to the school. Those attending on a full-time basis will pay one crown a day for board, lodging, bed etc., but will receive instruction free. Other students taking advantage of all the courses offered will pay twenty crowns a year. The types of needle work taught include dressmaking, hemstitching, various kinds of embroidery techniques, embroidery with gold or silver thread, crocheting and in the dark days before Christmas, knitting. The term lasts from October 1st to May 14th. Mrs. Thora Melsted is in charge of the school.[1]

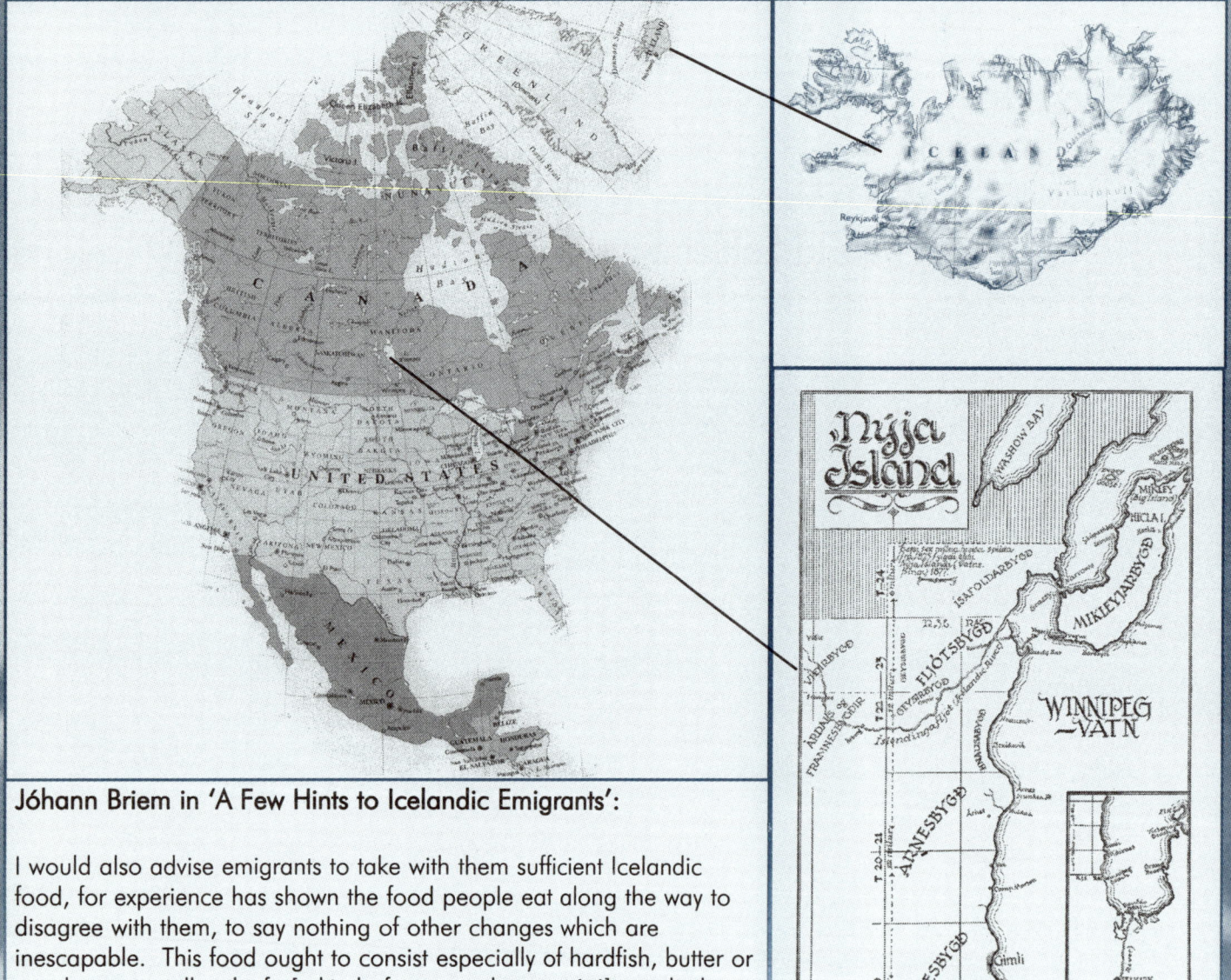

Jóhann Briem in 'A Few Hints to Icelandic Emigrants':

I would also advise emigrants to take with them sufficient Icelandic food, for experience has shown the food people eat along the way to disagree with them, to say nothing of other changes which are inescapable. This food ought to consist especially of hardfish, butter or good mutton, tallow kæfa [a kind of seasoned meat pâté], smoked lamb and biscuits; in addition, pure and good sour whey, rock candy, and a little good akvavit made from grain.[1]

(Framfari January 4, 1878)

New World Settlements and the Founding of New Iceland

AS A DESCENDANT OF ICELANDERS WHO CHOSE EMIGRATION I CAN ONLY TRY TO IMAGINE THE HEARTACHE OF LEAVING THEIR LOVED ONES AND HOMELAND, KNOWING THEY WOULD NEVER RETURN. STANDING AT THE RAILS ONBOARD SHIP, THE SHORELINE GRADUALLY RECEDING AND FINALLY DISAPPEARING FROM VIEW, THEY MUST HAVE FELT MOMENTS OF REGRET AND LONGING FOR THE LAND OF STRANGE, WONDROUS BEAUTY THAT, FOR ALL THEY HAD ENDURED, WAS THEIR HOME. TIME FOR THESE FINAL MOMENTS OF REFLECTION WOULD HAVE BEEN SHORT-LIVED. WITH THE IMMEDIATE NEEDS OF THE VOYAGE DEMANDING THEIR ATTENTION, THEY WOULD HAVE BEEN SUSTAINED, I HOPE, BY THE VIKING SPIRIT OF OPTIMISM AND ADVENTURE.

It is estimated that just under 20,000, representing approximately 20-25% of Iceland's total population, joined the European migratory movement, mainly in the last quarter of the nineteenth century. The causes for emigration were many: years of harsh weather conditions, earthquakes and volcanic activity had been disastrous to farming; ongoing political conflict with the Danish government had created a climate of discontent -even in light of the 1874 constitution establishing self-government; and personal (and religious) reasons impelled some. Although every person who emigrated had their own unique reason for doing so, what they all shared was the hope that a better life awaited them and their descendants in the New World.

The journey itself was long and arduous, particularly for those emigrants who took passage on the first voyages when conditions were at their worst. Many arrived weak, exhausted and ill; for women with children, these voyages must have been even more demanding. Nevertheless, with increased emigration, conditions improved and advice through letters and articles in newspapers better prepared the next emigrants for the journey.

Early Immigration to North America

Utah

Previous to 1870 when immigration may be said to have begun in earnest there had been smaller groups who had already departed Iceland primarily for religious reasons. A small group of converts to the Mormon faith immigrated to the United States and founded a settlement at Spanish Fork, Utah, in 1855, followed by another small group in 1856. After 1870, there was a slow trickle of immigrants until almost 200 had settled in the area of Spanish Fork and Salt Lake City.

Brazil

In addition to Utah, Icelanders immigrated to Brazil, influenced by Einar Ásmundsson, a farmer from Nes. In 1861, Kristján Ísfeld departed for Brazil, settling in Curitiba. In spite of considerable interest, only 34 others reached Brazil due to costly and inaccessible transit. Although Ísfeld died of jaundice before their arrival, this group settled in the Curitiba area also.

IMMIGRATION TO NORTH AMERICA BEGINS IN EARNEST

Wisconsin

Correspondence from William Wickman, a Danish merchant who had lived in Iceland and then immigrated to the United States, is said to have influenced the growing emigration movement. He wrote letters from Milwaukee, Wisconsin, to his former employer Guðmundur Thorgrimsen in Iceland, praising the fertility of the soil and the potential of Lake Michigan.

In 1870 four young Icelanders departed for Milwaukee, marking the beginning of the immigration movement that was soon to escalate. They settled at Washington Island, Lake Michigan. Two other small groups followed in 1871 and 1872 with Páll Thorláksson, who became a well-known pastor, as the leader of the second group. By 1874, when the Icelandic Millennial Celebration was held in Milwaukee, numbers had grown to about 200. Most left Milwaukee and settled mainly on Washington Island and in Shawano County.

Ontario

In 1872, Sigtryggur Jónasson, acknowledged as the 'Father of New Iceland', landed in North America, targeting Ontario as his destination and becoming the first Icelander to settle permanently in Canada. Letters to Icelanders from their friends and relatives in America and from Sigtryggur Jónasson in Ontario encouraged larger scale emigration. The first sizeable group, about 150, disembarked at Quebec City in August, 1873. Some 40-50 proceeded to Milwaukee while the remainder continued to the Muskoka District near Georgian Bay in the vicinity of Rosseau. Known as 'Hekla', this was the first Icelandic settlement established in Canada.

In his letter written November 19, 1877, J. Lindal gives an account of settlement in the Muskoka district:

On the last day of August, 1873, weary and exhausted after a journey of almost a month from their fatherland, but full of hope and eager to begin a new life of progress in Canada, they arrived at Rosseau, where they held a meeting...

Of the 110 Icelanders who came to Rosseau in 1873, only 25 settled here. The rest moved away in the autumn, some the following spring, to seek employment, and most of them have now probably settled at New Iceland. Their having to leave Rosseau was for the most part, a consequence of the shortage of opportunities for employment...

Icelanders here have now cleared sixty acres for cultivation as well as about fifty acres of meadowland which they have burnt and cleared and since then mowed annually with a good crop of hay. Most of them have constructed good and commodious log houses as well as barns and shelters for their cows. There are thirty head of cattle altogether. Some people here also keep pigs and flocks of poultry. Our countrymen here still have no horses or sheep, although those who were used to

having them home in Iceland would very much like to have them here. The raising of sheep is probably profitable in Ontario, however, among those who have sufficient meadow or pasture land for them in the summer...

Those unfamiliar with pioneer life in America and its difficulties might think it strange that our countrymen here have not made more progress in farming in the long time they have been living here. It must be mentioned, however, that they arrived here only in the autumn and knew nothing of the English language nor of the types of employment to be had here. In addition, there was widespread unemployment, stemming from the bank failure in New York; only a few were able to obtain work, and the wages were very low. It is true that the Ontario government provided work for some on road construction through thickly forested country. Since no one could refuse such work, it went at a slow pace. Single men could do no better than work for their keep, but the fathers of families were unable to feed themselves and their dependants. This work lasted only a short time, so that most men were unemployed over the winter and the little money they had after paying the costs of the voyage was soon used up... In the spring, on the other hand, they got busy and found work wherever it was to be had, even though the wages were low... Little land was cleared that summer (1874)... The following year they made more progress along these lines and more and more each succeeding year... Now they have also learned some English, had experience working in the woods, and acquired some knowledge of the cultivation and productivity of the land...[2]

(Framfari January 4, 1878)

Language and work methods were the major obstacles for this group. Also the land was for the most part unsuitable for cultivation as it was heavily timbered and rocky and under water in spring and fall.

In the spring of 1874, Sigtryggur Jónasson visited Rosseau and became their interpreter, advisor and later liaison with the Ontario government. When the 'St. Patrick' sailed direct from Iceland to Canada with approximately 375 onboard, Jónasson met them in Quebec on Sept. 23, 1874. Many had intended to settle in New Brunswick or Nova Scotia but as the best lands there had already been taken, the majority continued on to Kinmount, Ontario, where employment in railway construction was available. The employment prospect as well as the land proved disappointing. Ill health due to the sudden changes in climate, water, diet —especially the lack of milk— and crowded living conditions added to their hardships. Approximately twenty died from a stomach disorder -mainly the young and the elderly.

Amazingly, Ontario was still viewed optimistically as a suitable settlement site by the spring, but as there was not a tract of free grant land available to accommodate a large Icelandic settlement, they would soon be looking elsewhere.

Nova Scotia

Some who had arrived onboard the 'St. Patrick' had gone directly to Nova Scotia. Later, discouraged by conditions in Kinmount, about 80 left Ontario to join their countrymen in the Mooseland District of Halifax County, Nova Scotia. The settlement known as 'Markland' was established in 1874-75. In the following years others from Wisconsin, Ontario and Iceland arrived. The colony grew to about 200, and some found employment in the fishing town of Lockeport. Dissatisfied with the land here, all but 35 families moved on (mainly to Manitoba and North Dakota) in 1881-82.

Sigurdur Johannesson reporting from Hljeskógar, Icelandic Settlement, Halifax County, Nova Scotia on December 8, 1877:

It may be said of us colonists here that we are making progress slowly, for we lack financial means, but our livestock is beginning to multiply little by little and we had a very good harvest last summer. Everything we planted grew well, wheat, oats, buckwheat, barley, potatoes and several varieties of garden vegetables, such as carrots, cabbage, squash, pumpkins, beets and others.

Some of our countrymen here went to sea this past summer on fishing boats, but did not meet with success, for this fishing season is said to have been the least productive and the catch the poorest men can recall in many years.

The people here have been and are enjoying excellent health. It is now two years since there has been a death among our group, and in the two years and a half we have been living in this colony only one individual has died. There are now about 100 of us here. At Lockeport and elsewhere in Nova Scotia, there must be about 40 people...[3]

(Framfari January 14, 1878)

Excerpt from 'The Icelandic Settlement in Nova Scotia' (translated from 'The Toronto Globe', December 14, 1877):

The Icelandic settlement, which is about five miles from Archibald's Mill in Upper Musquodoboit in Nova Scotia, comprises about twenty families, each of which has its own little log cabin. There are also several other houses. The soil is reasonably good...

In most of their houses are to be seen the Bible and other books. The houses, although small, are clean and neat. Many of them contain a separate room and all are provided with a shed, about six feet wide. There is a cookstove in every house. The men know how to knit, sew and weave. As yet, however, they have neither wool not sheep. Their spinning wheels are smaller than ours and lighter, while the hand grip and support are above them, toward the back. The wheel is underneath the spindle and it is possible to feed the thread through a special contrivance, designed specifically for this purpose...[4]

(Framfari January 14, 1878)

Minnesota

The Minnesota settlement was begun by Gunnlaugur Pétursson who arrived in the vicinity of Minneota, Minnesota, from Wisconsin in 1875. Others from Wisconsin joined him and his wife the following year. Later with arrivals from Ontario and Iceland, the settlement grew and prospered in four districts: Lyon, Yellow, Medicine, and Lincoln Counties.

In 'A Few Words about the Icelandic Settlements in Minnesota' by S(norri) Högnason from Nordland, Lyon County, Minnesota, January 25, 1878, he chronicles the beginnings of the settlement:

The first group of Icelanders came to Lyon County in Minnesota late in June of 1875; they were six altogether, one family and a single bachelor. The father of the family, Gunnlögur Pjetursson from Hákonarstadir in Jökuldal, took up land, 160 acres, [and] began by building a rough cabin for himself and later in the summer ploughed three acres. Now he has 25 acres under cultivation and 21 head of cattle. These people came from Wisconsin, where they had been living for nearly two years. The next to come arrived here in June,

1876, three families and two unattached men, eighteen in all. These people also came from Wisconsin. The heads of families took up land at once close to the first Icelander who had settled here. In the course of the summer they ploughed 12 acres, and two of them built cabins, but one did not build on his land until last spring...[5]

(Framfari February 27, 1878)

Nebraska and Alaska

In 1874-75 a small group settled near Firth, Nebraska, as a result of an exploratory trip to that state. By then a movement to find a colony site suitable for a large number of Icelandic immigrants had begun. This area was deemed unsatisfactory and the settlement remained small. At about the same time as the Nebraska expedition, three Icelanders led by Jón Ólafsson travelled to Kodiak Island, Alaska on another exploratory search for a colony site. While Jón Ólafsson considered this site favourable, others thought it was too remote.

The following is from an extract of a letter from Jón Halldórsson in which he recounts the inspection of land in Nebraska and the subsequent enticement of Alaska as a settlement site:

In May 1873, two brothers, Torfi and Larus Bjarnason, journeyed west to Nebraska, where Torfi spent the summer and settled on railway land; he returned home in the autumn but Larus stayed behind. On the way home, he passed through Milwaukee, where there were quite a few Icelanders at the time and they held a meeting while Torfi was with them. Among other things, the purpose of the meeting was to obtain Torfi's advice as to whether it was feasible for Icelanders to move west. Even though he was impressed with the quality of the land there, he considered that moving there would entail many difficulties, giving as his reasons the Icelanders' ignorance of agriculture and their lack of funds to get started.

At a meeting in Milwaukee the spring of 1874 two men were chosen to inspect land in Iowa and Nebraska, and it was the intention of most of those attending the meeting to move west if these men thought it advisable.

These two, Sigfús and Jón Halldórsson, set out on the 4th of May, 1874. As they were not pleased with the land they saw in Iowa, they continued on to Nebraska and settled in Lancaster County, 20 miles south of Lincoln (the state capital), 8 miles to the south of where Torfi Magnússon had taken land. There they took up railway land for which payment would not have to be made for another ten years, but stayed with local farmers. They rather encouraged their fellows to follow them, even though they pointed out for them the difficulties of pioneer life they would find there as well as anywhere else. Some of their associates had already made up their minds to make the journey when the glowing fancies of Alaska overwhelmed the 'people'. The Nebraska partisans immediately became partisans of Alaska, so that summer only one Icelander moved to Nebraska and Sigfús Magnusson returned home in the autumn...

Toward the end of the summer of 1875, six Icelanders moved to Nebraska... [6]

(Framfari May 31, 1878)

THE FOUNDING OF NEW ICELAND

Manitoba- 'New Iceland'

Sigtryggur Jónasson -the Father of New Iceland

Many had left the settlements at Rosseau and Kinmount and those who remained were interested in relocating to either the western states or Manitoba. The Kinmount group had been befriended by John Taylor, a Methodist preacher, who made representation on their behalf to the Federal government. Through Lord Dufferin, the Governor-General of Canada at that time, he was successful in persuading the government to provide financial aid, allowing them to re-establish out west. Lord Dufferin was favorably inclined toward the Icelandic people having enjoyed his visit to Iceland in 1856.

At a meeting in Kinmount on May 30, 1875, John Taylor's report was heard and delegates chosen to journey west and search for a site for 'New Iceland'. John Taylor, as representative of the Canadian government, Sigtryggur Jónasson and Einar Jónasson travelled to Moorhead, Minnesota, where they were joined by Kristján Jónsson, Sigurður Kristófersson and Skafti Arason, representing other groups in Ontario and Wisconsin. Together they proceeded to Manitoba.

Upon their arrival in Winnipeg they were shown a map of the province indicating available land sites. Of the land remaining they concluded that none was suitable. They decided to investigate the area along the western shore of Lake Winnipeg extending north beyond the then Manitoba boundary in what was then the Northwest Territories. For the expedition they were loaned a boat by the Hudson's Bay Company. Upon inspection of the proposed site -from the boundary of Manitoba up to and including Big Island (Mikley, now Hecla)- they reserved it for Icelandic settlement on August 5, 1875.

Information meetings were then held in Milwaukee, Kinmount and Rosseau in August of 1875. The Canadian government made free passage available to Icelanders in Ontario and Wisconsin and promised re-establishment provisions. The Kinmount group of 200-250 with about 50 from Rosseau and Milwaukee resolved to move that fall. Upon learning of the devastation from the eruption of Mount Askja in Eastern Iceland, Sigtryggur representing the government returned to Iceland to organize emigration to the new colony.

The Kinmount area group departed on September 21, 1875, led by John Taylor and assisted by Friðjón Friðriksson. They travelled by rail to Sarnia, boarding a

steamship there which carried them to Duluth where they connected with the Milwaukee group. They proceeded by rail to Fisher's Landing on the Red River. A paddlewheeler and barges then transported the group down river to Winnipeg where their landing caused some excitement in what was then a frontier town of 3000.

They were encouraged to remain in Winnipeg because it was already mid-October and to their dismay, no preparation had been made for their arrival in New Iceland. About 150-160 decided to continue on as housing and employment were insufficient for all.

Supplies were purchased and loaded on six large barges or 'flatboats'. After a day and a night they reached the mouth of the Red River where they quite fortuitously met the Hudson's Bay Steamer 'Colville'. The barges were then towed by the 'Colville' expediting their progress. They disembarked at Willow Point, near the south end of the settlement on October 21 at 4:30pm.

Originally their intention had been to establish a central town on the Icelandic River. En route possible names for this town had been discussed. Gimli, was suggested by Ólafur Ólafsson -from the ancient Norse poem Völuspá, Sybil's Prophecy, in which Gimli is a 'gold thatched hall' and the home of all worthy men (gim-fire, hlé-lee, shelter). Gimli was founded along the bay to the north of Willow Point and not on the Icelandic River because the captain of the 'Colville' would not tow them further -due to the unstable weather conditions of that time of the season. The settlers moved their encampment soon after landing along the shore to the present site of Gimli seeking better shelter than afforded on Willow Point.

That winter, without adequate provisions, dairy products or fresh meat beyond some fish and rabbits, scurvy and illness took its toll. About 35 died, mostly children and those with infirmity. Spring helped to bring a renewal of their spirits but this tragedy had saddened the hearts of many. With fortitude they persevered; lands were claimed, loghouses and stables erected. They formed their own government responsible directly to Ottawa and supplies and cattle were distributed.

Over 1000 Icelanders, known as the 'Large Group', arrived in New Iceland in July and August 1876. This group was comprised of many from the ash stricken districts of the East mobilized through the efforts of W.C. Krieger and Sigtryggur Jónasson, acting as agents of the Canadian government. There were three parties and all departed Iceland in July, 1876. About 750 from the North and West of Iceland were the first group to leave. From Eastern Iceland about 378 departed soon after. Last to follow was a smaller group of about 20 from Southern Iceland.

There had been only three settlers at Icelandic River previous to the arrival of the 'Large Group' and very few elsewhere in New Iceland, most having settled in the Gimli and Arnes District. The 'Large Group' claimed lands and New Iceland became a vibrant, bustling colony. In the midst of all the positive activity -land clearing and building- tragedy loomed. A smallpox epidemic broke out that fall and continued through the winter, claiming 102 lives. With about one-third to one-half of the population believed to have contracted smallpox, the setback was serious. There were delays in building and cultivation of land, loss of employment, and the restricted communication and transport of supplies due to the quarantine were further impediments. Disillusionment due to the suffering and heartache of losing loved ones was widespread in the aftermath of this epidemic. The Canadian government provided assistance with loans that were used to purchase supplies, equipment and cattle.

LORD DUFFERIN'S ADDRESS

Lord Dufferin's visit had been a celebratory occasion for the New Icelanders and extensive preparations had been made to receive him. The following is an excerpt of Friðjón Friðriksson's address to Lord Dufferin, the Governor-General of Canada, on the occasion of his visit to Gimli, September 14, 1877:

It is still not quite two years since the first group of our people moved into this colony. The prospect was not a happy one when they arrived at this uninhabited and almost unknown tract of land, where they had to prepare for a long winter of cold and snow. Since then it has been a hard battle against shortages, illness, hard work which produced no results, and rainy weather which spoiled the crops. Most recently we had to contend with the depredations of the smallpox epidemic, which worked even more hardships on us because the quarantine was extended far beyond reasonable limits.

Now, however, conditions have improved and we can take pleasure in the hope that the dark days of adversity have finally come to an end, and a brighter future begun, giving us the opportunity to take into account the advantages of New Iceland, which are far superior to anything we might have expected at home.

We acknowledge with gratitude the great assistance the Canadian Government has extended to us and hope to be able to repay this loan with interest promptly. Although it is a great pity that unfortunate circumstances have prevented us from cultivating more land than has been the case, at the same time we are grateful that the excellent soil now appears to provide a good harvest from the seed sown last spring. We consider it a great advantage to have such extensive meadow and pasture land for our livestock; in time it can become a great source of prosperity for us. The abundance of fish we have caught in Lake Winnipeg has also been of inestimable benefit. We have here sufficient timber for building, fencing and firewood; we are therefore not so susceptible to the cold of winter as we would be otherwise. We have a good winter road, sheltered by the forest; it makes no little contribution to communications among us. [7]

(*Framfari* November 17, 1877)

Lord Dufferin's reply to Friðjón Friðriksson's address:

When it was my good fortune twenty years ago to visit your island I never thought that the day would come when I should be called upon as the representative of the British Crown to receive you in this country; but the opportunities I have thus had of becoming acquainted with your dramatic history, with your picturesque literature, and the kindness I have experienced at the hands of your countrymen now enable me with the greater cordiality to bid you welcome. I have learnt with extreme sorrow of the terrible trials to which you have been exposed so soon after your arrival by the unexpected ravages of a terrible epidemic...During a hasty visit like the present I cannot pretend to acquire more than a superficial insight into your condition, but so far as I have observed, things appear to be going sufficiently well with you. The homesteads I have visited seem well built and commodious and are certainly far superior to any of the farmhouses I remember in Iceland, while the gardens and little clearings which have begun to surround them show that you have already tapped an inexhaustible store of wealth in the rich alluvial soil on which we stand. The three arts most necessary to a Canadian colonist are the felling of timber, the plowing of land, and the construction of highways, but as in your own country none of you had ever seen a tree, a cornfield, or a road, it is not to be expected that you should immediately exhibit any expertness in these accomplishments, but practice and experience will soon make you the masters of all three, for you possess in a far greater degree than is probably imagined that which is the essence and foundation of all superiority —intelligence, education, and intellectual activity. In fact I have not entered into a single hut or cottage in the settlement which did not contain, no matter how bare its walls or scanty its furniture, a library of twenty or thirty volumes; and I am informed that there is scarcely a child amongst you who cannot read or write... I have learned with great satisfaction that numbers of your young women have entered the households of various Canadian families where they will not only acquire the English language, which it is most desirable you should all know, and which they will be able to teach their brothers and sisters, and —I trust I may add, in course of time, their children- but will also learn those lessons of domestic economy and housewifely neathandedness which are so necessary to the well-being, health, and cheerfulness of our homes. I am also happy to be able to add that I have received the best accounts from a great number of people of the good conduct, handiness, and docility of these young Ingeborgs, Ragnhildas, Thoras, and Gudruns, who I trust will do credit to the epical ancestresses from whom they have inherited their names. Many of the houses I have visited today bore evident signs in their airiness, neatness, and well-ordered appearance of possessing a housewife who had already profited from her contact with the outer world... I need not tell you that in a country like this the one virtue pre-eminently necessary to every man is self-reliance, energy, and a determination to conquer an independent living for himself, his wife and children by the unassisted strength of his own right arm. Unless each member of the settlement is possessed and dominated by this feeling, there can be no salvation for anyone. But why need I speak to Icelanders —to you men and women of the grand old Norse race- of the necessity of patience under hardship, courage in the face of danger, dogged determination in the presence of difficulties. The annals of your country are bright with the record of your forefathers' noble endurance. The sons and daughters of the men and women who crossed the Atlantic Ocean in open boats, and preferred to make their homes amid the snows and cinders of a volcano rather than enjoy peace and plenty under the iron sway of a despot may afford to smile at anyone who talks to them of hardship or rough living beneath the pleasant shade of these murmuring branches and beside the laughing ripples of yonder shining lake... Nor do we forget that no race has a better right to come amongst us than yourselves, for it is probably to the hardihood of the Icelandic navigators that the world is indebted for the discovery of this continent. Had not Columbus visited your island and discovered in your records a practical and absolute confirmation of his own brilliant speculations in regard to the existence of a western land, it is possible he might never have had the enterprise to tempt the unknown Atlantic... I trust you will continue to cherish for all time the heart-stirring literature of your nation, and that from generation to generation your little ones will continue to learn in your ancient Sagas that industry, energy, fortitude, perseverance, and stubborn endurance have ever been the characteristics of the noble Icelandic race. I have pledged my personal credit to my Canadian friends on the successful development of your settlement. My warmest and most affectionate sympathies attend you, and I have not the slightest misgiving but that in spite of your enterprise being conducted under what of necessity are somewhat disadvantageous conditions, not only will your future prove bright and prosperous, but that it will be universally acknowledged that a more valuable accession to the intelligence, patriotism, loyalty, industry, and strength of the country has never been introduced into the Dominion. [8]

(Framfari November 17, 1877)

These were distributed by the government of New Iceland.

A rivalry began to develop between Séra Jón Bjarnason and Séra Páll Thorláksson based on their very different religious beliefs, creating a building tension in New Iceland that was to impact the colony irrevocably. Séra Páll had arrived, as requested by his followers, just before Séra Jón who took up his post as pastor in November, 1877. The majority, including most of New Iceland's leaders supported the more liberal, Séra Jón. Séra Páll advocated a fundamentalist and conservative perspective, believing in a strict and literal adherence to the teachings of the Lutheran faith. Thus the settlers found themselves divided into two factions based on their religious beliefs.

The situation was provoked further when Séra Páll solicited financial aid from the Norwegian Synod in January, 1878. The Norwegian Synod responded with a contribution of $1300. Séra Jón's followers were outraged, thinking it was a disgrace to New Icelanders. The letter was dubbed the 'Beggar's letter'. As a result of the hostility, incited meetings were held in March 1878 and again the following year to debate the issues. Although an understanding was ultimately reached, members of Séra Páll's group had already begun leaving for available land in North Dakota. Séra Páll himself intended to relocate there as well. There were other reasons contributing to their decision to leave but their religious orientation was pre-eminent. New arrivals from Iceland in 1877-79, however, balanced the loss of those who had begun departure for Winnipeg and North Dakota.

The 'Great Flood' occurring in the late fall of 1880 contributed to a growing discontent. Flood waters, in the wake of an icy storm, flowed inland over the marshes affecting the settlers inhabiting the low lands. Despite the overall progress that had been made in the foundation of New Iceland, this flood compounded with general disillusionment over hardships and strife already endured perpetuated a widespread desire to relocate.

Further Settlements

North Dakota

Pembina County, North Dakota became the destination for many following the inspection of lands there in the vicinity of Cavalier by Magnús Stefánsson and Sigurður Joshúa Björnsson in April, 1878. They registered for homesteads as did Jóhann Hallsson with others soon joining them. A great increase in numbers during the spring and summer of 1879 established that settlement conclusively.

The most populous Icelandic settlement in Dakota is about 30 miles southwest of Pembina. The following information was obtained from Palmi Hjalmarsson, who recently came north from there. The Tongue River, which flows northeast from the Pembina Hills, passes through a corner of the settlement, but mainly to the north of it, flowing northeast into the Pembina River, which flows in an easterly direction into the Red River. In the eastern area there are a few sandy hills, but towards the north they are wooded, and the Tongue River flows through them. There are 40 homesteaders in the settlement, all told, six of whom have chosen land along the Tongue River. In a few localities there are streams with good water, but in most

places it is necessary to dig wells. An acre of land can be cleared for 3-4 dollars, or 3-4 days' work for the older settlers. One man working with two oxen can, as a rule, clear 1¼ acres a day. The largest wheat producer in the settlement is Johann Hallsson, who moved there in the spring of the year before last; he had about 4½ acres planted in wheat this year and expected to harvest about 30 bushels from each acre. The Icelanders have altogether about 120 acres cleared for the planting of wheat and other varieties of grain next year. The closest town to the settlement is St. Joe, about 40 miles west of Pembina and 12 miles northwest of the settlement on the Pembina River. A little trade is carried on there, mainly with the Indians and half-breeds. There is also a flour mill, operated by water power. The new settlers are well pleased and anticipate a good future. They are all in the Rev. Pall Thorlaksson's congregation. –In addition to these people, Icelanders have also settled here and there around Pembina in northeastern Dakota, but how many of them, we do not know.⁹
(Framfari September 23, 1879)

Manitoba -'The Argyle Settlement'

Others who became known as 'Loyalists' because they did not wish to cross the border in respect of the support the Canadian government had given them, selected the Argyle District in south-western Manitoba as their settlement site. Sigurður Kristófersson and Kristján Jónsson inspected the lands to the north and west of Pilot Mound in August, 1880, in the vicinity of present day Baldur and Glenboro. They filed for homesteads and by the fall of 1881 there were 8 families residing in the settlement. Many more followed in the ensuing years and the Argyle Settlement flourished. During the years 1889-94, an extension of the settlement -which was called both Skalholt and Holar (Hills) was formed in the South Cypress Hills close to the Assiniboine River about 10 miles northeast of Glenboro.

Saskatchewan -'Thingvalla-Logberg' and Foam Lake Settlement

During the early years, another significant Icelandic settlement had its beginnings in the present-day Canadian Prairies. The first Icelanders to settle further west in the North West Territories in what is now the province of Saskatchewan arrived there in 1885, having spent 2 or 3 years in Winnipeg or elsewhere. The first known homestead entry was in a district which is known as 'Thingvalla', (slightly north-east of Churchbridge, forty miles south-west of Yorkton). A few more settlers followed in 1886. In 1887 five homesteads were chosen a few miles east of the present village of Tantallon. In 1890, Icelandic settlers moved into a district reaching as far as the present town of Calder and called it 'Logberg'. Over time the two districts merged. In search of an area with more hay for their stock six men moved their families to the Foam Lake and Fishing Lake area in 1891. The turn of the century brought a new wave of settlers, most coming from North Dakota but some from Argyle and other settlements in Manitoba. At this time the area settled extended west of the original Foam Lake Settlement, making it the largest settlement site in Saskatchewan.

Alberta

Sigurður Björnsson settled along the Red Deer River in 1889. He was followed by others from North Dakota and a small settlement was established. At the same time there were some who went further west to settle on the west coast.

RESURGENCE OF NEW ICELAND

New Iceland's population had been reduced dramatically by the end of 1881. The government of New Iceland had been disbanded, the newspaper the Framfari had folded, log homes and fields had been abandoned and neglected. Through the commitment of those who remained -some 30 families at Icelandic River, 12 settlers in the Gimli area, 5 families in both South and North Árnes and in Mikley about 10 families- New Iceland eventually expanded beyond its original boundaries. The knowledge they had gained of the land and the lake was to stand them in good stead. They were also motivated to persist by their desire to preserve their language and culture. Outside employment provided by the fisheries and freighting, seasonal farm labour and domestic service work in Manitoba, and a logging and lumbering enterprise at Icelandic River contributed greatly to their success.

Immigrants arriving from Iceland between 1883 and 1893 settled on the abandoned farms along the lakeshore supplementing their farming livelihood with fishing as they were accustomed to in Iceland. During those years, adversities were experienced in Iceland which led to new waves of immigration including: 1882 -unseasonal storms and pack ice around much of Iceland; 1886 -a severe winter and cold wet summer forced farmers to slaughter their sheep and cattle; 1887 -violent spring storms and drift ice. Substantial immigration continued through 1889 -less through 1890-1892 but in-creasing again in 1893. By 1893 most of the homesteads had been reclaimed.

New Iceland's foundation having been restored, the settlement prospered and became the most populous of all the Icelandic communities in North America. For the immediately ensuing generations of New Icelanders, a gradual lessening of concentration on basic survival made possible an increasing emphasis on the restoration of their culture.

Of particular note is New Iceland's Íslendingadagurinn ('Icelandic Celebration'), which was intended as a means to unite Icelandic immigrants as well as to help foster preservation of Icelandic heritage and culture. The Celebration has been a special highlight each year since its inception on August 2, 1890, in Winnipeg, Manitoba, where it was held annually until 1931. In 1932, Gimli became the permanent centre for the Icelandic Celebration. In the early years there were always speeches, recitals, athletic events and a dance. It has grown in size and significance over time and is now a three day festival with a wide array of entertainment and activities. It has become an opportunity for Icelandic descendants to return "home" to Gimli to reunite with their friends and relations and honour their shared heritage.

The first Icelandic Celebration in North America took place in Milwaukee, Wisconsin, on August 2, 1874, to mark one thousand years of settlement in Iceland. On that same date, the King of Denmark presented a new constitution to Iceland. Festivals were also held separately in various communities in New Iceland. At Icelandic River, the first celebration was August 8, 1896. For the next two years, the Icelandic National Holiday, June 17th, was selected as the date for the occasion. In 1923, all the communities in the Bifröst Municipality amalgamated and held an Íslendingadagur at Hnausa.

Recently, New Icelandic culture has been imbibed with a rejuvenated spirit. Several historical time-markers have promoted this renewed interest and excitement, including millennium celebrations which put the Vikings on the world stage with the replica Viking ship 'Íslendingur' making the voyage from Iceland to L'Anse aux Meadows, Newfoundland, commemorating 1000 years since Leifur Eiriksson became the first European to cross the Atlantic. The year 2000 also marked the 125th anniversary of the New Iceland settlement and the openings of the Betel Waterfront Centre and the New Heritage Museum in Gimli. These occasions come at the end of a long line of centennials (100 years since New Iceland joined the province of Manitoba -1981; RM of Gimli -1987; and Islendingadagurinn -1989). The descendants of the original settlers have had much cause to celebrate, and it is with great optimism that they greet the twenty-first century.

New Icelanders and the Lake Winnipeg Fisheries

Lake Winnipeg was a natural draw for the men who selected the site for New Iceland in 1875. The lake teemed with a variety of fish that the Icelanders anticipated to be an important food source and a useful trade item. As fish had been a staple food for Icelanders since medieval times, this opportunity must have seemed auspicious given the uniqueness of a lake of this magnitude on the prairies.

Generations of New Icelanders have made their livelihood from the Lake Winnipeg fisheries. Tales abound of perils faced by fishermen on the stormy lake. There has always been a respect for Lake Winnipeg's very unpredictable nature. Lake Winnipeg has been described as one of the most treacherous bodies of water on the North American continent. It is the twelfth largest lake in the world and is long, narrow and shallow with a strong undercurrent -making it dangerous in a storm. As it runs north-south, a gale from either direction combined with the strong undertow can turn it into an angry boiling cauldron. Outlying reefs, shoals and half-submerged islands further add to its dangerous potential. In the days before lights and lake markers, a confident captain with good eyesight and an intimate knowledge of the lake was essential.

Survival was the utmost concern of the fishermen who pioneered commercial fishing on Lake Winnipeg. They fished to feed their families and to trade for necessities, demonstrating great determination in overcoming many challenges. Although Icelanders have a very long history of fishing ocean waters, the New Icelandic fishermen needed to adapt to local conditions such as thick winter ice, previously unknown to them. Explorations of the lake using small boats -to seek out the best fishing grounds- was precarious at best and could be perilous in bad weather. When fishing grounds were found north of 'New Iceland' and camps set up, fishermen were absent for weeks and even months at a time, creating hardship for the women and children who assumed sole responsibility for chores on the homestead.

Gradually and with increased proficiency, fishermen were rewarded with catches providing a surplus beyond their immediate food requirements. By 1877-78 fish were being hauled to the Winnipeg market. The demand for whitefish, in particular, encouraged venturesome men to become fish buyers, and by the winter of 1879-80 fish was being sold in markets as distant as St. Paul, Minnesota. Increasing fish sales resulted in a need for winter freighting services. Transportation routes developed over the frozen waters of lakes and rivers. Fish was hauled by oxen and horse teams to Grindstone, Gimli, Selkirk, and Winnipeg. Dogsleds were commonplace for light cartage.

The Diary of Sigurður Erlendsson

Sigurður Erlendsson's diary provides striking insight into the difficulties and hardships associated with the early days of fishing on Lake Winnipeg during the late 1870's. Sigurður Erlendsson and his family were members of the 'Large Group' who immigrated in 1876 to New Iceland. His diary, written originally in Icelandic, has been translated by Mr. Olafur Johnson of Eriksdale, Manitoba, and Professor Solli Sigurdson of the Faculty of Education, University of Alberta. The following is an excerpt from his diary in which he recounts his fishing experiences on Big Island (Mikley) -today known as Hecla Island- where he and his family had settled.

When I came from Iceland I brought with me a short net, 14 mesh deep, which I had bought there. Small floats were threaded on the top line and sinkers, made out of sawed leg bones, threaded on the bottom line. This net was not exactly suited for Lake Winnipeg, yet I managed to catch some jackfish in the fall which I rationed at half a fish each day for dinner.

Shortly after the new year my stomach ailment began to ease up and I recovered remarkably soon.

When I went through Winnipeg I bought one pound of net twine and I now made a net 19 fathoms in length; that was the usual length of nets in those days. The next fair day my Stefan and I took the nets and tools needed to set it in the lake about a mile north of the mill houses. The snow was deep, and we pulled a clumsy hand sleigh with our equipment on; the ice was close to three feet in thickness, but two days later we had the net in the water. Fishermen of this day and age will realize that here things were badly lacking, technique, proper tools and warm clothing.

In the first lift we caught three whitefish. Those who have experienced hunger will understand how much we relished the first meal after the whitefish was cooked. From then until spring we had plenty of whitefish to eat, either boiled or fried, and were able to share some of it with others less fortunate.

...During my second winter here a man came to the island on a team of horses selling flour. He wanted 56 whitefish for each bag. The third winter another man came who paid seven cents apiece for whitefish, in cash.

The fourth winter I made my first trading trip to Winnipeg, on one ox, and had 220 whitefish and 160 tullibees in a bag to sell. I had difficulties selling the tullibees, but finally sold them for one dollar for the bag. How much I got for the whitefish per pound, I don't remember, but everything considered, I felt I had made a successful trip and returned with more and better supplies for the home than I had known before.

I walked every step of the way, the going was heavy, the weather was frosty, and most of the time I was cold. I made a trip like that for several winters, and in that way improved my lot the most.[1]

By the mid-1880's, Icelanders were establishing fish companies. "The first of these were the Hanneson brothers, Hannes and Jóhannes, who as merchants at Gimli also dealt in fish as a matter of course. Around the same time, Jón Jónsson of Grund in Mikley with his son, Jón H. Johnson, together with Stefán Jónsson of Jónsnes and his son, Kjartan Stefánsson, went into business at Gull Harbour, building an ice house and later a ship called the Ida. Meanwhile not far away, at Skógar in Mikley, the Sigurðsson brothers, Stéfan and Jóhannes Sigurðsson, also got their start as fish buyers. The Sigurðsson Brothers, as they became known, relocated at Hnausa in 1890, however, establishing a thriving business there and eventually getting a government dock built nearby in 1895. They also acquired a large boat, *The Lady of the Lake*, in 1897."[2]

The partnership of the Sigurðsson brothers, Stefán and Jóhannes, eventually led to S.V. and S.R. Sigurdson's establishment in 1921 of Sigurdson Fisheries, one of the longest-lasting of the independent fishing companies on Lake Winnipeg. During this same period, other local men also became outfitters and fish buyers, owning and operating fish stations. With the Icelanders firmly established in the commercial fishing industry, operations continued with fluctuations through the years until the formation of the Freshwater Fish Corporation in 1969. The FFC is a system which required all fish to be sold through one desk. The industry was re-organized and has since been very productive.

'On Opening the Colony' by Johann Briem in 1878:

...We have here water transportation, which is as efficient as any other form of transport with the exception of railways; Lake Winnipeg provides transportation almost the year around and when the lake is ice-free there are also people from here travelling on both steam- and sailboats, and we can have everything we require shipped to us almost whenever we desire, if we have the financial means, and at the same time we can send to the Crossing or to Winnipeg at all times of the year whatever we have to sell, in addition to the fact that we also have vehicles and draught animals, although only a few at present. Even in winter we have no reason to complain over the lack of roads in existence now and of the isolation from markets (the Crossing), which as most people are aware, is no greater than that between most other places in this country, 25 to 30 English miles, two or three days by rowboat or driving with draught animals.[3]

(Framfari July 31, 1878)

Lake Winnipeg Vessels

Originally sailboats conveyed fishermen to and from the fishing grounds. Small row boats built by the settlers called 'byttur' or 'dallar', canoes and York boats were all utilized for various purposes. Steam boats, providing a more reliable service, were employed in the early years when they became affordable. By the 1920's gas engines were in general use; the introduction of diesel engines followed. Fishing vessels evolved to 40 to 60 foot steel, aluminum or wood hulled gill-netters powered by diesel engines and 16 to 20 foot fibreglass or wood yawls powered by outboard motors. When the lake froze over, oxen and horse teams which pulled 'trains' of a number of sleighs were replaced by tractors. Eventually, as today, bombardiers, 18 foot long two tracked snowmobiles resembling vans, and recreational-type snowmobiles provide transportation to the fishing grounds.

The boats that were essential as a means to provide a food source and a livelihood played an integral role not only for the fisheries but also the development of New Iceland. Rail lines and roads gradually evolved and it is eminently true that the viability of Lake Winnipeg fisheries increased in direct relation to improved transportation networks. However, before the rail and roads were built, boats brought supplies, outside news, passengers and mail. The first mailboat of the season bringing newspapers and letters from Iceland was particularly anticipated following the long isolated months of winter.

The attachment felt by New Icelanders for generations to Lake Winnipeg and the boats who sailed her waters is very strong. A brief description of some of the boats who served New Icelanders well follows. There are many more Lake Winnipeg vessels deserving of recognition and if space allowed, they would have been included.

SS Colville: The steamer Colville was built in Grand Forks in 1874 for the Hudson Bay Company and towed the barges or flatboats of the first group of Icelanders to settle in New Iceland, from the mouth of the Red River, dropping them off at Willow Point on Oct. 21, 1875. Their destination had been the Icelandic River but the Captain of the Colville -fearing weather conditions- would not tow them further.

HBC sold the Colville in 1882 to the Winnipeg and Western Transportation Company, who sold her two years later to the North West Navigation Company. She burned at Grand Rapids in 1894. The Colville operated out of Colvile Landing (later spelled Colville) on the East Slough of East Selkirk.

SS Victoria: The Victoria, a small paddle wheeler, was the first Icelandic-owned steamboat on Lake Winnipeg. She was built in St. Catherines, Ontario, in 1878 and transported to the Red River before being purchased by

Sigtryggur Jónasson (the 'Father of New Iceland'), Friðjón Friðriksson and a Scotsman named Walkley during the winter of 1879-80. She sailed between the Icelandic River and Selkirk, transporting lumber by towing barges until 1886 when the operation of Jónasson-Friðriksson was transferred across the lake. The Victoria was sold in 1887.

The Tow Barge 'Aurora': She was built in Riverton in 1884 to enable the Victoria to transport lumber and registered as the 'Aurora' in 1885 (named for Friðjón Friðriksson's daughter). In 1888, the Aurora was taken over by the Lake Winnipeg Transport and Lumbering Company. A steam engine and a boiler were installed, and she was fitted out as a side-wheeler. She then saw service as a passenger and general freight vessel.

MS Goldfield: Originally a steam tugboat built in 1886 by Captain John Howell for the Reid and Tait Fish Company of Selkirk under the name 'SS Frank Burton', the Goldfield also sailed under the name 'Minerva.' As a fishing vessel, she served the Armstrong Gimli Fisheries and then Sigurdson Fisheries of Riverton. The Manitoba Freshwater Fish Marketing Board later took over ownership. There was a 100th Anniversary celebration for the MS Goldfield the summer of 1986.

SS Gimli: The Hannesson Brothers of Gimli bought her around 1892. She was used mainly to transport freight and passengers from Selkirk to Gimli and in return transported fish to Selkirk. Previously the people of Gimli had to rely on the sailboat. The Gimli was a godsend providing a faster more reliable means of travel. Jón Guðnason of Gimli was captain at one time and she made two runs a week to Selkirk.

SS Ida: The Ida was a small steamboat built in Mikley (Hecla Island, Manitoba) in 1894 by Stefán Jónsson and his son Kjartan Stefánsson. Helgi Tomasson of Mikley bought a two-thirds share of the Ida in 1896 for his fishing enterprise. Not long afterwards though, the Ida was said to have been damaged in a storm on Lake Winnipeg, and did not resume operation.

MS Douglas M/M.S. Black Hawk VI: She was originally built and launched in Buffalo, New York in 1896. Christened the 'Alert', she sailed under American Registry as a freighter on the Great Lakes. In 1916, she was transferred to British Registry, sailing out of Southampton, Ontario, and in 1944, she became a tugboat at Port Arthur, Ontario.

In 1951, her steel hull was transported overland to the Red River. The hull and superstructure were rebuilt by Riverton Boatworks, and she was renamed the 'Douglas M'. She served as a lake freighter for the

Northern Lakes Fisheries Company Ltd. until the late fifties, when she was laid up on the beach at Hnausa harbour.

In 1972 Ray Sneft, builder of the Paddlewheel Riverboats, completely rebuilt her as a private yacht. She was renamed the 'Black Hawk VI.' The present owner, Dr. Irvin Olafson, of Gimli acquired the vessel in 1977. Her 100th Anniversary was celebrated in Gimli the summer of 1996.

SS Lady of the Lake: She was the largest steamer built by Icelanders to sail on Lake Winnipeg. The Sigurðsson Brothers of Hnausa (Stefán and Jóhannes) owned the Lady of the Lake from 1897 to 1901. Later Stefán reacquired her. For some time she was also operated as a government boat for passengers and freight. The theatre in the Waterfront Centre at Gimli has been named the 'Lady of the Lake Theatre'; this facility is dedicated to the

Sigurdsons of Riverton and their involvement on Lake Winnipeg.

SS Viking: She was built around the turn of the century by Ármann Bjarnason, a Winnipeg Icelander, and owned by Stéfan Sigurðsson of Hnausa.

SS Mikado/SS Grand Rapids: She was built at Selkirk in 1905 and was then acquired by Stefán Sigurðsson of Hnausa to transport his fish production from Horse Island and Little Georges Island to Selkirk. She was then later taken over by the Winnipeg Fish Company, housed in and renamed the 'SS Grand Rapids'. Her subsequent owners were Robinson Fish Company, Manitoba Transport Company and finally Booth Fish Company. Her last year on the lake was around 1934-35 when she was beached and dismantled.

SS Amisk: She was built in 1908 for the Beaver Lumber Company. Later Stefán Sigurðsson of Hnausa acquired her for his fishing operation, and then later by the Riverton Fish Company which had its operation in Hnausa 1917-1918. The Gimli Fish Company took over the Amisk in 1919. In 1927, the Amisk was beached.

SS Montgomery: She was built in 1910 by the federal government. Sveinn Thorvaldson purchased her in 1927 for the Hecla Lumber Company. In 1942 she was retired.

SS J.R. Spear: She was built in approximately 1910-1912 and used as a tugboat on Lake Manitoba. Later she was moved to Lake Winnipeg (and spent 4-5 years in drydock at Selkirk). She was purchased by Sigurdson Fisheries in 1932-33, at which point she was completely rebuilt and sailed as a fish freighter. During a storm in May of 1969 she went aground off Poplar Point. Luckily there was no "loss of life".

MS Newton: The MS Newton was a tug boat built by Purvis Boat Works at Selkirk in 1929 for the Northern Fish Company. A very large gas engine powered her. When the Northern Fish Company went into receivership in 1931, Olafson's Transportation of Riverton took over the Nelson and used her on the river from Winnipeg to English Brook. A fish company that was a branch of Keystone Fish Company later purchased her. In 1952 with a load of fish, she collided with the MS Luana and sank in the south basin of Lake Winnipeg, opposite Grand Beach.

MS Suzanne E.: Built by Captain Ed Nelson in 1946 at Selkirk for the Selkirk Fish Company, the MS Suzanne E was later acquired by the Booth Fish Company. On the night of Sept. 24, 1965, she was northbound in a strong northwest storm close to Berry Island when a terrific gust of wind sprang up and capsized the boat. Sole survivor Clifford Everett of Berens River reported that a pilothouse broke loose and the Captain, a deck hand, and he clung to it all night while it slowly drifted south past Deer Island. That was where the deck hand let go and perished. The Captain died just after they past Deer Island. Everett hung on to the pilothouse until it finally drifted ashore at Black Island. He walked the rocky shoreline for a number of miles before he eventually found a fishermen's cabin.

Fiskimatur
Lake Winnipeg Fish

Lake Winnipeg fish has always been a food staple for New Icelanders. Traditional accompaniments for fish dinners in New Iceland were and still are boiled potatoes, cabbage and apple slaw, beets, pickles and bread. Today there is an ever increasing respect for the ready availability of all varieties of local freshwater fish. When purchasing fresh fish, look for a mild, pleasant and characteristic odour; bright, clear eyes; a sheen on the scales; and flesh that is firm and elastic. For frozen fish, look for solidly frozen moisture-proof packaging with no signs of discoloration due to drying, freezer burn or a build-up of ice crystals; if the fish is ice glazed, be sure that the glaze is unbroken. Fish should never be overcooked and should always be served immediately for optimum enjoyment.

Lake Winnipeg Fiskur

Carp

Cyprinus carpio

Introduced to southern Manitoba waters in 1885, carp have spread to many regions of Manitoba, including Lake Winnipeg. They can be identified by their large scales and dorsal fin as well as the barbels at the corner of their mouths. Carp may reach sizes of up to 22 lbs. or more. Although carp are an important food fish in Asia and Europe, they have become undesirable in Manitoba. A growing market in the United States has encouraged commercial harvesting.

Channel Catfish (Kattfiskur)

A popular game fish, catfish commonly reach sizes of over 20 lbs. and are identified by its dusty grey colour and its long barbels which it uses like a nose. Their flesh is white, flaky and quite rich (making it very versatile for cooking).

Ictalurus punctatus

Fiskimatur

Hiodon alosoides

Acipenser fulvescens

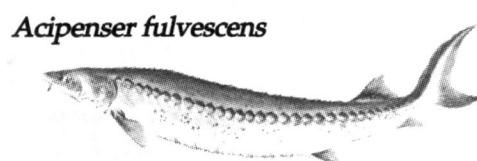

Coregonus clupeaformis

Lota lota

Esox lucius

Stizostedion vitreum

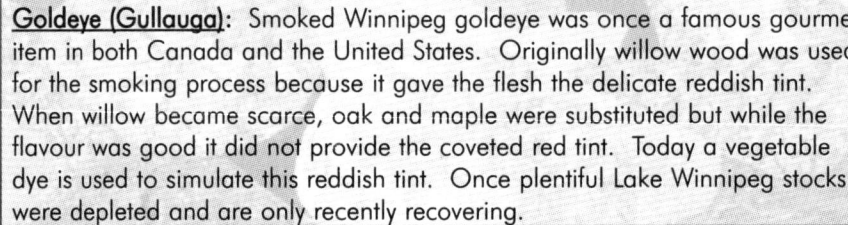

Goldeye (Gullauga): Smoked Winnipeg goldeye was once a famous gourmet item in both Canada and the United States. Originally willow wood was used for the smoking process because it gave the flesh the delicate reddish tint. When willow became scarce, oak and maple were substituted but while the flavour was good it did not provide the coveted red tint. Today a vegetable dye is used to simulate this reddish tint. Once plentiful Lake Winnipeg stocks were depleted and are only recently recovering.

Lake Sturgeon (Styrja): Lake Winnipeg's largest fish, its skeleton is made of cartilage rather than bone, and it can live over 100 years. There are reports of fish that are 400 lb. and 7 feet long. Sturgeon became very popular and because of its slow reproductive rate and the adverse affects of man on its habitat, stocks once plentiful were destroyed decades ago. Now only found in Northern rivers such as the Nelson and the Saskatchewan and the Winnipeg River in the south. Today there is only a limited fishery allowed.

Lake Whitefish (Hvítfiskur): Found in cooler or deeper waters, lake whitefish has always been a popular fish for consumers and has maintained good commercial value. It is marketed fresh, frozen and also smoked. Whitefish roe is made into a type of caviar.

Maria (Burbot) (Keilur): This is the only freshwater fish of the codfish family. It has an unappealing eel-like appearance which has hindered its acceptance for the consumer but its meat is white, tender and flaky. It is also one of the best fish for smoking.

Northern Pike (Jackfish) (Pækur): Northern Pike is the most common game fish with hundreds of Master Angler fish caught each year. It is also an important commercial fish. There are numerous bones in the fillets which can be avoided by filleting methods or by cutting into steaks, keeping the bone attached to the spine.

Pickerel (Pikkur): Pickerel (also known as "walleye") is in great demand commercially and by anglers. Its overwhelming popularity with chefs and home cooks is due to its versatility and white and flaky flesh. When caught, most pickerel weigh between one and two kilograms (two to five pounds).

Lake Winnipeg Fish

Stizostedion canadense

Aplodinotus grunniens

Coregonus artedii

Castomus commersoni

Perca flavescens

Saugers: Saugers belong to the same family as walleye and perch. Their flesh is so similar to walleye that commercially they are sold as one and the same. They are an important commercial fish but less popular than walleye with anglers due to their smaller size.

Sunfish or Silver Bass (Freshwater Drum) (Sólfiskur): Sunfish is not commercially harvested and is often overlooked by anglers. It has a rich oily flesh -good poached, in chowders, on the grill, or smoked.

Tullibee (Cisco or Lake Herring): Tullibee are primarily a commercial species found in deeper cooler waters. It is identified by many as a type of small whitefish. Distinguishable from whitefish by a lower jaw that is longer than the small upper jaw. It is also suitable for smoking.

White Sucker (Sögfiskur): White suckers are harvested by commercial fishermen and mainly exported from Canada. Suckers can be filleted and pan-fried. They can be ground for fish patties or canned.

Yellow Perch: Yellow perch, a cousin of the walleye and sauger, is also an important commercial fish. The flesh is tender and tasty and is good pan fried or barbecued whole with the skin on.

Fiskimatur

Lois Olafson's Baked Lake Winnipeg Whitefish

<u>Stuffing:</u>
1/3 lb. bacon, cut in 1/2 inch pieces
1/2 cup diced celery
1/2 cup chopped onion
1/2 cup chopped green pepper
3 cups bread crumbs
1 tbsp. chopped fresh parsley, or
1/2 tsp. dried parsley
1/2 tsp. basil
1/2 tsp. thyme
1/2 tsp. sage
salt, pepper to taste

For a 3-5 lb. whitefish, baking time with stuffing would be approximately 40-60 minutes. To crisp the skin, open up the tin foil for the last 15 minutes or place under the broiler.

Dress fish by removing guts, fins and scales (head and tail may be left on). Rinse under cold running water. Pat dry with paper towel. Cut 1/4 inch deep slits every 2 inches along top side of fish, vertically. Sprinkle inside of cavity with salt. Place fish on a sheet of tin foil on rack in shallow roasting pan (a sheet large enough to bring up and over fish to cover loosely). Stuff loosely. Fill slits with softened butter and sprinkle top of fish with salt and pepper. Bake at 400° F for 10 minutes per inch of stuffed thickness (at thickest depth).

Stuffing

1. Fry bacon until crisp. Add celery, onions, and green pepper. Sauté together until softened.
2. Toss bread crumbs together with seasonings. Stir in bacon-vegetable mixture with a fork.

I did not use the bacon but liked the celery, onions and green pepper. Will make again...

*Joyce Benedictson
Gimli, Manitoba*

Mrs. G. F. Jonasson's Fish Fillets with Dressing on Top

2 lb. whitefish or pickerel fillets
1 quart (or less if preferred) stale bread crumbs as for stuffing
1 tsp. mixed poultry spices (thyme, marjoram, savory, etc.)
1/2 cup sautéed onions (colourless)
butter or oil to mix dressing
salt and pepper

1. Cut fillets into small servings. Place in oiled baking dish suitable for table service. Sprinkle with salt and pepper.
2. Mix ingredients for dressing together and sprinkle over top of fish.
3. Place in a hot oven, 500° F for 15 minutes. Cover fish for first 10 minutes to prevent dressing from browning too rapidly. Remove cover for last 5 minutes. Serve at once with tartare sauce.

Fiskur á Fati (Fish on a Platter)

Original quantities followed by conversions in ¼ amounts:
6kg, 3⅓ lb fish
salt, butter, breadcrumbs
250g, ⅓ cup browned butter
2½ kg, 1½ lb (approx.) potatoes

The fish is cleaned, flattened, and cut into suitably sized pieces and sprinkled with salt; then dried after 20-30 minutes. Pieces of butter are put on the platter (baking pan) here and there, rusk (dry bread) crumbs sprinkled over that. The pieces are arranged on the platter without overlapping. Pieces of butter are dotted here and there and then the rusk crumbs are sprinkled over the top. When the oven is well heated, the fish is allowed to bake for 30-45 minutes. Browned butter is poured over this and it is served with potatoes.

This recipe is similar to Mrs. G. F. Jonasson's Fish Fillets with Dressing on Top. Both offer a simple way to bake fish, topped with bread crumbs. The addition of spices and onions in Mrs. G. F. Jonasson's recipe would have been a later adaptation due to the availability of spices and changing tastes. It can be assumed that the New Iceland version would also have been served with potatoes and also possibly the browned butter (see Notes – Steiktur Fiskur -Fried Fish).

Pan-Fried Pickerel Fillets

2 lb. fish fillets
1 egg beaten
2 tbsp. milk
½ cup flour
salt, pepper
½ cup breadcrumbs, rolled
2 tbsp. butter
1 tbsp. oil

Bread crumbs may be omitted. Just dip fillets into eggs and milk and then into seasoned flour.

1. Clean fillets and cut into serving portions.
2. Beat egg and mix together with the milk.
3. Combine flour and season with salt and pepper to taste.
4. Toss fish in flour; dip into egg and milk and then into breadcrumbs.
5. Heat pan. Melt butter with oil in the pan. Fry fish on each side just until golden and fish flakes with a fork. (If desired, add one chopped onion to the pan while frying the fish.) Serve immediately.

This recipe works great. I tried a few variations. Instead of breadcrumbs- I use cornflake crumbs (very fine)-you can buy them in a box. I use butter only and lots of it. I mix lemon pepper in the flour and breadcrumbs or cayenne pepper or cajun spice for more zip!

Val Dryden
Selkirk, Manitoba

Steiktur Fiskur (Fried Fish)

Original quantities followed by conversions in ¼ amounts:
6kg, 3⅓ lb fish
salt, flour and a pinch of pepper
or egg and breadcrumbs
Fat to brown in
about 375g, 5 tbsp. browned butter
2½ kg, 1½ lb potatoes

The fish is cleaned, head removed, flattened and cut in suitably sized pieces. Sprinkle salt over them and let stand for 20-30 minutes. Then the pieces are dried well, coated with the flour with the pinch of pepper mixed in, or with beaten egg and breadcrumbs or just crumbs, then browned well on both sides.

The fish is arranged in two rows on a platter with the browned butter poured over, or it is served separately and served with boiled potatoes.

Pan-fried fish was a staple dish when the fish was fresh in Iceland and New Iceland. Each cook developed their own method and preference for flouring or coating with crumbs with an egg, an egg and milk or none at all and the fat to fry the fish in. Seasonings were just salt and pepper. A hot heavy pan was essential. Of interest when examining this recipe from the New Iceland standpoint is the salting of the fish and letting it stand for 20-30 minutes. This is an unfamiliar practice in New Iceland as the fish is freshwater.

While potatoes are the customary accompaniment for fish in New Iceland, 'browned butter.. poured over or served separately with boiled potatoes' has lost favour over time but was common with earlier generations. The butter was browned in a heavy pan over low heat or added to the scrapings in the pan in which the fish was fried in order to add flavour (as in deglazing). Then the butter was served poured over the fish and potatoes or in a gravy boat.

Recipes or references to pan-fried fish are rare in New Iceland cookbooks because it was considered everyday cooking. The preceding recipe for Pan-Fried Pickerel Fillets records what I learned at the side of my mother and Amma and the following tip is one they neglected to teach me.

Food Hints: *'Shake salt in the fat when frying fish, the fish will retain its shape and not break up.'*

(<u>Tried and True</u>, circa 1950)

Lake Winnipeg Fish

Ingibjorg Sigurgeirson McKillop's Boiled Whitefish, Sunfish and Goldeye

Place whitefish or sunfish in a pan of cold water, scrape off scales, cut off head, tail and fins, slit down soft centre, clean out insides. Place in fresh cold water, rinse and towel dry. Cut into 4 or 5 pieces depending on the size of the fish. Place in a pot of cold water to cover fish adding 1 tbsp. of salt. Boil rapidly for approximately 20 minutes.

Place several goldeye, one or two per person in a pan of cold water. Scrape; slit down centre of soft side; wash thoroughly. Place whole in a pot of cold water to cover fish, add 1 tsp. salt to water. Bring to a boil and boil briskly for 10 minutes. Lift with draining ladle, serve whole.

It was common practice to boil all variety of fish available but most particularly sunfish (silver bass), whitefish and goldeye.

Today it would be more usual to: Fillet or cut the fish into pieces and place in a pan with just a small amount of lightly salted water to barely cover. A few peppercorns, bay-leaf and parsley may be added. Simmer covered at medium heat just until the fish flakes with a fork (only a few minutes depending on the size of the fillets or pieces).

Oven Steamed Smoked Fish

1. Heat oven to 400° F.
2. Lay large pieces of foil over bottom of baking pan (size depending on how many fish or pieces you are steaming). Butter foil where you will place the fish. Pour a small quantity of water around the fish (about ½ cup for 4 goldeye). Fold up foil to seal, leaving a few small openings for steam to escape.
3. Place in hot oven and steam for 15-20 minutes.
4. Serve immediately or debone and chill for serving as an appetizer.

Fiskimatur

Mrs. J.G. Johannsson's Fiski Hveitbollur (Fish Dumplings)

2 cups fish (to be made of any kind of fish)
1 egg
2 tbsp. melted butter
½ cup flour, approximately
1 tsp. baking powder

1. Run fish through a food chopper so that there will be enough for 2 cups.
2. Add the egg and the melted butter. Sift the flour and baking powder. Stir into fish mixture to make a stiff dough.
3. Have ready a pot of boiling water and drop fish mixture from a spoon and boil for ½ hour.

Serve with drawn butter or white sauce.

If using raw fish, put through a food processor in the frozen state.

It was absolutely delicious! I did some variations - cooked the pickerel before measuring it, but I guess you could do it raw as well. I fried the pickerel in butter and it gave a nice flavour. Also I used chicken stock in the boiling process. I recommend making it this way as it was very tasty. I served it with a basic seasoned white sauce - I made one batch and everyone was looking for more! It was a terrific success and a great addition to the Icelandic foods section of our New Year's Eve Feast!

Connie Magnusson Schimnowski
Winnipeg, Manitoba

Laurie (Olafson) Jervis's Djúpsteiktur Fiskur (Deep-Fried Fish in Batter)

1 lb. pickerel, catfish or sunfish cut into serving size pieces
1 cup flour
1 tsp. baking powder
salt, pepper to season
½ tsp. paprika
1 cup beer

1. Combine dry ingredients and add beer. Mix well.
2. Dip fish into batter and deep-fry a few at a time until golden brown. Drain on paper towels.

I liked the easiness of the recipe and the idea of doing fish differently. The only problem was that the batter seemed to stick to my deep fryer. We loved it, calorie wise and all!!!

Marla Olafson-Karr
Winnipeg, Manitoba

Lake Winnipeg Fish

Plokkfiskur (Fish Stew)

4 tbsp. butter
4 tbsp. flour
2 cups milk
salt, pepper
½ cup diced celery
¼ cup diced onion
1-2 potatoes, boiled and cubed
(optional)
1½ cups flaked cooked fish

1. Sauté celery and onion in a little butter until softened or simmer in fish stock to cover. Set aside.
2. Prepare white sauce: Melt butter, add flour. Heat stirring for a few minutes. Add milk all at once stirring until sauce is well thickened.
3. Season with salt and pepper to taste.
4. Add celery, onion, potatoes and fish to the sauce. Heat through and serve with brown bread.

Roy and I thought it was delicious! I would make it again.

June Gilbart
Selkirk, Manitoba

Plokkfiskur (Fish Stew)

Original quantities followed by conversions in ⅓ amounts:
125g, ¼ cup margarine
225g, ½ cup flour
1¾ litres, 2¾ cups fresh milk
pepper, salt, sugar
1½ kg, 1 lb. leftover fish
2 kg, 1½ lb. or 3-4 medium potatoes

The white sauce is made from the margarine and flour, thinned with hot milk. Pepper, salt and sugar are added to taste. Then the fish, in small pieces, and lastly the potatoes, boiled and cut up, are all allowed to heat through well. Bread and butter are served with the stew.

Both recipes are basically the same with the exception of the celery and onion in the New Iceland version which is probably a later adaptation. Guðrún Ágústsdóttir (granddaughter of Guðrún Jónsdóttir- the writer of this recipe) adds the following advice: 'Rúgbrauð (a very dark, dense rye bread) and butter is essential. I make this plokkfiskur with 3 chopped green onions, that I put into the margarine before adding the flour. I don't use sugar. Some people serve with chopped green onions sprinkled over top and a little dijon mustard on the side.'

Fiskimatur

Helga Gerrard's Stappa (Hashed Fish and Potatoes)

whitefish, boiled in salted water until tender
potatoes, enough for the family, boiled and drained
hot milk
salt and pepper
butter

1. After the whitefish has been cooked, remove all skin and bones.
2. Mash the fish to flake.
3. Mash the potatoes and add enough hot milk to make them creamy and light.
4. Add the fish to the potatoes (one cup of fish to 2 cups of potatoes, approx.).
5. Season with salt and pepper. Add a pat of butter per serving.

I am writing you regarding the Icelandic dish which I had always called 'Stappa' which in my Icelandic dictionary is defined as 'hashed fish and potatoes'. Having mentioned this dish to several friends, I get the answer 'Yes, they remember having this dish' but no one really has a definite recipe. Probably this dish did not turn out the same each time it was made, depending on the size of the fish. It seems sensible to me now that when there were several small children in the family that boning the fish ahead of time like this would save a lot of time at the table when each child's portion of fish would have had to be cleared of bones. I think this recipe was probably used to extend the fish and like many 'homey' kinds of dishes was not deemed fancy enough for cookbooks.

Helga Gerrard
Strathclair, Manitoba

Mrs. Helga Jonsson's Novel Way of Serving Fish

2 cups fish (boned and flaked leftover or finely chopped or ground raw)
1 large onion
3-4 medium sized potatoes
salt, pepper
flour
1 cup milk (approx.)

1. Spread ½ the fish in a buttered baking dish. Cover with thin slices of raw onion and on this place a generous layer of thinly sliced raw potatoes. Sprinkle with salt and pepper and dredge well with flour. Repeat these three layers, then pour in enough milk to show through the top layer.
2. Dot with butter, and bake at 375° F for about 45 minutes for raw fish or until potatoes are cooked (uncovered for the last 10-15 minutes).

An excellent dish to serve for a family supper.

Johanna Wilson
Winnipeg, Manitoba

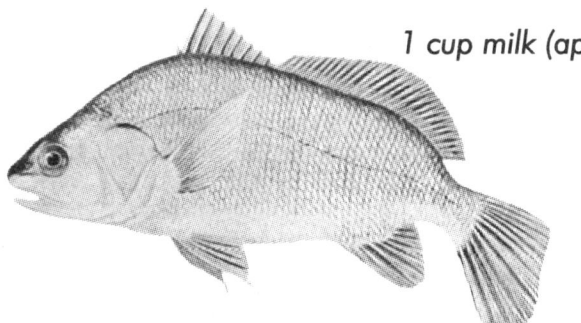

Mrs. L. Stevens's Fish Scallops

1 cup tomatoes
1 small onion, minced
1 bay leaf
salt, pepper
4-6 strips bacon, sliced in ½-inch pieces
1 tbsp. flour
1 cup flaked fish
1 cup grated cheese
buttered breadcrumbs

1. Heat tomatoes, onion and bay leaf with about ¼ cup water. Add salt and pepper to taste and allow to simmer.
2. Fry bacon and in the fat thus rendered stir in 1 tbsp. flour.
3. Add to hot tomato mixture and cook until thick.
4. Remove from heat and pour one layer in buttered baking dish. Then alternate with fish and grated cheese. Cover with breadcrumbs and more cheese if desired.
5. Bake at 375° F until crumbs are brown (20-30 minutes).

It was delicious as well as very easy to make. Great Brain Food!

Shannon Stefanson
Winnipeg, Manitoba

Fiskgratin í Skeljum (Fish au gratin in Shells)

Original quantities followed by conversions in ½ amounts:
180g, ⅓ cup margarine
180g, ⅔ cup flour
1⅛ litre, 2½ cups milk
8, 4 eggs
salt, sugar, pepper, mustard
approx. 1kg, 1lb. boiled fish
approx. 200g, ½ cup melted butter

Light (white) béchamel sauce is made and thinned with hot milk- placed in a bowl and allowed to cool. Stir in the egg yolks one at a time; beat 4-5 minutes with each addition. Salt and sugar are added to taste and a pinch of pepper and dry mustard and lastly the well beaten egg whites. The shells are rubbed well with melted butter or margarine, spread with breadcrumbs, then a layer of the béchamel sauce, then the fish in small pieces, then again with sauce, breadcrumbs spread over this, and melted butter drizzled over here and there. Bake at good heat 20 to 30 minutes. (Suggestion for good heat: 350°-375° F.)

The specification for baking in shells infers a sophistication in cooking and presentation. However as Guðrún Ágústsdóttir (granddaughter of Guðrún Jónsdóttir, the writer of this recipe) states, 'The gratin can also be baked in a bigger baking pan (or casserole). Wrap a napkin around the pan and serve immediately. Serve melted butter with this.' Prepared this way a comparison can be made with New Iceland dishes such as- Mrs. Helga Johnson's Novel Way of Serving Fish and Mrs. L. Stevens' Fish Scallops. All are variations for baking fish, either flaked or in small pieces with a sauce.

AÐ BÚA TIL FISKSÚPA (TO PREPARE FISH SOUP)　　　April 23, 1879

One plump whitefish or other similar fish shall be scaled and thoroughly cleaned, cut into small pieces and dropped into three or four quarts of boiling water with as much salt as required for flavour. The foam must be skimmed off and when the fish is boiled, it should be removed and placed in a bowl with a little of the broth or boiling water, salted well and let stand until it is to be used. Then the broth is strained in order to clarify it, poured back in the pot, with the addition of finely chopped onion together with cooked turnips, carrots, parsnips, or whatever else may be at hand, and boiled again until the onions are done. A small amount of potatoes can also be added. Just before taking the pot off the stove, a paste should be added, consisting of flour stirred into sour cream or milk, but it is not well to have it thick. If sour milk is not available, sweet milk may be used, and if there is no milk at all at hand, the thickener may be made of flour and water, but in that case the soup is not as good. After the thickening is added the soup should be just let come to a boil. Vinegar and pepper may be served with this soup for those who desire them ("sweet milk" refers to "fresh milk".)

　　If one wants to use a good deal of root vegetables it is better to cook them in a separate pot, or the soup will taste too strongly of them and that will detract from its flavour. The same is true of the preparation of meat soup; if root vegetables are to be added they should be boiled separately so the flavour of the turnips does not overwhelm that of the meat. Onions should not be added until 15-20 minutes before food is removed from the heat, for otherwise they lose their flavour.

　　Fish should be boiled briskly and placed in boiling water, never cold water.

Mrs. Petrina Eggertson's 'Grandma's Fish Soup'

2½ lb. fish
2 qts. water
½ cup prunes
1 tbsp. vinegar
1 cup brown sugar
2-3 bay leaves
½ cup flour

Boil fish till very soft. Strain, add other ingredients to the broth. Work flour into paste with a little cold water, stir into broth, and then boil (simmer) until prunes are cooked. Serve hot.

Serve the fish separately or return to the broth for reheating just prior to serving. I would suggest that the fish be cooked only until it has lost its translucency.

Fiskisúpa (Fish Soup)

Original quantities followed by conversions in ¼ amounts:
- 5kg, 2¾ lb. halibut
- 6 litres, 6-7 cups water
- 6 tsp., 1½ tsp. salt
- 300g, ½ cup flour
- 12-15, 3 bay leaves
- 275g, ⅓ cup sugar
- about 3 tbsp, 1 tbsp vinegar
- 250g, 3 oz. prunes (½ cup)

The halibut is cleaned and cut into rather large pieces, put into the water as well as the salt and vinegar. When this boils, remove the froth and then the pot is removed from the heat and kept in a warm place (on the stove) for 20-30 minutes.

The pieces are removed, salt sprinkled over them and kept warm. Strain the stock and add the bay leaves and the prunes which were previously washed. The flour is mixed with cold water and when the soup has boiled for 10 minutes, the flour mixture is stirred in bit by bit. When it comes to a boil, cook for another 10 minutes. Then the sugar and additional vinegar if needed.

Comparing this recipe with the one that appeared in Framfari (April 23, 1879) is especially interesting as the New Iceland recipe predates it. Guðrún Jónsdóttir's recipe does not include vegetables but the fish 'cut into rather large pieces' may indicate a common preference to serve the broth on its own. The fish and accompanying vegetables would then be served on a plate. This was a preference in New Iceland also, particularly with the men, and extends to other meat based stews and soups as well. This was very thrifty as the benefit was that from the fish or meat cooked in the water a tasty broth was also produced. In the Framfari recipe, it is recommended that 'if one wants to use a good deal of root vegetables it is better to cook them in a separate pot, or the soup will taste too strongly of them and that will detract from its flavour.' This suggests not only the preference for a stock that is concentrated in flavour from the fish but that it is understood that it may be served separately if vegetables were plentiful at the time. Both recipes are thickened with flour with the difference being that the New Iceland recipe uses milk or sour cream instead of water.

The sugar, vinegar and prunes in this recipe indicates a sweet sour taste to the broth. Sugar is not included in the Framfari recipe but the addition of root vegetables like turnips, carrots and parsnips would add sweetness and it is stated that 'vinegar and pepper may be served with this soup for those who desire them.'

The best comparison is to Mrs. Petrina Eggertson's 'Grandma's Fish Soup' from **Cook Book** (1930). The recipes are almost identical. The inclusion of prunes in both recipes is of particular interest because today this combination would be considered unusual.

Fiskimatur

Fiskibollur (Fish Balls)

The recipe variations for fiskibollur are unlimited. Some cooks begin with raw fish and others with cooked, flaked fish, which is a tasty way to make use of leftover fish. They can be boiled, pan or deep fried. Sometimes vegetables are added, especially potatoes and onion. These recipes are very basically seasoned, but today we might consider using other spices and herbs. Serve for dinner with rice or potatoes and sautéd onions. Tomato, curry, tartare and white are the customary sauces. Again there is an opportunity for innovation with spicy sauces, salsas or chutneys. They may also be served as an hors d'oeuvre with a dip.

Mrs. J.G. Christie's Fiskibollur

1 lb. fresh fillets
2 tbsp. flour and 2 tbsp. potato flour
(or 4 tbsp. flour)
2 tbsp. melted butter
½ cup milk
1 tsp. mace
1 tsp. salt, ½ tsp. pepper (or to taste)

1. Scrape fish to a very fine pulp (mince fish) or put through the food chopper. (Today a food processor with a steel blade could be used.)
2. Mix the remaining ingredients together with the fish, combining well.
3. Form into balls, using about 1 tbsp. of the mixture and drop into boiling water. Boil for 10 minutes (or pan fry in butter).

I did not use any potato flour. For #3 in method I pan-fried rather than boiling them. I also put all the ingredients in the food processor-it would be better just to mince the fish in the food processor and then mix it into the other ingredients in a bowl by hand.

I froze some and heated them later in the microwave. They would be good when entertaining. I plan to make the recipe again.

Margaret Eyolfson
Winnipeg, Manitoba

Fiskfriggadellur

Original quantities followed by conversions in ¼ amounts:
6 kg fish = 2 kg ground fish,
3⅓ lbs. ground fish = 1 lb. ground fish
1, ¼ medium onion
4-5 tsp., 1 tsp. salt
8 tbsp., 2 tbsp. flour
8 tbsp., 2 tbsp. potato flour
1 tsp., ¼ tsp. white pepper
½ tsp., pinch of nutmeg
75 g, 1-2 tsp. melted butter
1-2, 1 egg
about ¾ litre, ¾ cup milk
lard or butter for browning
browned butter potatoes

The fish is washed, skinned and flattened, then put through the meat grinder 6 or 7 times with the onions. The ground fish is thoroughly cut in with the salt until it is viscous; then the flour, potato flour and spices are cut in. Place the fish mixture into a bowl and mix for ½-¾ of an hour. The egg and milk mixture is added a bit at a time. Shape into balls using a tablespoon and fry until light brown, either in butter, lard or margarine, 8-10 minutes over low heat. Place on a platter. Serve with potatoes. Pour browned butter over the fishballs.

The Danish word 'Friggadellur' (instead of 'bollur') is used here in reference to oval-shaped meatballs. This recipe is most similar to Mrs. J.G. Christie's Fiskibollur. Mace was specified in Mrs. Christie's recipe. However, nutmeg, as in this recipe, was also used in New Iceland as a matter of personal preference. Another difference is that Mrs. Christie adds another alternative for cooking the fiskibollur (dropping them into boiling water). Guðrun Agústsdóttir (granddaughter of the writer of this recipe) considers it very important to mix the fish for the length of time stated in the recipe. However, she finds it easier to add the salt and the beaten egg whites at the end of the mixing rather than the beginning.

Fiskibollur

1½ cups cooked, flaked fish
1½ cups mashed potatoes
1 egg well beaten
salt, pepper to season
fine breadcrumbs (optional)

1. Mix all ingredients together well. Form into balls or cakes.
2. Optional: Roll in breadcrumbs.
3. Fry in melted butter on all sides or deep fry until golden.

Delicious! Add a little Hy's if you like more zip to the taste. Fast and easy!

Alanna Goodman
Winnipeg, Manitoba

Fiskimatur

Joyce Benedictson's Fiskibollur

1 lb. fresh pickerel fillets
3-4 tbsp. flour
1 medium carrot, shredded
1 small onion, minced
salt, pepper to taste
1 egg

1. Mince fish fine or put through a meat grinder (today a food processor with steel blade could be used).
2. Mix remaining ingredients together with the fish. Combine well.
3. Form into balls, using about 1 tbsp. of the mixture. Pan fry in butter.

This recipe is great as an appetizer or as a main course. After forming the balls I placed them on a sheet of waxed paper and chilled them for 1 hour. They browned nicely. I served them with tartare sauce. They were a big hit!
Lenore Good
Winnipeg, Manitoba

FISKKÖKUR (FISHCAKES) — April 30, 1879

Cold leftovers of boiled fish are frequently thrown away or are unusable. We shall explain here a way of using them profitably. The skins, fins and bones shall be carefully cleaned from the fish, the flesh then shredded and mixed with potatoes with a spoon in a bowl, preferably a good wooden spoon. Salt should be added, finely chopped onion and pepper if available, and a little flour. A little milk may also be added along with one or two eggs depending upon the size of the fish, but then more flour is required. The mixture should be thick enough to form small cakes, then add flour so they don't stick to the fingers. Fry in butter or fat over a slow fire.

Lake Winnipeg Fish

Canning Fish

It is possible to can all varieties of fish using the following recipes. It is important to use a pressure canner and to bring to a temperature of 118° C. Different canners have varying fish canning process times. These recipes are here presented as originally written and therefore the times given may be ignored. Use glass jars in good condition with new metal lids and sealing rings. A perfect seal is very important. For metal lids -tighten as much as possible before placing in the canner. For glass lids with separate sealing rings -tighten as much as possible, then release one quarter turn before placing in the canner. When removed from canner, tighten up again.

Pack clean jars loosely leaving a 1-inch head space which allows the fish to boil and not disturb the seal. Jars packed with raw fish should be placed in a boiling water bath until the contents reach 78° C. Then tighten lids appropriately and place in canner.

Ingibjorg Sigurgeirson McKillop's Canned Fillets

2 tbsp. vegetable oil
1 tbsp. vinegar
1 tbsp. ketchup
1 tsp. salt

Clean fillets (saugers or pickerel). Cut into 2 inch cubes and place in pint jars. Pack, then place the ingredients in each pint. Seal jars and steam 90 minutes in preserving canner.

Fish may also be cut into steaks or rounds; halve or cut into smaller pieces if necessary. Tomato juice is an alternative for the ketchup. For 1 quart of fish: 3 tbsp. vinegar, 3 tbsp. vegetable oil, 1 tsp. salt (heaping) and 3-4 tbsp. tomato juice.

Fiskimatur

Ingibjorg Sigurgeirson McKillop's Canned Fish

1 tsp. pickling salt
¼ tsp. dry mustard
¼ tsp. pepper
1 onion, sliced
4 tbsp. tomato soup
7 tbsp. vinegar

Clean sunfish, whitefish or pickerel. Cut into small pieces, pack into sterile sealers. Combine all ingredients and add for each quart. Seal, turn back half turn (glass lids), steam for 3 hours. After steaming do not invert, just screw lid on tight.

Original recipe states pickling salt, I have read a similar recipe which calls for just salt in the same quantity.

Harðfiskur (Hardfish)

Harðfiskur is dried fish. Cleaned whole fish are split and hung up to dry on racks. The practice of drying fish in this fashion has diminished to a virtual non-existence here today and so most harðfiskur is imported from Iceland. Many might balk at the chewing required to consume harðfiskur but most Icelanders and New Icelanders consider it a delicacy. To eat, the fish is beaten and then torn into narrow strips spread with butter. The flavour is faintly fishy. Highly nutritious it must be credited with keeping Icelanders nourished for centuries.

Al Dryden's Harðfiskur

The following method of making harðfiskur was taught to me by my uncle, Gunnar Helgason, as taught to him by his father, Helgi Helgason. The best fish to make harðfiskur out of is Pickerel (Walleye Pike) but Saugers or Jackfish (Northern Pike) may also be used for this process. The best size of fish is 1.5 to 2 lbs. Jackfish can be larger.

The fish should be scaled. The old boys always said that a fish was not cleaned properly until it was scaled. This also helps to keep the fish from curling up in the drying process.

Once the fish is scaled the proper way of cutting the fish is a little different than most are accustomed to. Take the cheeks out now if you

want to save them. The fish is then held belly up and cut high on the gullet. Then cut back and down, removing the gills and the rest of the head leaving the gullet in tact. The next step is a little tricky the first few times so don't be scared to try it as it really is not hard once you get used to it. The backbone is filleted out leaving the belly in tact.

Clean out all the guts. When you get all your fish cut and cleaned, wash fish thoroughly.

The last step is to hang the fish. To do this properly a notch is cut into the end of the gullet and a hole is made in the gullet approximately 1 inch from the top. String the fish on a rope or rod, whichever you prefer. If the notch and hole are in the proper spots, the fish will hang perfectly for drying. The notch allows the fish to lay back and open.

Hanging the fish in a shed will keep birds and cats away. I do not use any salt. The fish should be hung in early spring when there are not flies and it is still freezing at night. Once the fish has a hard skin on it and the drying process has started the flies will not bother the fish. When the fish turns white, enjoy.

If you want to make harðfiskur in the summer, then you will have to salt it and hang it in a screened box to keep the flies off. I find that this process does not make the best harðfiskur. When you are satisfied that the harðfiskur is ready to eat, it should be kept in the freezer as it may turn yellow if left outside too long.

Ingibjorg Sigurgeirson McKillop's Harðfiskur

As many pickerel as desired, wash thoroughly, cut off heads, fins and tails. Slit down centre soft side. Clean out, wash inside of fish. Spread open, cut 2 inch slit in top of spine part, 1 inch down. String onto 7 or 8 foot long wooden slab, 1 inch deep, ¼ inch wide. Hang out to dry, away from flies, crows and rain. The spring is an excellent time if there is a verandah. The drying takes a good 3 weeks. To serve, place skin side on a stone and with clean hammer, pound meat soft. It is eaten with the hands, chunk at a time, dipped in hard butter.

Fiskimatur

Ingibjorg Sigurgeirson McKillop's Platfiskur (Flattened Fish)

Several large pickerel, remove heads, fins and tails. Slit down centre soft side, wash clean, spread flat and salt real well. This should be done in early spring, spread (skin down) on house roof and let dry 10 days. Wash again, cut in serving pieces and boil 20 minutes. Do not add salt.

Ingibjorg Sigurgeirson McKillop's Fish Liver Sausage

25 fish livers
1½ tsp. sage
½ tsp. pepper
1½ tsp. salt
4 cups milk
3 cups oatmeal
1 cup flour

Soak liver overnight in a little salt water, skin and mince twice. Add ingredients as given, add more flour and oatmeal to make a smooth consistency. Ladle into cotton bags, 4 x 8 inches sew top, place in boiling water, boil 2-3 hours.

Ingibjorg Sigurgeirson McKillop's Soured Catfish Heads

Clean any number of catfish heads, remove insides and eyes. Boil in well-salted water, 20 to 30 minutes. In a 5 gallon stone crock put 3 gallons buttermilk, into this place the boiled catfish, making sure they are completely covered. Cure 10 days, serve cold.

Forrétir (Hors d'oeuvre)

Smoked Goldeye Pâté

2 medium sized smoked goldeyes
1 8oz. pkg. cream cheese, softened
2 tsp. drained horseradish
juice of ½ lemon
a few drops of worcestershire sauce

1. Wrap goldeyes loosely in foil with ¼ cup water. Steam in 400° F oven for approximately 15 minutes. Debone fish while warm (retain 1 tail and set of fins for presentation).
2. Combine flaked fish with remaining ingredients, beating until smooth.
3. Chill in bowl for several hours or overnight.

To present pâté: Empty contents of bowl onto a sheet of waxed paper, fold waxed paper over top and shape mixture into a fish shape with your hands. Lift fish-shaped pâté on to a serving platter. Smooth with a knife if necessary. Place rinsed and dried tail and fins appropriately. Place a thin slice of a pimento stuffed olive for the eye. Arrange flaked almonds to resemble scales. To complete the presentation, slice a lemon thinly. Cut slices in half. Arrange fanned around pâté. Garnish with parsley. Refrigerate until serving time.

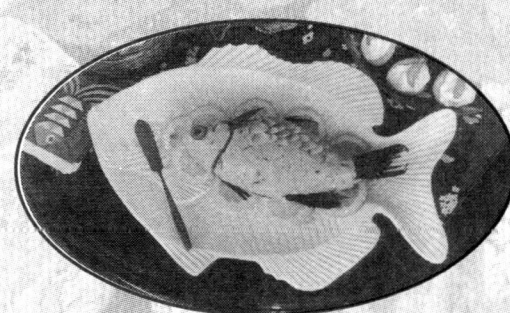

Smoked Fish Appetizers

Arrange steamed and deboned smoked fish, thinly sliced dark breads such as Icelandic Brown and crackers on serving platters. Complement with your preference of tomato butter, dilled cream cheese and mustard dill and horseradish sauces in small bowls. Guests prepare their canapes by spreading the tomato butter or dilled cream cheese on the bread and laying fish on top or by placing the fish directly on the bread and spooning a little of the mustard dill or horseradish sauce over. Cocktail picks or forks may be provided for simply dipping the fish.

Fiskimatur

Tomato Butter

8 tbsp. butter
2 tbsp. tomato paste
pinch of salt and sugar
freshly ground pepper, to taste

1. Cream butter. Beat in remaining ingredients.
2. Transfer to serving bowl and chill.

Dilled Cream Cheese

1 8oz. pkg. of cream cheese, softened
2 tbsp. green onion, finely chopped
1-2 tbsp. fresh dillweed, snipped fine
or
½ -1 tsp. dried dillweed
generous squeeze of lemon juice
dash of worcestershire sauce
2 tbsp. pimento-stuffed olives, finely chopped (optional)
salt, freshly ground pepper to taste
cream (optional)

1. Combine all ingredients except cream. Beat until smooth. Add a little cream if you prefer a thinner consistency.
2. Transfer to a serving bowl and chill.

Mustard Dill Sauce

½ cup dijon style mustard
2 tsp. dry mustard
⅓ cup sugar
¼ cup white vinegar
⅔ cup olive oil
½ cup fresh dillweed, snipped fine
pinch of salt

1. Combine the mustard, dry mustard and sugar in a small mixing bowl.
2. Whisk in the vinegar. Continue to whisk as you gradually add the oil.
3. Stir in the dillweed and salt.
4. Transfer to a serving bowl and chill.

Horseradish Sauce

1 8oz. pkg. of cream cheese
¼ cup horseradish
¼ cup celery, finely chopped
1 tbsp. parsley, snipped fine
1 green onion, finely chopped
½ cup sour cream
2 tbsp. lemon juice
dash worcestershire sauce

1. Combine all ingredients together, blending well
2. Transfer to a serving bowl and chill.

Pickerel in Orange-Tarragon Marinade

2 lb. pickerel fillets

Marinade
⅓ cup freshly squeezed orange juice
peel of one orange, cut into very fine strips
¼ cup olive oil
3 tbsp. white vinegar
1½ tsp. dried tarragon leaves
1 tsp. salt
⅛ tsp. white or lemon pepper
¼ cup chopped green onion
1 clove garlic, minced
2 bay leaves
1 green pepper, cut into very fine strips
juice of lemon to taste

1. Day before: Steam pickerel fillets and arrange in shallow glass dish.
2. Blend marinade ingredients together and pour over fish. Cover tightly and refrigerate at least 12 hours, basting occasionally.

Fiskimatur

Fish Seviche

¾ cup lemon juice
¾ cup lime juice
¼ cup olive oil
2 tsp. salt
½ tsp. minced garlic
freshly ground pepper to taste
2 lb. fish fillets,
cut crosswise into ½ inch strips
2 fresh hot peppers, seeded and
chopped (optional)
1 pint cherry tomatoes, halved and
seeded
1 red onion, chopped
1 green pepper, coarsely chopped
¼ cup fresh coriander, minced

1. Combine juices, oil, salt, garlic and pepper in a shallow ceramic or glass bowl.
2. Add the fish and peppers to the bowl. Chill, covered, stirring occasionally to coat fish with the marinade for 2 hours or until the fish is opaque.
3. Add the tomatoes, onion, green pepper and coriander. Toss lightly to mix well. Chill, covered for one hour. Drain and serve with cocktail picks or forks.

Profiteroles with Wild Rice and Fish Salad

1 cup water
½ cup butter
1 cup flour
4 eggs

1. Heat water and butter in medium sized saucepan until butter melts and water comes to a boil.
2. Add flour all at once. Continue cooking and stirring until dough forms a ball and clears sides of pan. Remove from heat. Place dough in a small mixmaster bowl. Cool for 5 minutes.
3. Beat in eggs, one at a time, beating well after each addition.
4. Drop by ½ teaspoonfuls onto a lightly greased baking sheet.
5. Bake at 350° F for 15-20 minutes or until puffed and lightly golden brown. Cool.

To fill: Split each puff horizontally, but not through one side. Spoon filling into the opening. These puffs may be baked ahead, and frozen. The day you are serving, remove from freezer and cut and fill while still cold.

Wild Rice and Fish Salad Filling

1 cup wild rice
½ -¾ cups steamed and flaked smoked fish
1 tbsp. lemon juice
¼ cup green pepper, finely chopped
¼ cup pimento, finely chopped
⅓ cup mayonnaise
1 tbsp. Russian style dressing
salt, freshly ground pepper to taste

1. Cook rice, cool.
2. Sprinkle lemon juice over fish and toss lightly. Add remaining ingredients and toss together to combine well. Add more mayonnaise if the mixture is dry.

Makes approximately 6 dozen hors d'oeuvre.

Pönnukökur with Tomato-Artichoke Heart and Fish Salad

<u>Tomato-Artichoke Heart and Fish Salad</u>
2 medium-sized tomatoes, seeded and finely chopped
½ cup green pepper, finely chopped
2 green onions, finely chopped
2 tbsp. capers
¼-½ tsp. dried oregano
¼-½ tsp. dried basil
1 cup artichoke hearts, drained and chopped
2-3 tbsp. grated parmesan cheese
1 tbsp. lemon juice
dash of Worcestershire sauce
freshly ground pepper to taste
1 cup smoked or cooked fish, flaked

1. Pönnukökur: Prepare as directed in Kaffibrauð (Sweet Breads and Fried Cakes), omitting sugar, spices and flavourings.
2. Prepare tomato-artichoke heart and fish salad. Toss all ingredients together lightly and combine well. Chill.
3. Fold pönnukökur in half, and then fold again in thirds to form a cone-shaped triangle; open up centre folds and fill. Or cut the pönnukökur in half. Fold in half, then in quarters. Fill opening.

A smaller-sized pönnukökur is daintier and easier for guests to pick up. Crisp folded pönnukökur by standing up in muffin pan cups at 350° F for 10-15 minutes before filling; cucumber sauce may be served alongside to spoon over individually (see "Cucumber Sauce" p. 67). Spices and herbs may be varied in the salad or batter, e.g. dillweed is wonderful in the batter, and numerous other fillings may be used. If you have a filling that would be best served hot, fill and bake at 400° F for 5-10 minutes depending on size.

Fiskimatur

Golden Whitefish Caviar on Rosettes

1. Rosettes: Prepare as directed in Kaffibrauð (Sweet Breads and Fried Cakes), omitting the sugar.
2. Recrisp just before serving: Place upside down on a baking sheet. Heat in 400° F oven for 2-4 minutes depending on how many you are serving.

To serve: Spoon a dollop of whipped cream on each rosette. Sprinkle a small amount of crumbled hard cooked egg, finely chopped red onion and then a small spoonful of caviar in the centre. Set out lemon wedges.

Fiskréttir (Fish Entrées)

Garden Medley Pickerel

1 – 1½ lb. pickerel fillets
1½ tbsp. butter
1 medium green bell pepper, or ½ green and ½ red bell peppers; sliced in fine rings
2 medium tomatoes, cut in ½ inch chunks
2 green onions, chopped
1-2 tbsp. fresh parsley, minced
½ lemon
1 tsp. worcestershire sauce
salt, pepper (freshly ground)

Serves 4-6.

1. Preheat oven to 400° F.
2. Arrange fillets in buttered baking pan just large enough to hold fish in a single layer. Dot with 1 tbsp. butter.
3. Layer over fillets in the following order: bell pepper rings, tomato chunks, green onion and parsley.
4. Squeeze lemon and sprinkle worcestershire sauce over all. Season to taste.
5. Cover loosely with foil and bake for about 20 minutes or until fish flakes easily.

To serve: With a flat spatula lift fillets covered with vegetables onto plates. Spoon sauce from baking pan over each serving. Pass Cucumber Sauce. <u>As a filling for Dill Pönnukökur</u>, lift fillets as above onto right side of pönnukökur. Spoon baking sauce over fillets. Fold left half over. Spoon Cucumber Sauce over.

Dill Pönnukökur (Thin Pancakes)

Prepare pönnukökur as directed in Kaffibrauð (Sweet Breads and Fried Cakes), omitting sugar, spices and flavourings. Add approx. ¼ cup fresh dill, snipped finely. Use 1 tsp. dried if fresh is not available.

Suggestion: As the pönnukökur recipes will yield more than is required for this dish, you may choose to divide the batter in half. Add dill to one half and sugar, spices and flavourings according to the recipe to the other, or freeze remaining dill pönnukökur for another time.

Cucumber Sauce

1½ cups skyr or plain yogurt
3-4 inches cucumber, halved lengthwise,
each half cut into 3 lengths and sliced fine
2 green onions sliced fine
½ tsp. minced garlic (or to taste)
1 tsp. lemon juice
¼ tsp. salt

1. Combine all ingredients together.
2. Chill for several hours allowing flavours to blend.

Pickerel Amandine

1- 1½ lb. pickerel fillets
2½ cups fine breadcrumbs, made from day old bread
1 cup sliced blanched almonds, toasted lightly
¼ cup fresh parsley, minced
3 eggs whites
½ cup clarified butter
(instructions following recipe)

1. Combine crumbs, almonds and parsley in shallow bowl.
2. Beat egg whites lightly in another shallow bowl.
3. Dip fillets into the egg whites and then into the crumb mixture (Tip: Press down on the fillets with waxed paper under your hand. Lift out of crumbs and flatten between sheets of waxed paper pressing gently but firmly to insure that the crumb mixture will stick).
4. Arrange fillets on a dinner plate lined with waxed paper in a single layer. Lay waxed paper over and top with another dinner plate for weight. Chill for 30 minutes.

5. Heat butter in large skillet over medium high heat. Sauté for 1-2 minutes on each side or until fillets are golden and fish flakes easily.
6. Transfer to heated platter or serve immediately. Garnish with a sprig of parsley and lemon slice or wedge.

Serves 4-6.

Clarified Butter
1. Melt ¾ cup butter over low heat.
2. Remove from heat; let stand for 3 minutes; skim the froth.
3. Strain through a sieve lined with cheesecloth leaving milky solids in the bottom of the pan.

Yield: approximately ½ cup.

Tomato-Mushroom Stuffed Whitefish

1 whole whitefish, about 3-5 lbs.
4 slices bacon, cut in ¼ inch pieces or 2 tbsp. butter
1½ cups fresh mushrooms, sliced
3 medium sized firm ripe tomatoes; cut in quarters, remove seeds and chop coarsely
2 tbsp. fresh parsley, minced
2 tbsp. green onions or chives, finely sliced
juice of ½ lemon

1. Dress fish by removing guts, fins, scales (head and tail may be left on). Rinse under cold running water. Pat dry with paper towels and sprinkle lightly with salt and pepper inside cavity and out.
2. Fry bacon until crisp or melt butter in medium-sized skillet (olive or vegetable oil may also be used).
3. Add mushrooms and tomatoes. Sauté until the mushrooms have lost some of their water content and the mixture is thick. Add parsley, onions and lemon juice. Season with salt and pepper to taste.
4. Lay the fish in a buttered shallow baking pan or on a wide sheet of heavy-duty foil (buttered under fish) set on a shallow baking pan for oven baking or doubling the foil for the barbecue.
5. Stuff the fish with the tomato-mushroom mixture. Place any excess stuffing along side the fish.

1-2 tbsp. softened butter
salt, freshly ground pepper
3 tbsp. fine bread crumbs (optional)

6. Cut slashes across the fish ¼ inch deep and about 1½ inch apart. Pat a little softened butter into each slash. Cover baking-pan with foil or wrap up foil package securely.
7. Bake in oven at 375°-400° F or grill over medium heat for 10 minutes per inch of stuffed thickness (at thickest depth -approx. 30-40 minutes) or until fish has lost its translucency and flakes easily. Test by inserting a fork into the fish. Cooking time will vary with the size of the fish and the heat intensity of the barbecue, if grilling. Optional: Remove foil or open up foil package; sprinkle with bread crumbs and broil until crumbs are lightly browned.
8. Serve fish from baking pan or move gently from foil to a heated platter. Spoon pan juices and hollandaise sauce over each serving.

Serves 6-8 (depending on the weight of the whitefish).

Hollandaise Sauce

¼ cup soft butter
2 tbsp. flour
3 eggs yolks
1½ cups fish broth*
¼ tsp. sugar
juice of ½ lemon
salt, freshly ground pepper
*Substitutes: dried seafood stock concentrate (prepare as directed); or bottled clam juice

1. In the top of a double boiler, mix the butter and flour together until smooth. Add the egg yolks one at a time, stirring until well combined.
2. Place over, not in, boiling water and slowly whisk in the fish broth; keeping the sauce smooth.
3. Cook, stirring, until thickened and add the sugar, lemon juice and salt, pepper to taste. Remove from heat and serve immediately.

Fiskimatur

Provençal Sauce for Fish

2 tbsp. olive oil
1 medium sized green pepper, cut into fine strips
1 medium onion, sliced fine
1 tsp. sugar
1 28oz. or 796ml. can of tomatoes, drained and chopped, reserve juice
1 garlic clove, minced
strips of peel from 1 orange
¼ cup anise liqueur
2 tsp. Herbes de Provence*
1 tsp. dried thyme leaves
1 tbsp. fresh parsley, chopped
salt and freshly ground pepper to taste
*Substitute: ½ tsp. dried lavender, ½ tsp. dried rosemary and ½ tsp. crushed fennel seed

1. Heat oil in skillet. Add green pepper and onion. Sprinkle with sugar. Sauté for about 5 minutes.
2. Add tomatoes and cook on high heat for about 3 minutes to thicken.
3. Reduce heat to low. Add the reserved tomato juice and remaining ingredients. Cover partially with lid and simmer for about 30 minutes until sauce has thickened and vegetables are soft.

For serving over 4-6 portions of broiled or pan-fried fish steaks or fillets.

Pickerel Chowder

6 slices bacon
1 garlic clove, minced
1 celery stalk, chopped
¼-½ cup each of red and green bell peppers, chopped
1 medium sized onion, diced
2 cups potatoes, diced
1 cup mushrooms, sliced
2-3 tbsp. flour
½ cup dry white wine

1. Sauté bacon in a large soup pot (do not allow the pot bottom to become too browned).
2. Add the garlic, celery, peppers, onion, potatoes and mushrooms. Sprinkle the flour over the vegetables and sauté, tossing for about 15 minutes.
3. Add the wine and the fish stock to cover and simmer until the potatoes are just barely tender.
4. Add the pickerel and herbs. Cover and steam until the fish is opaque, about 8 minutes.
5. Add the corn, cream and milk to cover: Simmer on low heat, below

1½-2 cups fish stock, or to cover*
1½ - 2 lb. pickerel fillets, cut in chunks or pickerel cheeks
½ tsp. dried thyme, crumbled
1 can kernel corn, drained, optional
1 cup heavy cream
1½-2 cups milk, or to cover
salt and freshly ground pepper to taste
*Substitute: dried seafood stock concentrate (prepare as directed).

Serves 6-8.

boiling, until the flavours have blended, about 30 minutes. Season to taste.

Tip: Prepare a day ahead- Remove from heat after adding corn, cream and milk. Next day, simmer gently, until the flavours have blended and the chowder is hot.

'Fish on the Grill'

For the methods of grilling fish described I would emphasize you avoid overcooking. The common rule of ten minutes per inch of thawed fish thickness is only a guideline. Fish weight and texture, varying heat intensities and distance from the heat will have an effect on the cooking time. Test by inserting a fork into the fish. The fish is ready for serving as soon as it as lost its translucency and flakes easily.

Barbecued Whole Fish Using a Fish Grilling "Cage"

The wire fish "cage" or "basket" is designed to allow you to turn a whole fish easily to cook both sides. Oil the cage well to prevent sticking; lay the dressed fish inside and place on the barbecue grill.

To dress a whole fish: Remove guts, fins, scales (head and tail may be left on). Rinse fish quickly in cold water and dry with paper towelling.

Fiskimatur

Blackened Fish with Creole Sauce

1 whole fish: The recipe was tested using whitefish and northern pike (jackfish). Other varieties will be equally good. Approximate fish weight: 3-5 lbs. as determined by the size of the grilling cage.

¼-⅓ cup butter
juice of ½ lemon
½-1 tsp. minced garlic clove
Cajun Blackened Seasoning*
*Substitution: 1½ tsp. cayenne, 1 tsp. salt, 1½ tsp. freshly ground black pepper, 1 tbsp. dried leaf thyme — adjust quantities to your own preferences

This recipe is a summertime adaptation of Acadian (Cajun) and Creole cuisines originating in southern Louisiana. More typically the fish would be cooked in a hot iron skillet. The skin becomes crisp and very tasty. Regarding the seasonings: serious cooks would avidly discuss the ideal combinations of herbs for Cajun and Creole cuisines. However, there are pre-combined seasonings available. Later you may wish to develop your own blend. Creole Sauce, recipe following, may be prepared ahead. See also Fish Creole. Suggested accompaniments: rice and tossed green salad. Serves 6-8 (depending on the weight of the fish).

1. Dress fish and oil the grilling cage.
2. On low heat melt the butter in a small saucepan. Add garlic and lemon juice. To blend flavours stir occasionally for 5 minutes or so.
3. Brush the inside cavity with the butter mixture and sprinkle generously with the blackened seasoning. Optional: Stuff fish with onion, green or red pepper rings, or if you like it "hot" with green onion (lengths of 3-4 inches) and hot red pepper strips. Skewer and lace or sew shut.
4. Brush one side of the fish with the butter mixture and sprinkle generously with the blackened seasoning. Lay fish, buttered side down in the grilling cage and repeat on the other side. Close cage.
5. With barbecue at medium heat, place on the grill. Turn every 5-10 minutes, cooking time dependent on fish size. Test often.
6. Transfer to a heated platter and serve with Creole Sauce.

Creole Sauce

6 medium sized firm ripe tomatoes cut in quarters, remove seeds, and chop coarsely
¼ cup olive oil
¾ cup each of onion, green pepper, celery; coarsely chopped
½-1 tsp. minced garlic clove
¼ cup water
1 bay leaf
1 tsp. Cajun Creole Seasoning or to taste*
1 tbsp. cornstarch mixed with ¼ cup water

*Substitution: 1 tsp. paprika, ¼ tsp. cayenne, salt and freshly ground pepper to taste

1. Heat oil in skillet. Add onions, green pepper, celery and garlic. Cook, stirring about 5 minutes or until tender.
2. Add tomatoes, water, bay leaf and seasonings. Bring to a boil over high heat. Reduce heat to low and simmer partially covered for 20 minutes.
3. Add the cornstarch mixture. Stir for a few minutes until sauce thickens slightly. Discard bay leaf and season to taste. Serve at once or reheat while fish is cooking.

<u>Fish Creole</u>: Cut a firm fleshed fish such as catfish into chunks (approximately 1lb.) and add to Creole sauce during the simmering stage (2). Serve with rice and salad. Serves 4.

Fiskimatur

Fish Fillets Barbecued in Foil

This is a practical method for barbecuing pickerel and whitefish fillets as both tend to flake apart when placed directly on the grill. Use heavy duty foil; wrap folding the edges and turning them up at the ends to retain the juices. Even the simplest combination of butter, onions, and fillets wrapped in foil is delicious.

White Wine and Herbs

1-1½ lb. pickerel or white fish fillets
¼-½ lb. shellfish such as shrimp, scallops or mussels (cleaned, steamed and shelled), optional
1-2 tbsp. butter
1 small onion, sliced in rings
½ cup mushrooms, sliced
juice of ½ lemon
¼ cup dry white wine
1 tbsp. fresh parsley, chopped or ½ tsp. dried
½ tsp. tarragon
salt and freshly ground pepper to taste

Serves 4-6.

1. Spread one half of the butter in the centre of a large foil sheet where you will lay fillets in a single layer. Package only as many fillets as you can wrap up securely.
2. Layer shellfish, onion, mushrooms over fillets. Sprinkle herbs and seasoning over top. Moisten with wine and lemon juice. Dot with remaining butter. Seal up foil package.
3. Barbecue on medium high heat. Approximate cooking time: 8-12 minutes. Unwrap foil carefully to test. Suggested accompaniments; boiled new potatoes or rice and fresh garden vegetables.

Greek Fillets: Prepare as above layering chunks of tomato, zucchini, eggplant, onion rings and black olives over fillets. Season with oregano, rosemary and garlic and drizzle with lemon juice.

Lake Winnipeg Fish

Marinades for Grilling Fillets and Steaks

Silver Bass (Sunfish) fillets and catfish steaks are excellent fish to marinate and grill. Baste with marinade while cooking and turn to grill both sides. Pickerel and white fish fillets can be used as well if you place them on a sheet of foil on the grill and turn carefully. Approximate cooking time: 3-5 minutes each side for steaks depending on size.

An alternative to marinating before grilling is to baste with fresh lemon juice and melted butter (or oil). Variations: Add herbs to the basting mixture or after basting, sprinkle with caraway or sesame seeds while fish is grilling.

Note: marinated or fish basted with lemon juice and butter may be broiled as well.

Marinate fish for 3-6 hours, covered and refrigerated.

Hoisin

(makes 1 cup, sufficient for 1 - 1½ lb. fish)

Combine, stirring until well blended and sugar is dissolved: ½ cup hoisin sauce or sweet bean sauce, ¼ cup dry vermouth or dry white wine, 2 tbsp. sugar, ½ tsp. ginger or 1 tsp. finely grated, fresh ginger root, ½ tsp. minced garlic clove, juice of ½ lemon, 2 tbsp. green onion sliced thinly.

Mustard Dill

(makes 1½ cups, sufficient for 2 lb. fish)

Combine: ¼ cup dijon mustard, ¼ cup fresh lemon juice, 1 tsp. minced garlic clove, 2 tbsp. fresh dill, chopped or 1 tsp. dried dillweed, dash salt and freshly ground pepper. Add 1 cup olive oil in a stream whisking until well blended.

Lime and Ginger

(makes 1 cup, sufficient for 1 - 1½ lb. fish)

Combine, stirring until well blended and sugar is dissolved: ½ cup fresh lime juice, ⅓ cup olive oil, 3 tbsp. brown sugar, 2 tbsp. onion thinly sliced, ½ tsp. minced garlic clove, ½ tsp. ginger or 1 tsp. finely grated, fresh ginger root, dash salt and freshly ground pepper.

Kjötmatur og Súpur

Meat and Soups

Sunnudagssteikin - The Traditional Sunday Roast

In Iceland the traditional Sunday roast would be lamb as well as the most common kinds of wild game-reindeer, ptarmigan, geese and ducks. In earlier times, fresh mutton would have been eaten only occasionally and more likely than roasted was boiled with cabbage, turnips and potatoes, if available. In winter, mutton was eaten dried or hung. Sheep were the mainstay of the farms in Iceland, and they were also raised in New Iceland. Sheep raising gradually declined from the turn of the century and by the mid-1900's was quite unusual. Cows became predominant as they were better suited to the land in the region.

In New Iceland, the traditional Sunday roast came to include a greater variety of domesticated animals and fowl as they were acquired than was common in Iceland. Furthermore, the settlement area provided a greater variety of wild game: deer and moose (venison), geese, turkey, ducks, grouse, pheasants and prairie chicken.

The meat, poultry and wild game recipes included and this applies to the fish recipes as well, represent the everyday home cooking style that began in Iceland and continued in New Iceland. Out of necessity the cooking was -by our modern standards- plain with very little seasoning. However, many still favour this simple home cooking to more sophisticated cuisine when well-prepared and served with the traditional accompaniments.

Kjötmatur og Súpur

Sunnudagssteikin - Ofnbakað Lambalæri (Roast Leg of Lamb)
Ofnbakaður Lambahryggur (Roast Saddle of Lamb)

Serve with sugar browned potatoes (Brúnaðar Kartöflur), red cabbage, green peas and rhubarb conserve. Recipes for these accompaniments to be found in 'Grænmeti, Pækill og Niðursoðnir Ávextir (Vegetables, Pickles and Preserves)'.

1. Place in a roasting pan on a rack or grease under the meat with butter (excess fat can be removed).
2. Season the meat with salt and pepper. Dot with butter on top of the roast.
3. Roast at 450° F for 15-20 minutes, then lower to heat 350° F. Pour hot water or lambstock into the pan and roast for about 15 minutes per pound; basting with the stock. Additional water or stock may have to be added during the cooking.
4. While making gravy, place the roast under the broiler for 3-5 minutes for browning. Make gravy from the stock. If stock is fatty, skim. Thicken with flour and butter. Cream can be added. Season with salt and pepper to your liking (see also the currant jelly sauce recipe that follows).

We hosted an Icelandic dinner and invited some people of Icelandic descent as well as others (eight of us in total) but two couples had to cancel suddenly so there were four of us in the end. Needless to say there was so much food around we decided to repeat the performance the next day with Ernest's Mom, Dad his brother Eric and wife Barbara plus the three kids. I am saying all this because despite the number of people the comments were similar.

    The lamb was considered 'succulent'. We did a leg of lamb with the bone. The butcher had offered to butterfly it for us but I hesitated because I did not think they would have done that in the old days. A seven-year-old's comment: 'It's great!' He ate enough to convince me.

    I made the spiced rhubarb conserve. I did not plan to keep it forever, plus I did not have enough rhubarb, so I made a limited version of it. It tasted very good but no one believed it belonged with the lamb. It tasted too different to most people. Individually people liked the conserve.

    The red cabbage was a huge hit. Everyone loved it. It went well with the lamb. We did the potatoes too. They were good. I also served fresh garden peas. In the end we did not make gravy. We could have though as there were lots of good scraps.

Claire Gillis
Gimli, Manitoba

Roasting Meat

The following directions, time table, gravy and currant jelly sauce are all from the Gimli Lutheran Church cookbook *Tried and True* (1950). Oven temperatures are not provided. Recipes included descriptives such as very slow oven (200°-300° F), slow oven (300°-325° F), moderate oven (325°-400° F), hot oven (400°-450° F), very hot oven (450°-550° F).

Roasting Meat: Wipe, trim, tie or skewer the meat into shape. Place on a rack in a pan and place pieces of fat from the meat over it. Rub meat over with salt and dredge meat and pan with flour. Place in the hottest part of the oven to sear the outside and brown the flour; then move to lower shelf and reduce the temperature; baste meat every ten minutes until done, or use a covered roaster. (Suggestion: searing temperature of 425°-450°F and a roasting temperature of 325°-350°F.)

Time Table for Roasting:

Beef (rare)	10-12 min. per lb., 15 min. extra
Mutton	20 min. per lb., 20 min. extra
Veal	25-30 min. per lb., 20 min. extra
Chicken	3-4 lb. 1-1½ hours
Goose (7-8 lb.)	2½ -3 hours
Turkey (10 lb.)	3-4 hours
Duck (6-7 lb.)	2-2½ hours
Wild Duck	30 min.-1 hour

Gravy

In any roast pour off all but ¼ cup of fat for every ¼ cup flour used, cool a little and add flour, ½ tsp. salt, ¼ tsp. pepper. Add 2 cups boiling water or vegetable water slowly, stirring constantly. Boil 3 minutes.

Currant Jelly Sauce

To 1 cup gravy made to serve with roast lamb, add ½ cup currant jelly and 1 tbsp. lemon juice.

Mrs. M. Brynjolfson's Roast Stuffed Shoulder of Lamb with Brown Potatoes

3½ -4 lb. shoulder of lamb

<u>Dressing</u>
2 cups stale bread crumbs
1 tbsp. finely cut onion
1 tbsp. drippings
1 tbsp. chopped parsley
1 tsp. salt
⅛ tsp. pepper

1. Wipe lamb with damp cloth; debone and fill this pocket with dressing and sew up.
2. Put into hot oven (425° F) for 20 minutes. When well-browned, season with salt and pepper, add one cup cold water, and roast 45 minutes.
3. Add 1 qt. white potatoes, which have been washed, pared and boiled, and roast until potatoes are brown. Remove to a platter.
4. Add water to pan to make 2 cups of gravy. Thicken gravy by adding 1 tbsp. flour mixed with a little cold water. Season and cook until smooth.

Að Salta Kjöt til Reykingar (To Salt Meat for Smoking)

To smoke it is best to use the legs and sides, and it is best to salt it the day after slaughtering. A sharp pointed knife is used to poke holes in the thickest portion of the muscle in 2 or 3 places for putting in the saltpetre. The sides are put into boiling water and allowed to just come to the boil again; then taken out and cooled quickly; then rubbed well with salt. The meat is then put into a vessel or crock, salt and saltpetre in between the layers. Let it remain there for 6 – 7 days. Thin linen or gauze is sewn over the parts and then later smoked.

These directions are applicable for Hangikjöt (smoked lamb or mutton). Smoking was an essential method of meat preservation for centuries. Traditionalists still enjoy Hangikjöt particularly at Christmas and þorrablót (Winter feast – see Þorramatur p. 93)..

Traditional Christmas Eve Dinner

Soðið Hangikjöt (Boiled Smoked Lamb)

Serve hangikjöt with boiled or mashed potatoes, and green peas in white sauce (or cut the potatoes up small in the white sauce with the peas). Mashed turnips and Red or Browned Cabbage were also common accompaniments. The traditional dessert is Jólahrisgrjónagrautur (Christmas rice pudding).

In a pot bring water to boil (enough to immerse hangikjöt). Add meat. Boil for 45 minutes to 1 hour. Let meat cool in stock.

> This meal was a tradition on Christmas Eve in our home for as long as I can remember. We always had company, new and old friends were invited to take part in this wonderful event. The aroma of Christmas was evident everywhere in our home. Lots of love and friendship and always happy times.
>
> Brian Jakobson
> Winnipeg, Manitoba

A Christmas Eve in Iceland

We had the wonderful opportunity to spend Christmas 1995 in the home of good friends in Akureyri. The evening started about 6pm. with the entire family gathering in their finest clothing in a formal dining area.

The main course was Rjúpa or ptarmigan (wild chicken). These ptarmigan are highly sought after in the north for just this occasion. They had been skinned and the breasts were separated and removed from the bone. The legs became a delicacy in the kitchen later that night! The breasts were laid in fan shape around the platter and a creamy mushroom sauce accompanied this. They had been slightly seared and then poached, so that they remained a very light colour. They do not take much cooking, 1 hour or less. There were also the little potatoes, red cabbage (sweet and sour), cabbage coleslaw, and green peas to accompany this. It was wonderful! The dessert was the traditional rice pudding with one almond meant to allow someone to open the first gift. I did sense this was added at the last minute as the youngest member of our table received the almond. There was plenty of chocolates after and a drink of cognac.

Lorna and Terry Tergesen
Gimli, Manitoba

Kjötmatur og Súpur

Beef Pot Roast with Prunes

4 lb. pot roast
flour for dredging
3 tbsp. fat for browning
3 medium onions, sliced
½ lb. uncooked prunes
1 tsp. salt
⅛ tsp. pepper
1½ cups water
¼ cup vinegar
4 whole cloves

1. Soak prunes overnight.
2. Dredge roast in flour and brown on all sides in hot fat. Remove roast to heavy baking dish.
3. Cook onion in hot fat until golden and add to roast together with the fat.
4. Sprinkle with salt and pepper. Arrange the prunes around the roast. Add water, vinegar and cloves.
5. Cover tightly and bake in a 325° F oven until tender, about 3½ hours.

The recipe was easy to prepare. The meat was very tender and tasted very good. The gravy has a very distinctive taste and everything tasted just as good as leftovers. It's a keeper!

Kathy Kristjanson
Winnipeg, Manitoba

Kálfsragout með Sveskjum (Veal Stew with Prunes)

sliced veal, roasted or boiled
roast gravy
300g prunes
sugar, chutney

It is usual to use leftover roast. The prunes are washed, allowed to soak with a little water and cooked until they are soft. Usually the roast gravy is available, the cooked prunes are added with the sugar and chutney to taste. Then the veal slices are laid down and the whole is allowed to heat thoroughly without boiling. The meat is placed on a platter with the cooked potatoes around the meat.

The flavour outcome of this recipe would be very similar to Beef Pot Roast with Prunes. The prunes, gravy and chutney combination compares closely to the prunes, vinegar and cloves cooked with the pot roast.

Saddle of Venison

5-6 lbs. saddle of venison
4-6 strips of bacon
salt, pepper, powdered or minced garlic (if desired)
crushed juniper berries (optional)

1. Rub seasonings and berries into the meat; lay bacon slices over.
2. Roast at 450° F for 10-15 minutes. Pour some boiling water into the pan. Reduce heat to 325° F for about 1½ hours. Baste often.
3. Make gravy from stock using cream and some red currant jelly.

A saddle is the equivalent of a standing rib roast in beef. It is the middle section of chops left in tact to make the premier roast.

Venison Pot Roast

3-4 lb. venison roast
flour for dredging
3 tbsp. fat, oil for browning
salt and pepper
garlic or minced garlic (optional) to taste
1 onion, sliced
1 cup hot water

1. Dredge roast in flour and brown on all sides in hot fat. Remove meat to roaster pan.
2. Sprinkle with salt, pepper and garlic. Add the onions. Pour water over. Cover roaster and bake at 325° F for about 3 hours. Add water if necessary.
3. Muke a sauce from broth in the pan, scraping up any brown bits, thickening with flour and butter and then adding some cream and red currant jelly.

Ingibjorg Sigurgeirson McKillop's Roasted Wild Goose

1 wild goose
1½ tsp. salt
¾ tsp. pepper
1 tbsp. vinegar
1 onion
½ cup flour

1. Rub goose with salt, pepper and vinegar. Place peeled onion in cavity and let stand overnight.
2. Remove onion, dredge with flour and fill cavity with stuffing. Place in roasting pan, uncovered at 325° F. Roast 20-25 minutes per pound. Baste with juices in roaster.

Savoury Stuffing for Goose

8 cups bread crumbs
2 cups grated apples
1 cup drippings (fat)
1 cup diced celery
1½ tsp. poultry seasoning
1 small onion, minced
1½ tsp. salt
¼ tsp. pepper
¼ tsp. sage

1. Add onion, celery and seasonings to melted fat in heavy frying pan.
2. Brown slightly. Toss in bread crumbs until well combined. This will stuff a 10 lb. bird.

I followed the recipes for roasted wild goose and savoury stuffing exactly. It's actually as I have always prepared wild goose, with the exception of the vinegar. My family enjoyed the stuffing - especially with the addition of the grated apples.

Gail Thorvaldson
Thunder Bay, Ontario

Mrs. S.W. Sigurgeirson's Roast Turkey

Clean, stuff and truss the turkey. Rub entire surface with salt, brush with soft butter and dredge with flour. Place in hot oven (425°-450° F) and when well-browned reduce the heat (325°-350° F). Baste with fat in pan and add 2 cups of boiling water, to which ½ cup of melted butter may be added. Continue basting every 15 minutes until turkey is cooked, which will require about 4 hours for a 10 lb. turkey. During cooking process turn turkey frequently so that it may brown evenly.

Baked Grouse or Pheasant

Minced garlic, chopped green onions or shallots, mushrooms and thyme would be good additions.

Cut 2 grouse or pheasant into serving pieces and wash and dry. Dredge with flour, salt and pepper. Brown well in 3 tbsp. cooking oil. Place in baking dish in a single layer. Pour 1 qt. half and half cream over and sprinkle with parsley flakes. Bake at 325° F for 2 hours, adding a little more cream if necessary.

Mrs. O. Bjornson's Baked Chicken

Clean and cut up a young chicken. Roll in flour, brown in butter and place in rack of roaster. Pour a little water into the pan in which chicken was browned; season and pour into bottom of a roaster. Season chicken, cover and bake in a hot oven (375°-400° F) for 30 minutes to 1 hour, adding a little water if necessary. Add a cup of milk or cream to gravy and thicken with flour.

I followed the exact recipe. There were 6 of us for dinner. I only used salt and pepper and probably did not use enough because we found it extremely bland. The chicken was nice and moist but we all felt it needed more spices. We added stock such as oxo to the gravy and preferred it before we added the milk which added to the blandness. We felt this was no doubt tasty when eaten years ago but because our tastebuds are now more accustomed to herbs, spices and garlic in the 90's we found it bland!

D. Johanna Sigson
Saanichton, B.C.

Mrs. J.P. Markuson's Prairie Chicken "Icelandic Style"

1. Pluck and remove skin of chicken. Soak 4-5 hours in 1 part vinegar and 2 parts water, liquid to cover. Wash well and soak in milk overnight. Dry carefully.
2. Skewer legs to body and thread breast with strips of fat, salt pork or ham. Fry in butter.
3. Place in baking dish and pour over the following sauce: Melt 2 tbsp. butter and cook until light brown. Stir in 2 tbsp. flour. Add whole milk gradually to make a thin sauce. Add salt to taste and a pinch of sugar. This sauce should cover half of the chicken.
4. Bake at 325° F for 1 hour. Baste often. For more gravy add cream and butter.

Steiktar Rjúpur (Roast Ptarmigan)

Original quantities followed by conversions in ¼ amounts:
- 16, 4 ptarmigan
- 200, 50g side pork (bacon)
- milk plus water
- 1 tsp., ¼ tsp. pepper
- 3 tsp., ¾ tsp. salt
- approx. 200g, ¼ cup fat (skimmed from water in which hangikjöt is cooked)
- 1 litre, 1¼ cup milk
- a little bit of butter
- 3 tbsp., 1 tbsp. flour
- red currant jelly sauce
- approx. ⅛ litre, ¼ cup whipping cream
- 2½ kg, 1½ lbs. browned potatoes

Brúnaðar kartöflur ~ Sugar Browned Potatoes; Rauðkál ~ Red Cabbage; see recipes Grænmeti, Pækill og Niðursoðnir Ávextir (Vegetables, Pickles and Preserves).

The ptarmigan are washed. Be careful to wash away all the blood. The side pork (bacon) is best fresh but it could be smoked or salted, which is cut into thin slices and put into slits in the breast (larding), 4 slices on each side of the bird. The ptarmigan are then arranged in a bowl. Boiled milk is poured over them and they are allowed to soak until the next day; then they are removed and allowed to drain, dried well and rubbed inside and outside with the salt and pepper blended together. The fat is put into the heated pan, when it smokes, the ptarmigan are put in the pan and browned well on all sides, beginning with the breast. Milk and butter are heated together, then a little bit of boiling water is added and then the ptarmigan are arranged in the pan (may be layered if necessary). Half of the milk is poured over them and then covered with a tight fitting lid and they are allowed to cook slowly for 1¼ to 1½ hours. In the last half hour, the ptarmigan are removed to another pan and kept warm, while the sauce (gravy) is made. The flour is mixed with cold milk and added, when it boils again in the pot let it simmer for 8-10 minutes. The red currant jelly is added to taste (if you do not have red currant jelly, use sugar). Lastly the whipped cream is stirred in carefully. The ptarmigan are cut up, first the legs, then the breast in two pieces; the back is not served. They are arranged on a platter on a little bit of the sauce, while the rest is placed in a sauce dish (gravy boat). Sugar-browned potatoes are served as well as preserves or a compote such as pear compote or red cabbage.

Ptarmigan resemble grouse and are identified by the covering of short feathers on their feet. Ptarmigan in Iceland are light brown with dark specks in summer and white specks in winter. As they are hunted in early winter until Christmas, they are served for traditional Christmas dinners in many homes (see Lorna and Terry Tergeson's comment – "A Christmas Eve in New Iceland" p. 81, and the following recipe, a modern version of Rjúpa). In New Iceland, prairie chicken was substituted for ptarmigan although the meat of the prairie chicken is lighter and more mildly flavoured. In early years when fresh meat was prized, prairie chicken would often be served at Christmas.

There are definite similarities between this recipe and Mrs. J.P. Markuson's Prairie Chicken 'Icelandic Style' (interesting to note that 'Icelandic Style' was included in the original title). In both recipes the method of cooking is basically the same. Most significant is that both employ a milk-based baking sauce.

Guðrún Ágústsdóttir's Steiktar Rjúpur (Roast Ptarmigan) – A Modern Version

1-2 ptarmigan per person
prunes, 1-2 per ptarmigan
salt
pepper

Fry the ptarmigan in butter in a frying pan. Put in a pot with the breast side down, pour water over, just enough to cover. Add prunes. Cook for one hour. Use the stock for the sauce. Serve the breasts only with the following sauce.

Sauce
3 tbsp. butter
3 tbsp. flour
5 dl., 2 cups ptarmigan stock
50g blue cheese (gorgonzola may be used)
50g mysuostur (or Norwegian goat cheese)*
50g red currant jelly
salt and pepper
½ dl., 1 cup cream

*Mysuostur -see recipes in Búðingur(súpa) og Desarar (Puddings and Desserts).

Sauce

Melt the butter in a pot, stir in the flour, add the stock, slowly, stirring constantly. Cut the blue cheese and mysuostur and melt in the sauce together with the red currant jelly. Season to taste with the salt and pepper, and add the cream.

Guðrún adds, "As you can see, the sauce is very important –the blue cheese is a recent addition that not everyone likes. I have two containers on my Christmas table, one with the blue cheese and one without. I frequently use whipped cream in the sauce. I always serve red cabbage (sweet and sour) and Waldorf salad along with the browned potatoes."

It is possible to use "Gjetost", a Norwegian brown cheese made of goat's milk instead of the mysuostur. "Gjetost" is available in many supermarkets and may be melted with some milk to the consistency of mysuostur if desired or may be added to the sauce as it comes in the package.

Roasted Prairie Chicken or Wild Duck

Wash chicken and pat dry. Stuff cavity with celery stalk pieces (with leaves) and apple. Roast at 425° F for 30-40 minutes, basting often with butter. Remove stuffing before serving (the cavity could also be filled with onion, bread stuffing or a knob of butter with juniper berries). Make gravy adding some red currant jelly if you desire.

Kjötmatur og Súpur

Ingibjorg Sigurgeirson McKillop's Braised Duck (Wild or Domestic)

½ tsp. salt
½ tsp. pepper
1 large carrot, sliced
1 medium onion, chopped
2 cloves garlic, minced
⅓ cup butter
1 can apricots
cornstarch

1. Clean and dry ducks inside and out.
2. Brown ducks in butter; season with salt and pepper. Remove duck to baking dish. Sauté the onion and garlic until the onions are translucent. Add to the baking dish.
3. Parboil the carrots for 10 minutes. Drain the cooking water into fry pan to loosen any brown bits. Add carrots and liquid to the baking dish along with the apricots including juice. Add a little water if necessary while baking.
4. Bake for 1½ hours at 375° F. Remove duck(s) and thicken broth with cornstarch before serving.

Mrs. Halldora Bardal's Fars (Cabbage and Ground Steak)

1 medium sized cabbage
1 lb. ground round steak
1 small onion, chopped
1 egg
2 tbsp. flour
1 tbsp. water
1 tsp. salt
½ tsp. pepper

1. Remove a slice from the top of the cabbage; scoop out centre.
2. Combine remaining ingredients. Stuff mixture into cabbage and replace the top slice. Wrap in a cheesecloth and place in a deep pot. Bring to a boil in salted water; reduce heat, and simmer until the meat is done and the cabbage is cooked (it should not lose its colour or become mushy) -approximately 1 hour. (The original recipe gives instructions to boil for 2½ hours.)
3. Serve sliced into wedges with melted butter.

Thank you for the recipe - it brought back childhood lunch times. We used to have two hot meals a day and the Fars was a standard lunch dish. The melted butter is essential to bring out the flavour.

Viola Johnson
Winnipeg, Manitoba

Beef Stew with Dumplings

1½ lb. round steak or stewing beef
3 cups potatoes, diced
1 onion, sliced
¼ cup flour
½ tsp. salt
¼ tsp. pepper
1 cup carrots, sliced

<u>Dumplings</u>
2 cups flour
1 tsp. salt
4 tsp. baking powder
3 tbsp. shortening
¾ cup milk

1. Cut meat into small pieces, dredge with flour seasoned with salt and pepper. Brown in well greased frying pan. When browned put in kettle (heavy saucepan).
2. Rinse pan with 1 cup boiling water and add to kettle. Add 3 more cups of water to the meat. Boil 5 minutes then simmer at lower temperature until meat is tender. Add potatoes, carrots and onions; continue to simmer for approximately 1 hour.
3. Add dumplings 15 minutes before serving.

To make the dumplings: Mix flour, salt and baking powder. Cut in shortening or rub in with the fingertips. Add milk to make a soft dough. Drop by tbsp. into stew and cover tightly. Cook 10-15 minutes without lifting the lid (¼ tsp. nutmeg may be added to the dry ingredients).

The stew recipe was 'plain old-fashioned cooking' -but good. My only suggestion would be the addition of a few herbs, spices and possibly a few more veggies.

Joyce Peterson
Gimli, Manitoba

Mrs. S. Johnson's Kjötsúpa (Meat Soup)

2 qt. water
1 lb. lamb or mutton
1 lb. beef shanks
½ cup rice
½ cup rolled oats
3 carrots, peeled and cut
1 onion, chopped
3 celery stalks, chopped
1 tomato

1. Bring to boil- then simmer meat, rice and rolled oats for 2 hours.
2. Add vegetables, except tomato. Continue simmering for nearly 1 hour.
3. Add tomato and simmer a few minutes longer.

I made the recipe as stated. It tasted good and hearty. But then I added some fresh herbs and other vegetables I had on hand. My daughter and I both really enjoyed it.

Vivienne Jakobson
Winnipeg, Manitoba

Kjötsúpa (Meat Soup)

Original quantities followed by conversions in ¼ amounts:

4kg, 2¼ lbs. meat (lamb or mutton; veal, beef, pork)
7 litres, 2 qt. water
7 tsp., 1½ tsp. salt
3-4 kg, 1 small-medium turnip and 6 medium carrots
250g, ½ cup flour, ground rice or rice
Soup herbs ("Bouquet garni")

The meat is washed and cut into reasonably large pieces, added to the boiling water along with the salt, skimming off the froth as necessary. The carrots and turnips are washed and scraped, cut up and added in with the meat (the vegetables are removed when cooked). The soup herbs are wet in cold water and added ½ to ¾ hours before the soup is ready. Lamb is cooked for 1 hour, mutton for 2, beef for 3 hours, and old beef for 4 hours.

Before the rice is added to the soup it is washed well and added an hour before the meat is cooked, stirred in either during or when it comes to a boil again. If ground rice is used then it is first stirred into cold water and added 20-30 minutes before the meat is cooked. Flour is similarly mixed into cold water and added 15 minutes before the meat is cooked.

Kjötsúpa is a "homey" basic- tasty and nourishing soup that thrifty cooks would prepare to utilize tougher cuts of meat and available root vegetables. Mutton was the traditional meat; however, meats other than mutton were substituted.

In this recipe the meat which is 'cut into reasonably large pieces' is removed from the broth when cooked. There is no directions provided for cutting the meat in Mrs. S. Johnson's recipe. This ambiguity suggests that the same preference for removing the meat when cooked and serving the meat and vegetables and also potatoes separately from the broth could be presumed (see also Notes -Fiskisúpa, Fish Soup).

Mrs. S. Johnson's recipe does not include herbs or seasonings while Guðrún Jónsdóttir's Kjötsúpa calls for soup herbs ('bouquet garni'). Vivienne Jakobson when testing Mrs. S. Johnson's recipe added herbs. Her desire to add herbs may be attributed simply to changing tastes over time but justification for this is perhaps limited if you view both of these recipes as a base to which any variety of vegetables, herbs or seasonings would be added according to preference and availability. (When confronted with a simmering soup pot a cook's natural inclination is to add whatever is on hand – this would hold true through the generations).

There is some question regarding soup herbs. My interpretation of 'Bouquet garni' is fresh herbs such as parsley, dill or cumin bound together with leafy celery pieces and tied with string or dried herbs in a small cheesecloth square, tied up to make a bag (this makes removal before serving easier). However, Guðrún Ágústsdóttir (granddaughter of Guðrún Jónsdóttir, the writer of this recipe) describes the soup herbs as 'dried tiny pieces of turnip, carrots etc. not necessary when lots of wonderful vegetables are available. I add one leek, it does wonders, and also potatoes.'

The broth is thickened similarly in both recipes; Mrs. S. Johnson's with rice and rolled oats and Guðrún's with flour, ground rice or rice.

Loa Johannson's Baunir Súpa (Bean Soup)

1 lb. brisket of beef
2 cups white navy beans
4 cups water
1 large onion, chopped
salt to taste

1. Wash the white navy beans; drain and add 4 cups of water, soak overnight.
2. The next day, cut the beef brisket into 1 inch slices. With a little oil on the bottom of a dutch oven or heavy soup pot brown the brisket pieces. When the meat is well browned add 4 cups of cold water and bring to a boil. Reduce the heat so that the mixture remains at a simmer and allow to simmer for 45 minutes or so.
3. Drain the beans and add to the pot. Return to a boil and again allow to simmer until the beans begin to soften. Add the onion and salt to taste (about 1 tsp. to start). Continue to cook until the onion is transparent. It may be necessary to add water depending on how the beans swell during the cooking. The beans should remain whole and not be puréed.

My mother used to serve this often on cold blustery days especially in the late fall or during stormy winter days, and of course, she was always taking fresh bread out of the oven just as we were getting home from school at noon. I still think of her comforting soups whenever I am chilled and wish I could go back in time.

Elva Jonasson
Winnipeg, Manitoba

Baunir (Beans)

Original quantities followed by conversions in ⅓ amounts:
1 kg, 350g or 12 oz. beans (split yellow peas is intended)
3-4 kg, 2-3 lb. salted meat
6 litres, 2 quarts water
5 tsp., 1½ tsp. salt (if meat is fresh, not salted)
celery, onions, carrots, turnips

The beans (yellow split peas) are washed well first in hot water and then cold water and allowed to soak overnight. If the water is hard, then you may have to add baking soda or use boiled water. The beans in the same water are brought to a boil and allowed to simmer for 2½-3½ hours or longer. The meat is washed and cut up, added with the salt. Lamb, an hour before the beans are cooked; mutton, 2 hours before; and beef, 2½-3 hours before. The vegetables are washed and peeled and cooked with the beans and meat, then removed when they are tender and still hold together.

This recipe is included because today in Iceland it is a tradition to have saltkjöt og baunir (salted meat and split pea soup for Sprengidagur (Bursting Day) which is the Tuesday at the beginning of Lent. Earlier, it was a feast to celebrate and perhaps overeat (to the point of bursting) before the fasting of Lent. In **Cook Book** (1930), there are two recipes for split pea soup (which were omitted in the 1950 edition). Mrs. S. Palmason contributed a Cream of Split Pea Soup, with no meat. The other one, with meat, contributed by Mrs. J. Dalman is as follows:

Mrs. J. Dalman's Split Pea Soup

2 lb. shank meat and bone
2 quarts cold water
1½ cups split peas
2 tsp. salt

Put meat in water and salt, and let boil for ½ hour. Then add the peas and allow to boil for 1½ hours.

Sprengidagur was a custom that did not survive in New Iceland. However, the tradition of sewing little bags of ash to pin on someone who might not see the humour involved continued in New Iceland for Oskudagur (Ash Wednesday). These pranks were popular with school children who found much glee in attaching the bag of ash to their unsuspecting teachers.

Ingibjorg Sigurgeirson McKillop's Hangikjöt og Baunir (Smoked Lamb and Beans)

½ lb. white beans
1 lb. smoked lamb
1 tsp. salt
½ tsp. pepper

1. Cover beans with water, boil slowly 1 hour, stirring and add water when necessary.
2. Cut smoked lamb into 2 X 2 inch chunks, add to beans and continue cooking slowly until beans are softened.

> Brian and I tried this recipe and found it to be very tasty. We used leftover smoked lamb-Hangikjöt.
>
> Susie Erickson-Jakobson
> Winnipeg, Manitoba

Þorramatur

These are the foods that, combined with some dairy products, sustained the Icelanders for centuries. Hangikjöt (smoked lamb) and especially the diet staple Harðfiskur (dried fish) are also included in this group. They are reminders of the days in Iceland when almost all foods were dried, smoked or pickled in whey on the premise that food preserved in the summer months would have to keep through the long months of winter.

Þorrablót is the winter feast that begins on the first day of the ancient Norse month of Þorri (Thor) which is Friday in the 13th week of winter, January 19-25. As it was associated with heathen or pagan times it was not celebrated for a long period of time in Iceland but then it was revived. It is still celebrated in Iceland with singing, dancing, drinking (Brennivín, an Icelandic schnapps, being an essential accompaniment for many) and feasting on these unique foods that represent the most traditional of all Icelandic cuisine.

The first day of Þorri is called Bóndadagur – Farmer's or Husband's Day. A feast at home of the best foods available, frequently hangikjöt was the old custom. Organized festivities outside the home began with the Þorri celebration revival.

The Þorri celebrations continued in North America and the foods are still prepared and enjoyed by many. In the past it has been celebrated in Gimli but not on an annual basis. Every year in Arborg, Winnipeg, Brandon and intermittently in other areas of Manitoba, several areas in Saskatchewan; also in Seattle, Vancouver, Victoria, Edmonton, Calgary, Toronto; and more recently in Minneapolis, Boston, New York and in California.

The methods and ingredients in some recipes are much the same as in ancient times. Of course, long-term pickling in whey is no longer necessary.

Súr (Pickled) Pork Hocks

6 pork hocks (5 lb.)
3 tbsp. mixed pickling spice
15 each of whole cloves and allspice
1 cup chopped onion
1 clove garlic, minced
1 cup vinegar, cider or malt
3 tbsp. brown sugar
2 tsp. salt

Pickled Pork Hocks were also served without deboning.

1. Cover the hocks in salted water and boil until the meat falls off the bones. Lift out the bones and set aside to cool.
2. When cold remove all fat and return to stove and add the spices tied in a cloth, onion and garlic and let simmer for an hour. Remove the spice bag and the rinds. The rinds may be discarded or put through a blender.
3. Turn half into molds about 1½ inches thick, and to the other half add the rinds and turn into molds. The latter will be of a somewhat smoother texture.
4. Cut into 1-1½ inch cubes, and serve on toothpicks, or slice and serve on crackers, or dark brown bread.

I followed the recipe except I did not dice the meat. I put it through a blender. It all turned out very well.

Brian Jakobson
Winnipeg, Manitoba

Rose Helgason's Kjæfa (Headcheese)

2 beef heads
1 pork head (optional)

4-5 cups meat stock
(more if needed)
1 tsp. pepper
1 tsp. marjoram
1 tsp. sage
1 tsp. paprika

1. Cut heads in half and wash well. Soak overnight in cold water and 4 tbsp. salt.
2. Next day, cover with fresh water and 2 tbsp. salt. Boil until tender (meat leaves the bones). Cool. (Save the meat stock to use in the ingredients.)
3. Remove meat from the bone and put it through a meat grinder.

2 cloves garlic or garlic salt
(All spices should be added according to own taste)
2 large onions (that have been put through meat grinder)
salt to taste

4. Put all the remaining ingredients, including the ground meat and the meat stock, in a large pot and simmer until fairly thick; stir occasionally.
5. Place into loaf pans or form to cool.

Kjæfa (Headcheese)

3 lb. shoulder of lamb
3 lb. veal from the shank
2 small or 1 large onion, chopped
2 tsp. ground cloves
2 tsp. ground allspice
2 tbsp. salt
1 tsp. pepper

Spice variations from other recipes:
1 tsp. ginger, 1 tsp. allspice; 1/2 tsp. ground cloves, 1/2 tsp. cinnamon., 1 tsp. poultry seasoning.

1. Boil the meat in water to cover until the bones can be easily removed.
2. Put the meat through a meat grinder (grind very fine).
3. Boil the stock down until it measures about 2 cups. Add the ground meat, the onion and the seasonings. Bring to a boil, stirring constantly.
4. Remove from the fire (heat), turn into a loaf pan, rinsed with cold water and chill thoroughly. Slice very thin for sandwiches.

I tried this recipe a few times. The first time I didn't like the colour so I soaked the meat in salt petre the next time and decreased the cloves and increased the garlic times two. I also found if you put the meat in cans it is nicer on a tray and lays better on the buns. You can choose the size can - example 1 lb. coffee tin for hamburger buns or kaiser buns or corn or soup cans for a tray. When you want to remove the kjæfa cut the bottom out of the can and push it through.

If you are using salt petre for the colour I would recommend decreasing the amount of salt. This recipe takes four hours from start to finish. I did once on the stove but felt it boiled away too much of the essence of the meat. I cooked the meat in the oven in a roaster after that. It cooks differently but doesn't take any longer and there is less chance of boiling dry.

Edna Johnson
Winnipeg, Manitoba

Kjötmatur og Súpur

Shirley Sigurdson's Kjæfa (Headcheese)

3 lb. pork hocks
3 lb. beef shank
1-2 medium onions, chopped fine
salt to taste
1 tsp. ground ginger
¼ tsp. cloves
¼ tsp. pepper
pinch of allspice

1. Boil pork hocks (skin on) and shanks until meat falls off the bones in salted water. Drain, saving broth. Allow meat to cool and then remove skin and bones. Chop meat finely.
2. Put meat in a saucepan with enough broth to moisten well (not quite to cover). Add onions and salt to taste (make a little saltier than you would expect as salt seems to disappear when cold). Simmer.
3. When onions are cooked (translucent), add the ginger, cloves, pepper and allspice. Boil uncovered for 15 minutes, being careful not to burn.
4. Pour into oiled loaf pans. Cool. Refrigerate.
5. Slice as any cold meat. Serve in sandwiches or as cold cuts, open-face.

Finally got everyone's opinion on the Kjæfa that I made. Brian (my son-in-law) liked it. My husband Tenno made the mistake of telling our daughter Korine it was headcheese so she wouldn't try it. I asked her if she really thought I would cook heads! Gave some (almost half) to friends of ours and they really liked it and asked for more. No wonder you had a hard time getting someone to cook it. I started about 11 am and it was 4:30 pm when I finished washing the dishes and cleaning up. I'd forgotten how much work it was, but we did like it!

Diane Kortesluoma
Sudbury, Ontario

Kæfa (Headcheese)

Original quantities followed by conversions in ⅛ amounts:
20 kg, 5 ½ lb. meat
200g , 1 onion
25g, ¾ tsp. allspice
600g, 4 tbsp. salt
25g, ¾ tsp. white pepper
water

The meat is washed and cut up and put into cold water with 200g salt (⅛ amt = 4 tsp), this then is boiled together until it is possible to remove the bones. The excess fat is skimmed from the surface of the liquid and allowed to cool. Then the meat is put through the meat grinder. The bones are put back in the pot as soon as the meat has been removed. While the meat is put through the grinder, the bones are brought to a boil in the stock and allowed to cook (simmer) until the stock begins to thicken, then removed. The salt and chopped onions are added, followed by the excess fat and spices. When the excess fat is melted, the meat is stirred in until it is well cooked. The Kæfa is put into clean containers and patted down well in them. After 2-3 days melted pork fat or suitable fat is poured over to seal. When cool, it is good to sprinkle salt on the top. Keep in a dry cool place.

Overall similarity to the New Iceland Kjæfa recipes. Kjæfa, being the older spelling, was retained in New Iceland. The spices vary in all the recipes but the allspice in this kæfa is also called for in two of the New Iceland recipes. The meat is not specified but I would assume that lamb or mutton is intended. Of the New Iceland recipes two specify pork and beef and the other a lamb and veal combination. Likely whatever meat was available would have been used in early settlement days. It was critical not to waste any part of the animal and this is documented in Rose Helgason's Kjæfa which uses the heads. Fat is not added in the New Iceland recipes. The bones in the stock were relied on to provide the gelatinous requirement (gelatinous extractives present particularly in marrow bones and heads). The fat poured over to seal was important for storage in the years before refrigeration (also in New Iceland).

Kjötmatur og Súpur

Steindor Jakobson's Rúllupylsa (Rolled Spiced Lamb)

1-2 lb. lamb flank, boned
1 tsp. salt petre
¾ tsp. ground cloves
¾ tsp. allspice
¾ tsp. pepper
1 medium onion, chopped

1. Ask the butcher to bone the lamb but leave in one piece. Lay the flank flat on the table with boned side up. Mix the seasonings together and sprinkle over the flank. Sprinkle onion over top.
2. Roll as you would a jelly roll. Sew up both ends and loose edges with needle and thread. Wind string tightly around the roll.
3. Marinate rolls in the following brine. Make enough to cover the rolls with room to spare. Refrigerate for 10 days.

Brine:

1. In a large container combine: 1 gallon of water, ¾ cup pickling salt, ½ cup brown sugar and 1 tbsp. saltpetre. (A medium sized potato should float in the brine. Add more pickling salt if it doesn't.)
2. At the end of that time, remove rolls from brine and place in a large pot, covering with water. Bring to a boil and then turn heat down and simmer for about 1½ hours. Remove and cool.
3. Place between two surfaces and put a heavy weight on top. Leave overnight in the refrigerator.
4. Next day, remove string, slice thinly and serve on Icelandic Brown Bread, thinly sliced and buttered. Refrigerate to store.

This recipe is as my father's that he used when making it on a commercial basis. My father was the late Steindor Jakobson who owned and operated Westend Food Market at the corner of Victor and Sargent in Winnipeg. I followed the recipe as written, mine was very good. One other thing I did was to remove as much of the fat as possible at the start.

Brian Jakobson
Winnipeg, Manitoba

Anna Skaptason's Rúllupylsa (Rolled Spiced Lamb)

1 lamb flank, boned
2 tbsp. chopped onion
1 tbsp. salt
⅛ tsp. salt petre (used to keep meat slightly pink)
½ tsp. brown sugar
¼ tsp. pepper
¼ to ½ tsp. allspice
⅛ tsp. cloves

1. Lay flank on cutting board and remove as much fat as possible from both sides. Sprinkle flank with chopped onion.
2. Combine the remaining ingredients and sprinkle this mixture over the flank.
3. Wrap from the thick side to narrow edge and using a darning needle and grocery string, sew closely to seal roll. Then tie the roll firmly.
4. Place flank on a double or triple layer of wax paper. Sprinkle roll with mixture of 1 tbsp. brown sugar and 1 tsp. salt. Wrap roll closely in the wax paper and then put into sturdy plastic bag. Tie bag with string to keep covering tight.
5. Lay flat in a glass dish in the fridge and turn roll(s) once a day for 7-8 days. At this stage the meat is cured.
6. Remove plastic and wax paper wrapping and rinse roll in cold water. At this point it may be stored in the freezer uncooked (if so, wrap tightly in wax paper and a plastic bag before freezing) or it may be boiled and pressed.
7. Boil until fork tender (about 2 hours) in lots of water, adding water as it boils away. Remove from water and press in meat press (or under a heavy weight) until cool. Remove all string. Store in the fridge.

In 1949-51 I made rúllupylsa for the Sigurdson-Thorvaldson store in Riverton (Sveinn Thorvaldson was married to my Amma.) Lamb flanks came frozen in 40 pound boxes. I deboned them and removed as much membrane as possible and then Auntie Sella and I prepared them for curing. I bought the flanks for 9-11 cents a pound and sold the rúllupylsa for 35 cents. The profit margin excluding my penurious labour was about 15 cents a pound - this in the days when a living wage was 40 -50 cents an hour. The saving grace was that Aunty made all kinds of tasty dishes with the ribs. There wasn't a lot of meat on them but she made them taste great in her 'wearever' pots - stuffed and baked, sweet and sour, etc.

In later years I made rúllupylsa out of pork tenderloin, shoulder of pork, deer meat, leg of lamb, shoulder of lamb etc. None of these had the traditional flavour of the 'old style' rúllupylsa. The best and easiest substitute

Kjötmatur og Súpur

was alternate layers of leg of pork and lamb flanks. I think modern Danes do something like this -I bought some in Kingston and it was very good! The traditional spices carry it off and it makes a nice modern day version of a traditional recipe -who says we have to be authentic if it tastes better.

I like the recipe Johanna uses because I like everything she does and cooks!

Irvin Olafson
Gimli, Manitoba

Dee Dee Westdal and I have followed our Aunt Anna's recipe for a number of years and found it to be most reliable.

Johanna Wilson
Winnipeg, Manitoba

Mrs. Lydur Lindal's Lifrarpylsa (Liver Sausage)

7 lbs. liver
3 tbsp. salt
3 cups flour
3 cups ryemeal
6 cups oatmeal
5 lbs. kidney suet, chopped fine

1. Take 7 lbs. of liver. Wash and mince liver, using no water, only milk, about 2 quarts, then add the remaining ingredients and mix well. (Use a little more oatmeal if required.)
2. Then put in thin cotton bags and boil 3-3½ hours.

*This recipe is from **Cook Book** (1930). A similar recipe was given to me by Stefan Stefanson in Gimli. His recipe calls for 6 cups of whole wheat flour instead of 3 cups ryemeal and 1 cup raisins which are optional. Parchment paper bags is given as an alternative for the 'thin cotton bags', which also may be sewn by machine. He added the instruction to 'let it firm well before serving' following the boiling and also that 'it is very good when served while still warm'.*

Rose Helgason's Lifrarpylsa (Liver Sausage)

2 lb. beef liver
1 lb. beef suet
2 cups oatmeal
¾ cup graham flour
½ cup white flour
3 cups milk
1 tbsp. salt
1 tsp. each of pepper, ground cloves, and allspice

1. Put liver through food chopper.
2. Cut the suet in small pieces.
3. To the ground liver and suet, add the remaining ingredients. Mix thoroughly.
4. Make cotton bags about 4 X 8 inches. Fill them with the liver mixture about ¾ full, sew up and boil for 2½-3 hours in salted water.
5. Serve sliced, either hot or cold, also can be fried to reheat.

The recipe as it stands delighted my guests. Their comments were that it is truly a traditional form of lifrarpylsa. It was also delicious fried. The next time I make it I would increase the salt to 1½-2 tbsp, double up on the pepper, ground cloves and allspice as the spices were boiled out during the cooking process. Some additions to consider - a medium-sized onion ground in with the liver, minced garlic and oregano. The recipe is large. My yield was four bags full. The bags were easy to sew and worked well. I found placing the bags upright in a deep kettle helped them to keep their shape.

Judith Lehn
Winnipeg, Manitoba

Kjötmatur og Súpur

Sigrun Stefanson's Lifrarpylsa (Baked Liver Sausage Pâté)

2 cups milk
1½ tsp. brown sugar
1 tsp. salt
1 cup oatmeal
1 cup whole wheat flour, heaping
1 lb. beef liver
1½ cup beef suet

1. Mix milk into dry ingredients and let stand while preparing liver and suet.
2. Put liver through food chopper or use food processor.
3. Cut suet into small pieces.
4. Add liver and suet to milk mixture. Combine well and place in a greased casserole dish.
5. Bake in a pan of water at 300° F for 2 hours.

I used ground suet-difficult to get suet to chop. If you have a little more than 1 lb. of liver then use more of the other ingredients.

Claire Stefanson
Gimli, Manitoba

Leverpostej (Liver Pâté)

250g, ½ lb. liver
1 small onion
40g, ⅓ cup flour
175-200g, ⅓ -½ lb. fat bacon
35g, 2 tbsp. margarine
¼ litre, 1 cup milk
1 egg
salt, pepper, allspice, cloves

The bacon is cut into thin slices and then used to line the form or container (baking dish). If pork liver is used, it is recommended that it is first soaked in vinegar water, then washed, dried, any membrane removed, cut into slices and put through the meat grinder 2-3 times with the onion and whatever was left of the bacon. The margarine and flour are heated together thinned with the hot milk (white béchamel sauce), poured out in a bowl and the egg mixed in, and the spices are added to your taste, then the liver is added and stirred until it becomes light in texture. Place in a container (baking dish), which is placed in a pan of water for the first 30 minutes, do not fill the pan more than half full as it will have evaporated in that time. Allow to bake approximately 1¼ hours. (Taste to see if there is enough spice) This is not removed from the container (baking dish) until cold then the container is quickly set into hot water for ease in removing.

Leverpostej is as the original. This was due to the Danish influence of the time period. Leverpostej would be translated from Danish as Liver Paste. Lifrarkæfa (pâté) is the correct name in Icelandic, which differs from Lifrarpylsa as it does not include oatmeal and is not boiled in casings. Sigrun Stefanson's preceding recipe is a variation of Lifrarpylsa in that it is baked but it does include oatmeal. This recipe is lighter than Sigrun's as there is no oatmeal and an egg has been added. It is interesting to note that the spices associated with traditional New Iceland lifrarpylsa, cloves and allspice, are included and in Sigrun's there is none. After reading a lifrarpylsa recipe originating in Iceland I would conclude it is simply a matter of the cook's preference. This recipe boiled in casings was similar in ingredients to both New Iceland lifrarpylsa recipes and did include oatmeal but no spices.

Blóðmör (Blood Sausage)

2 qt. blood (sheep or cattle)
2 qt. water
7 lb. rolled oats
2 lb. whole wheat flour
1 lb. graham flour
1 cup sugar
¾ cup salt
7 lb. kidney suet, well chopped
2 cups rye meal
2 cups bran
2 cups shorts or vita B. flour
1 lb. seedless raisins

1. Combine all ingredients adding the raisins last and fill bungs or casings ¾ full, sewing them securely (casings may be sewn from thin cotton, 8 inches long and 3 inches wide).
2. Drop into rapidly boiling water, and prick with a large needle or hatpin to prevent the bungs from bursting. Boil 1½ - 2½ hours.
3. Serve blood sausage hot or cold or fried in slices; you can sprinkle a bit of sugar (white or brown) on each slice..

(Blood and Bungs may be purchased from an abattoir or packing plant; bungs are also called casings)

This recipe for blóðmör is in a larger quantity perhaps for blood from a larger animal. It is preferable to use milk rather than water because the blood sausage will be tough if water is used.

I don't remember having brown sugar on the slátur/ blóðmör. You sprinkled the sugar on at the table yourself. Some did not like it with sugar at all and others liked lots of sugar.

Elva Jonasson
Winnipeg, Manitoba

It is now about forty years since I made blóðmör with my mother, but I feel that this is the recipe that we used. And boy was it good! Here is another recipe that I found:

Blóðmör

Use sheep or cattle blood; strain well to remove fibrin (clots).
1 litre of blood
1 2/3 cups water
1 tbsp. salt
400g rye flour
600g oatmeal
1-1 1/2 kg coarsely cut suet

Method

Dissolve salt in the water.
Add the blood and the flour until the consistency of a rather thin cake batter is reached, and then stir in the chopped suet.
Boil at least 2 1/2 hours in a large pot or canner. Turn bags over 2 or 3 times during the boil.
Now to make the bags; perhaps you can obtain blood and casings (to use as bags) from an abattoir or use your favourite butcher to get this for you as they are constantly dealing with the abattoirs.

My mother and I made our bags up out of parchment paper. Folded the paper to the proper size and sewed them up on the sewing machine. Here again remember to prick very small holes in the bag. When you have made about three batches and observed how everything goes, trial and error will bring you the perfect product. Good luck. Authenticity not guaranteed!

Stefan Stefanson
Gimli, Manitoba

Steiktur Blóðmör (Fried Blood Sausage)

Original quantities followed by conversions in ⅓ amounts:
Blood sausage pieces, fat, butter or margarine

<u>Rófustappa (Mashed Turnip)</u>
3 kg, 2 ¼ lb. turnip
water, salt
3-4 tbsp., 1 tbsp. flour

<u>Mysuostasósu (Mysuostur Sauce)</u>
250g, ⅓ cup mysuostur
250g, ⅓ cup butter or margarine
milk

The blood sausage is sliced in ½ inch thick slices. Browned on both sides in the fat and arranged in 2 layers on a plate.

The turnip is washed and scraped. Boiled in salted water until soft (salted with 1 heaping tsp. in pot), the water is drained and then it is mashed well; the flour is mixed with cold water and added to the pot, put over the heat again and allowed to boil slowly for 10 minutes, stirring all the while. Sugar and nutmeg is stirred together and added if you wish.

Mysuost Sauce - the margarine and mysuost are blended together over medium heat, thinned with milk until the sauce is even and of the proper consistency.

The serving of fried blood sausage with the mashed turnip and mysuost sauce was more common for earlier generations in New Iceland. It is more usual to sprinkle sugar on blóðmör than serve with mysuost sauce. Notable that a sweetness was favoured on the sausage, overall. Recipes for Mysuostur – see Búðingur(súpa) og Deserar (Puddings and Desserts).

Guðrún Ágústsdóttir (Guðrún Jónsdóttir's granddaughter – the writer of this recipe) adds – ' The easy version from my friend Pastor Anna – Cut the blóðmör into ½ inch slices. Brown on both sides, sprinkle sugar on the slices (only a little), serve with turnip. Children love this.' This is consistent with the usual preference in New Iceland.

Hulda Johnson's Slátur (Blood Sausage)

8 cups blood
4 cups milk
1 cup oatmeal
⅓ cup salt
9 cups whole wheat flour
Suet - as much as you prefer

1. Mix blood, salt, milk and gradually add the whole wheat flour and the oatmeal. Stir well.
2. Add the suet that has been cut into small pieces.
3. Make bags of cotton material 4 x 8 inches. Wet in cold water. Put mixture in bags but leave about 1 inch space for expansion. Sew up opening.
4. Drop bags into boiling water. Boil about 2 hours.
5. Serve hot or cold. It may also be cut into slices and fried.

Ingibjorg Sigurgeirson McKillop's Súr Slátur (Soured Blood Sausage)

In Iceland, "slátur" refers to both "lifrarpylsa" and "bloðmör".

In a five gallon crock put 3 gallons of buttermilk. Now add your bags of already boiled lifrarpylsa and blóðmör, making sure they are completely covered. Let sit 10 days. Serve sliced, cold.

> Slátur or súrt slátur and blóðmör are not exactly the same thing. Slátur refers to the result of the slaughter - the meat product made from the fresh blood caught when the animal is slaughtered, an idiomatic or farm expression.
> Súr slátur refers to the end product which has been cured or pickled in brine (sour milk or buttermilk or whey) used to preserve the slátur through the winter. In Iceland freezing was not usual as the temperatures were neither cold enough nor consistent enough for the preservation of food.
> Blóðmör refers to the cooked end product (sausage) as is recognized as such by many ethnic groups, notably the Scandinavian and German countries, as well as the British Isles, particularly Scotland.
>
> Elva Jonasson
> Winnipeg, Manitoba

Ingibjorg Sigurgeirson McKillop's Svið (Sheephead)

Recipe as original. The usual reference is to 'singe' rather than scorch. Singeing refers to burning off all the hair or fleece from the surface of the head. This process also ensures that there will be no lingering wool taste to the skin.

As many sheep or lamb heads as desired. These are scorched completely all around for approximately one hour. Now the head is cut in half through the mouth. All insides are removed. Now it is scraped very thoroughly in cold water. Then boiled 1½ hours with 1 tbsp. salt added. Half a head is served to each person. (The eyes and teeth are removed.)

Grænmeti, Pækill og Niðursoðnir Ávextir
Vegetables, Pickles and Preserves

Brúnaðar Kartöflur (Sugar Browned Potatoes)

2 lb. potatoes, boiled and peeled
4 tbsp. sugar
4 tbsp. butter

1. Carmelize the sugar slowly to a light brown colour in a heavy skillet.
2. Add the butter, stirring until melted, and then the potatoes, sautéing until evenly coated. (Don't overcrowd the pan. Place hot carmelized potatoes in a heated serving dish and continue until all the potatoes are done.)

Small potatoes are best. If large, cut into uniformly sized pieces.

This is the way the potatoes are cooked when served with a slow roasted leg of lamb. They are excellent! The only thing I would add to this recipe is when serving the potatoes they are not served with the sauce, the sauce is discarded. The red cabbage recipe I am enclosing is served with the meal of lamb and sugar browned potatoes.

Susie Erickson-Jakobson
Winnipeg, Manitoba

KARTÖPLU-KÖKUR (POTATO CAKES) — May 31, 1878

The potatoes should be peeled raw, then boiled in well salted water. After boiling they should be mashed fine while still hot and mixed with about one third as much flour. The dough should then be rolled out flat or very thin with a rolling pin and cut into cakes with a glass or other utensil. These cakes should then be baked on a pan in the oven, and it is not necessary to cover the pan. The oven should not be very hot. Should soft cakes be desired, they may be baked wrapped in a thick cloth, otherwise not. They are good hot or cold, with butter or fat.

Susie Erickson-Jakobson's Rauðkál (Red Cabbage)

1 medium sized red cabbage
¼ lb. butter, approximately
2 tbsp. brown sugar
2 tbsp. white wine vinegar
⅓ cup red wine (approx.)

Good served warm (not too hot) with a roasted leg of lamb alongside brúnaðar kartöflur (sugar browned potatoes).

1. Shred cabbage.
2. In electric frying pan sauté cabbage in butter at 350° F until heated through. (Or use large frying pan) on element at medium heat.
3. Stir in brown sugar and white wine vinegar and then red wine to moisten.
4. Cover pan and turn heat down to 200° F (or reduce heat to low on element) and simmer until cooked, the cabbage should be limp.

Elva Jonasson's Brún Grænkál (Browned Cabbage)

½ head of green cabbage, shredded
¼ cup beef stock or 1 bouillion cube
2 tbsp. butter
salt to taste

1. In heavy or cast iron skillet, heat the butter over medium heat until it begins to brown slightly. Add the shredded cabbage and cook (still over medium heat). If the pan becomes dry add enough of the stock to keep the cabbage from sticking to the pan. Stir while cooking, adding stock as necessary until the cabbage is cooked and lightly browned.
2. Add salt to taste. I will often use ½ tsp. salt and ½ tsp. of sugar instead of just salt. Makes the cabbage taste more like it just came from the garden.

Kartöflur og Groengresi Hvítsósu (Potatoes and Green Peas in White Sauce)

potatoes, 4 to 6 approx.
peas

<u>White sauce</u>
2 tbsp. butter
2 tbsp. flour
1 cup milk
salt, pepper

1. Prepare white sauce -melt butter, blend in flour and cook on low heat for a few minutes, stirring. Gradually add milk, stirring and continue cooking (on medium low heat) until thickened. Add salt and pepper to taste.
2. Meanwhile boil potatoes and peas. Cut the potatoes into small pieces when cooked and add to the white sauce together with the peas.

The amount of white sauce you prepare will depend on the amount of potatoes and peas you require.

The following are all recipes contributed by Mrs. Gustaf Anderson to an older cook book from which I have only loose pages. Creamed Peas, Boiled Beets and Rutabaga were all commonly prepared vegetables in New Iceland.

Creamed Peas

Drain a can of green peas and put them with a tbsp. of butter into a saucepan; let them heat thoroughly, then throw a tbsp. of flour over them and mix so that every pea is well coated with flour. Gradually add milk until they are of the desired thickness. Then lift off the fire (heat) and add a beaten egg, salt and pepper. They should be so thick that they almost hold their shape when dropped from a spoon.

Today fresh or frozen peas could be cooked and used also. Canned peas would have been more readily available at the time.

Rutabaga

Pare, wash and cut into squares. Boil until tender in salt water, drain and mash with sweet cream (fresh), or the mashing may be omitted and a cupful of rich milk may be added, thickened with a little flour and butter and seasoned to taste with salt and pepper.

Boiled Beets

Wash the roots carefully, and put them into a pan of boiling water and boil until tender. When done, put them into cold water and rub the skin off and slice them. They may be sent to the table with a seasoning of pepper, salt and butter or they may be returned to the fire (heat) and a thin sauce of flour, butter and milk may be poured over them.

Grænmeti, Pækill og Niðursoðnir Ávextir

Judith Sigurdson's Sósu (Salad Dressing)

2 tbsp. flour
¾ cup sugar
1 tsp. dry mustard
2 eggs
½ cup vinegar
½ cup water

Cook together in double boiler until thickened.

Thought it might be good to add a few instructions - cook and stir constantly over hot (not boiling) water until thick. The dressing has a definite zing to it which we enjoyed.

Myrna Stefanson
Winnipeg, Manitoba

Kristin Thorvaldson's Sósu (Salad Dressing)

1 cup sugar
1 tbsp. dry mustard
2 tbsp. corn starch
4 eggs
pinch of salt
1 cup water
1 cup vinegar

1. Mix sugar, dry mustard, corn starch and salt together until well blended.
2. Add eggs one at a time beating well after each. Add water and vinegar.
3. Cook over medium heat stirring all the time until the mixture comes to a boil and is thickened.
4. Pour into a jar or container and cool. Keep in fridge.

You may mix this recipe in your blender with very good results. Also you may substitute other vinegars other than the usual white vinegar. This is particularly good with Hangikjöt or ham and it is great for potato salad especially for picnics as it keeps so well.

Elva Jonasson
Winnipeg, Manitoba

Kál og Epli Salat (Cabbage and Apple Slaw)

3 cups shredded cabbage
½ cup finely cut green onions, or chopped onions
1 apple, finely chopped
*cooked salad dressing and 2 tbsp. cream
salt and pepper

*See Judith Sigurdson's and Kristin Thorvaldson's Sósu (Salad Dressing).

1. Combine cabbage, onion and apple.
2. Toss with dressing and cream until well coated. Season to taste.

> Thought using green and red cabbage would give the slaw more colour. We enjoyed the apples in the coleslaw. I used a Royal Gala apple. I substituted half and half cream for the cream in the recipe. We enjoyed the recipe - had it with salmon. Thought it complemented this well.
>
> Myrna Stefanson
> Winnipeg, Manitoba

Sylvia Sigurdson's Súr Sykurrófu (Pickled Beets)

<u>Syrup:</u>
2 heaping cups brown sugar
2 cups vinegar
1 tsp. whole cloves
3 cinnamon sticks

1. Boil beets until tender. Peel and cut into pieces if beets are large (uniform small beets are best). Pack tightly into hot sterilized jars.
2. **Make syrup:** Combine ingredients and heat to boiling; then simmer slowly for 15 to 20 minutes.
3. Cover with boiling syrup. Seal jars tight. If more syrup is required make it using the same proportions of ingredients.

This was a favourite recipe of mine and made a wonderful accompaniment to pickerel fillets. I still miss that combination.
-Sylvia

> I found this beet recipe very nice - a little too spicy for my taste but that could be adjusted to one's liking.
>
> Gudrun Dryden
> Selkirk, Manitoba

Susie Erickson-Jakobson's Súr Sykurrófu (Pickled Beets)

<u>Syrup</u>:
6 cups vinegar
4½ cups brown sugar
3 cups water
3 tbsp. pickling spice
(tied in a cheesecloth bag)
(Remove bag before pouring syrup over beets.)

Prepare beets and make syrup as directed in the preceding recipe.

Wonderful recipe! I've used it for years. -Susie

Rööbeder (Red Beets)

1 kg, 2.2 lb. red beets
¾ litre, 3 cups vinegar
125g, ½ cup sugar (heaping)

The beets are washed and scrubbed with a brush being careful not to break the skin. They are placed in boiling water (salted with 1 level tbsp. to 3 litres of water) and boiled until they are tender. The pot is then removed from the heat and the beets are left to cool in the water. Then they are peeled and cut into thick slices, which are placed in a crock (mason jar). The sugar and vinegar is brought to a boil and poured over the beets until well covered. Parchment paper is tied tightly over the top of the crock (or the mason jar is sealed).

"Rööbeder" is as in the original due to the Danish influence of the time period. "Rauðrófur" is "red beets" in Icelandic.

There are no spices in this recipe. However this could simply be a matter of personal preference. Sylvia Sigurdson's recipe includes cloves and cinnamon sticks which Guðrún Dryden found too spicy and Susie Erickson Jakobson's recipe used pickling spices which would result in a completely different flavour.

There is a much higher ratio of sugar to vinegar in the New Iceland recipes and it is notable that both New Iceland recipes use brown sugar. I have read recipes from New Iceland that use white sugar but most have specified brown.

Vegetables, Pickles and Preserves

Helen Kristjanson's Sweet Green Tomato Pickles

6 quarts green tomatoes
6 large onions
½-¾ cup salt
3 cups vinegar
6 cups white sugar
3 tbsp. pickling spice

If you have a 4 cup measurer, fill with sliced tomatoes 6 times to make 6 quarts.

1. Peel the onions and place in cold water.
2. Wash tomatoes, remove ends, stems and blemishes. Slice or chop.
3. Put ¼ of the tomatoes in a large pot, a layer of thinly sliced onions, and sprinkle with salt. Repeat layers until tomatoes, onions and salt are used up.
4. Weigh down with a plate and let stand covered overnight. In the morning drain well and rinse with hot water twice.
5. Heat vinegar to boiling. Add sugar and pickling spice tied in cheesecloth. Add tomatoes and onions. Simmer on medium heat for 10 minutes until tomatoes are clear.
6. Remove spices and fill sterilized jars and store in a cool place.

I like the sweet, slightly tangy flavour of these pickles. They go very nicely with fish, roast beef and stew. -Helen

Grænmeti, Pækill og Niðursoðnir Ávextir

Mrs. F.A. Finson's Million Dollar Pickles

3 qt. cucumbers, wipe and slice thin
1 qt. onions, sliced
3 green peppers, chopped
2 tsp. turmeric
6 cups white sugar
1 tsp. mustard seed
1 tsp. celery seed
vinegar to cover

1. Cover the cucumbers, onions and green peppers with water and ⅓ cup salt. Let stand overnight.
2. Drain well and add the remaining ingredients.
3. Simmer until cucumbers are clear. While hot add 1 tin pimento.
4. Fill sterilized jars and seal.

Great! Delicious every time! They never fail!

Sella Benedictson
Gimli, Manitoba

That recipe is correct. I made them for years they were delicious with most dishes, very good with fish as well. This also appeared in a revised edition of the Dorcas Society Cookbook in 1950. Obviously all these recipes were used by Icelandic ladies from the earlier times.

Sylvia Sigurdson
White Rock, British Columbia

Nola Anderson's Dill Pickles

<u>Syrup</u>: Boil together ~
15 cups water
3½ cups vinegar
1 cup pickling salt
1 cup sugar

Fill quart sealers on bottom with 1 tsp. pickling spice, ½ tsp. alum, dill and 1-2 cloves garlic. Fill with cucumbers and put dill and 1 garlic clove on top. Pour syrup over. Place sealed jars in hot water (not boiling) in canner until they turn colour (not very long.)
Optional: Slivered carrots can be added to the jars with the cucumbers.

Taste is excellent. The carrots give colour. These stay fresh for a long time and will not get sour.

Helen Kristjanson
Gimli, Manitoba

Sigurros Palsson's Celery Sauce

1. Vegetables
1 head celery, chopped fine
1 qt. green cucumbers, peeled, seeded and chopped fine
1 qt. onions, chopped fine
1 green pepper, chopped fine
2 red peppers, chopped fine

2. Syrup
3 cups vinegar
2 cups water
3 cups sugar
½ tbsp. tumeric
1 tbsp. mustard seed
½ tbsp. curry
1 tbsp. celery seed

3. 3 cups sugar
¾ cups flour

1. Sprinkle all of the vegetables with 2 tbsp. pickling salt and let stand, covered, overnight. Do not drain.
2. Put all the syrup ingredients into a preserving kettle or large pot. Bring to a boil and add vegetables.
3. Mix sugar and flour and add to vegetable/syrup mixture. Combine thoroughly and bring to a boil. Simmer until it thickens (more flour may be required-if you mix flour with the sugar the mixture will not get lumpy).
4. Seal in hot sterile jars. Works well to double the recipe.

> I did make the celery sauce and with good results. I loved it. Have had friends enjoy it as well. The recipe is easy to understand. I did end up adding an additional ¼ cups flour after simmering for a long time (was still runny) I felt it needed it. I took out some sauce and added the flour, stirred well, then slowly added to the pickling pot and continued to boil again.
> Also the colour is so attractive. I loved it with grilled cheese sandwiches. I will decorate jars with Christmas fabric and ribbon on lids and give along with Christmas gifts.
>
> Sesselja Still
> Stonewall, Manitoba

Claire Stefanson's Chili Sauce

3 qt. ripe tomatoes
2 cups onions, finely chopped
½ cup sweet red pepper, finely chopped
¼ cup coarse pickling salt
2 cups celery, finely chopped
2 cups sugar
1 cups white vinegar
1 tbsp. celery seed
1 tbsp. mustard seed
pinch of cayenne

Yield: 5 pints. Doubles well.

1. Scald and peel tomatoes. Chop fine.
2. Combine tomatoes, onions and pepper. Mix in pickling salt. Let stand at room temperature for 2 hours. Drain off all juice.
3. In large heavy pot or preserving kettle, combine the celery and other remaining ingredients. Bring to a boil; cook uncovered about 15 minutes or until of desired consistency.
4. Pour into hot sterilized jars and seal.

Guess what!! We made some chili!! It was fantastic. The house had this wonderful celery aroma during the simmering stage. The spiciness is perfect for those who like medium-hot. Corn chips and crackers are the best dippers. The batch made 4 pints. Perfect size for gift giving.

Jane Pimm
Tulsa, Oklahoma

Mrs. G.O. Bergman's Rabarbarsúpa (Rhubarb Compote)

3 cups rhubarb, diced
3 cups sugar
3 oranges
1 lemon
¼ lb. almonds (optional)

1. Put all ingredients into preserving kettle and cook 30 minutes.
2. Add juice and rind of oranges, lemon and the almonds if desired.
3. Cook 5 minutes more.

Helen Kristjanson's Rabarbar og Fíkjusúpa (Rhubarb and Fig Compote)

6 cups rhubarb, chopped
1-14 oz (390ml) can crushed pineapple
(do not drain)
1 lb. figs (500g.), cut fine
4 cups white sugar (add more or less to taste and depending on tartness of rhubarb)

1. Place rhubarb, figs and crushed pineapple in a pot. Stir together and simmer covered 12-15 minutes.
2. Add white sugar and boil 10-12 minutes.
3. Put in hot sterilized jars and seal.

Very good! I made it using one package of frozen rhubarb (4 cups) and one package of figs (375g), one cup of sugar and omitted the pineapple. It is wonderful on my morning toast and on frozen yogurt.

Judith Sigurdson
Riverton, Manitoba

Gudrun Erickson's Kryddaður Rabarbarsúpa (Spiced Rhubarb Compote)

2½ lb. rhubarb
2 lb. sugar
⅞ cup vinegar
1 tsp. cinnamon
½ tsp. cloves

1. Wipe rhubarb skin and cut stalks into 1 inch pieces. Put in preserving kettle and add remaining ingredients, bring to boiling point and boil until soft and thick.
2. Put in sterilized jars and seal. Very good with cold meat.

Mrs. R. Marteinsson's Canned Crabapples

1. Wash, stem and quarter crabapples and put in sterilized jars.
2. Make a light syrup: 1 cup sugar to 2 cups water, let come to a boil. Pour over apples in jars and seal tightly.
3. Put sealers in hot water bath and boil for 30 minutes.

Grænmeti, Pækill og Niðursoðnir Ávextir

Mrs. B.W. Benson's Crabapple Jelly

1. Wash and core 8 lb. crabapples, put in preserving kettle, boil until pulpy.
2. Strain through jelly bag. Measure juice and boil 15 minutes.
3. Add 1 cup sugar to each cup of juice. Boil until it tests for jelly (when jelly forms on spoon).
4. Skim well and put into sterile jars and wax when set.

Helen Kristjanson's Cranberry Jelly

3-4 litre pail (approx.) cranberries to make 4 cups juice
3¾ cups sugar
1 box fruit pectin crystals

Helen freezes juice from cranberries in four cup amounts to make jelly when she wants.

1. Remove stems from berries, wash and drain.
2. Put berries in large pot and cover with water. Bring to a boil and simmer 20-30 minutes, crushing with potato masher.
3. Strain a little at a time through a large sieve (the liquid will be murkier than if dripped through a cheesecloth bag but tastes as good or better).
4. Mix fruit pectin crystals with juice in a large canner or pot. Bring to a rolling boil and then add sugar all at once. Return to a boil and boil hard one minute.
5. Remove from heat and skim foam. Put in hot sterilized jars and seal (or let cool, put lids on and freeze).

Ingibjorg Sigurgeirson McKillop's Choke Cherry Jelly

8 cups clean choke cherries, add 4 cups hot water, boil 20 minutes, drain through jelly bag. Add 1 cup sugar to 1 cup juice. Boil 5 minutes, counting from the time you have a rolling boil. Then test for jelly. Skim well so that jelly will be clear. Turn into sterile jars and wax when set.

Vegetables, Pickles and Preserves

Ingibjorg Sigurgeirson McKillop's Raspberry Jam

6 cups raspberries
4 cups sugar
1/3 cup lemon juice

Measure raspberries and sugar into preserving kettle. Let stand until sugar is dissolved. Stir frequently. Place on stove and boil slowly, approximately 2½ hours, stir frequently while boiling. Turn into sterile jars and wax when set.

Freezer Raspberry Jam

4 cups crushed raspberries (strain half of pulp through a sieve to remove some seeds if desired)
3 ¼ cups sugar
1 box fruit pectin crystals "light"

1. Combine ¼ cup of sugar with fruit pectin crystals; set remaining sugar aside.
2. Add fruit pectin mixture to prepared fruit in a large bowl. Mix well.
3. Let stand 30 minutes, stirring once or twice (mixture will be thick).
4. Add remaining sugar and continue to stir for 3 minutes.
5. Pour into clean dry jars or plastic containers. Cover and let stand at room temperature until set.
6. Freeze up to one year. Keeps in fridge for 4 weeks.

We love this 'not too sweet' jam as it always tastes like fresh picked berries. Delicious over ice cream or rosettes.

Helen Kristjanson
Gimli, Manitoba

Búðingur(súpa) og Deserar
Puddings and Desserts

Skyr

The seafaring Vikings brought this ancient dish with them when they settled in Iceland. Skyr is a smooth curd with a creamy texture and is classified as a cheese. It is made from 2% or skim milk and is very low in butter fat content. Protein rich, skyr was for centuries one of Iceland's most important staple foods and in earlier days was made from sheep's milk and preserved all winter in casks.

The traditional way to eat skyr is with milk or cream and a little sugar. (Crowberries or Juniper berries were mixed in as a sugar substitute in earlier times.) It is also delicious with fresh fruit. On farms in Iceland, it was also served mixed with porridge, which is called 'Hræringur'. It was served with milk and accompanied by the traditional 'black pudding' and 'liver pudding' which were made at slaughtering time in autumn.

Mrs. J.K. Johnson's Skyr

1. Take 4 quarts of milk and bring to the boiling point. Cool until lukewarm.
2. Stir 2 tbsp. skyr into ½ cup milk. If skyr is unavailable use the recipe for þjetti(starter). Stir this into the lukewarm milk.
3. Add 12 drops of liquid rennet, stir well. Set aside in a warm place for about 24 hours.
4. Drain off liquid through cheesecloth. Remove cloth, put in a bowl; beat well. Chill. Serve with cream and sugar if desired.

Þjetti: Beat together 2 eggs (well beaten), ½ cup sour cream and 1 tbsp. sugar.

Lyla Thorarinson's Skyr (An Alternative Method)

1 quart buttermilk
1 glass baking dish with cover

1. Make the night before at bedtime.
   Pour buttermilk into the baking dish. Cover and place in a preheated 325° F oven. Bake for 30 minutes. Shut oven off.
2. Leave dish in oven overnight, for at least 12 hours, after which the whey should be visibly separated from the curd.
3. Line a colander with cheese cloth or a new J-cloth and place the colander into another container.
4. Try to separate as much of the liquid from the curds before pouring the curd into the lined colander. Let it drain for about 4 hours or until the curd is fairly firm.
5. Put the curd into a bowl and beat until smooth.
   Add sugar to taste and serve with cream and/or fruit.

Terrific. I placed it in a j-cloth lined colander after 12 hours. I beat it with an electric mixer and had a bowl with brown sugar and cream. Janis suggested I put white sugar in at the time of beating but I didn't because it's not as sour as skyr I've had and brown sugar at serving offsets any sourness. Definitely a keeper.

Viola and Janis Johnson
Winnipeg, Manitoba

Fresh Fruit with Cardamom Skyr Dip

<u>Cardamom Skyr Dip</u>
1 cup skyr or sour cream
3 tbsp. honey
2 – 3 fresh strawberries (optional)
1 tsp. ground cardamom seeds

Prepare a selection of fruits and berries. Cut into bite size pieces and display attractively on a tray (lemon juice will keep pears and apples from browning). Serve with dip, providing cocktail picks.

<u>Cardamom Skyr Dip</u>

1. Blend altogether until smooth. If using strawberries, a food processor works well.
2. Transfer to a serving bowl and chill.

Puddings and Desserts

Ron Eyolfson's Skyr

1 4-litre ice cream pail of boiled water, cooled down to room temperature, 72° F to 75° F is okay (thermometer can be bought at beer or wine supply store)
1 - 5 litre bag of instant skim milk powder
1 cup of fresh buttermilk, for use as a culture (starter)
(The above amount should make between 40 - 50 oz. of skyr)

Ron Eyolfson is a professional skyr maker who was formerly with the Arborg Creamery.

8:00 am - Pour out about 1 litre of water from pail into a clean container to make room for powder and starter. Stir in powder until all is dissolved, then add starter and water to ½ inch from top of pail. Stir well and cover. Place in oven, leave undisturbed. At bedtime, turn oven light on. This will bring the temperature up to about 90° F and help to separate whey from curd. In the morning, test the curd for firmness and flavour. If okay, it is ready to be drained. This requires 3 ice cream pails or similar containers with cheese cloth held with clothes pegs.
Before scooping curd into the cloth, cut the curd into 1 inch squares with a long knife for better drainage and then scoop curd very gently to avoid breaking up curd too much for faster drainage. It takes about 1 day to drain before you remove from cloth to bowl and beat until smooth. I use my electric mix master for that. Good luck!

I have made skyr this way and find that occasionally the skyr will have very small granules that will remain unless you use a blender when you add the extra sweetener and milk or cream to bring the skyr to a nice soft pudding-like texture!

Elva Jonasson
Winnipeg, Manitoba

Hræringur (Skyr and Porridge)

2 cups skyr
1 cup porridge

Stir well together. Serve with brown sugar and cream if desired.

Skyr Cheesecake

Crust
- ½ cup flour
- ½ cup finely ground almonds
- ¼ cup sugar
- 1 tsp. grated lemon peel
- ½ tsp. vanilla
- 1 egg yolk
- ¼ cup butter, softened

Filling
- 3 cups (2 x 375g. containers) skyr
- 1 cup sugar
- 2 tbsp. flour
- 1 tsp. grated lemon peel
- 1 tsp. grated orange peel
- ½ tsp. vanilla
- 4 eggs
- ¼ - ½ tsp. ground cardamom seeds (optional)

1. Preheat oven to 400° F. Lightly grease inside of a 8 inch spring-form pan (2¼ inch high). Remove sides. Make crust: In medium bowl combine flour, sugar, lemon peel and vanilla; with pastry cutter blend in yolk and butter. Mix with fingertips until smooth.
2. On bottom of pan, form half of dough into a ball. Place waxed paper on top; roll pastry to edge of pan. Remove paper. Bake 6-8 minutes, until golden. Cool. Spreading with fingertips, line inside of pan (to ½ inch below top edge) with the remainder of the dough (smooth by rolling a glass over surface).
3. Preheat oven to 450° F. Make filling: In a large mixing bowl blend skyr, sugar, flour, peels, vanilla and cardamom. Beat in eggs, one at a time, until smooth. Pour into pan. Bake 10 minutes. Lower oven to 250° F. Bake one hour longer or until set. Remove to rack to cool-2 hours.
4. At this point you can spread the cheesecake with any fruit glaze you desire. Refrigerate until chilled-3 hours or overnight.

To serve: Remove side of pan. If you have not glazed, top each serving with a spoonful of preserves (e.g. raspberry or rhubarb).

Variation
- ¼ cup brown sugar
- ¼ tsp. cinnamon and nutmeg
- ½ cup slivered almonds

Combine and sprinkle over filling before baking.

Mysuostur (Whey Cheese)

Mysuostur was made from the whey, drained off from the curds used to make skyr. The whey was then boiled down and made into 'cheese' ('ostur' meaning 'cheese'). The whey was also kept to drink or to sour for the pickling of meats in barrels.

A caramel-coloured spread with a creamy smooth consistency, it has been dubbed 'Icelandic peanut butter', but this is misleading as only the texture is similar. It is delicious spread on Icelandic brown bread.

The first recipe is as it was made traditionally, starting from milk. From the curd, skyr could then also be made. Fortunately today we can purchase whey powder which greatly simplifies the process.

Mrs. B. Pell's Mysuostur (Whey Cheese)

2 gal. milk
1 tsp. liquid rennet
1 cup sugar
1 cup thick cream (or 4 tbsp. butter)

1. Warm milk and add rennet. When set break up curd and strain it off.
2. Boil whey down until there is about one pint left (this takes nearly a whole day), then strain.
3. Add cream or butter, or both may be added if desired. Simmer for ½ hour.
4. Beat thoroughly until cold. (If it is not well beaten it becomes coarse and sandy). Should be smooth and creamy, and thick enough to spread on bread like jam.

Doreen Guttormson's Mysuostur (Whey Cheese)

2 cups whey powder
1 385 ml. can of condensed milk
¼ cup butter, softened
1 cup brown sugar

1. Whip whey powder, milk and butter with beaters until smooth.
2. Place in microwave for 15 minutes on power level 4 (medium high). Stir every 2 minutes. Add brown sugar after six minutes.
3. Beat well and put into jars when cool.

Búðingur(súpa) og Deserar

Leslie Gislason's Mysuostur (Whey Cheese)

2 cups whey powder
1 385 ml. can evaporated milk or
1 500 ml. carton half & half cream
1½ cup brown sugar
½ cup butter

1. Mix all ingredients together in a 5 quart casserole dish. Combine well (use a large casserole to avoid mixture boiling over).
2. Microwave on high until mixture comes to a boil. Stir well.
3. Microwave on medium (enough heat to allow mixture to simmer, about 15 minutes) until it begins to thicken, stirring occasionally.
4. Once mixture has thickened beat continuously until cool (a mix-master may be used as it takes a long time to cool). Put into jars. Serve on brown bread (Should be the consistency of peanut butter).

It turned out wonderfully smooth in texture. Leslie's instructions emphasize the importance of beating it until it is cool (like making fudge) to avoid a grainy texture.

Shirley Schellenberg
Dundas, Ontario

Sætsúpa (Sweet Soup)

2½ qt. boiling water
1 cup sago (seed tapioca)
1 cup sugar
½ cup raisins
½ cup chopped prunes
2 sticks cinnamon
¼ tsp. oil of lemon
1 cup fruit juice
1 cup sherry (optional)

1. Add the sago and the sugar to the boiling water. Cook until sago becomes clear.
2. Add raisins, prunes, and cinnamon and boil for 10-15 minutes longer, until prunes are tender. Remove from the fire (heat) and add lemon flavouring, fruit juice and sherry. Serve hot as you would any soup.

The sago soup has been made and consumed. Comments of my dinner guests-'I like it!'; 'Good after a cold day'; 'Nice light dessert'; 'Very nicely spiced'; 'Great after skiing or sleigh ride'.

Carol Frederickson
Winnipeg, Manitoba

Sætsúpa (Sweet Soup)

Original quantities followed by conversions in ⅓ amounts:
6 litres, 9 cups water
400g, ¾ cup sago
150g, ½ cup raisins
2-3 prunes per person as desired
½ litre, ¾ cup fruit juice
cinnamon, sugar, salt to taste

The sago is added to the boiling water and stirred until it comes to a boil again. The raisins and prunes are washed well and added with the cinnamon and allowed to boil about 15-20 minutes. Then the fruit juice, sugar and food colouring, if necessary and 1-2 tsp. salt.

This recipe is very similar to the one preceding. The differences are that the New Iceland version includes sugar and the option of adding sherry. Fruit juice would typically be from berries. Berries available in Iceland are red currants, blackcurrants, blueberries, krækiber (crowberries) and strawberries although scarce. Apricot or apple juice could also be used. Dried apricots and dried apples were sometimes added to sætsúpa in New Iceland. (See the following recipe.)

Sætsúpa (Sweet Soup)

¾ cup dried apricots, cut in half
1 cup prunes
6 cups cold water
1 cinnamon stick
2 lemon slices
3 tbsp. sago (seed tapioca)
½ cup sugar
½ cup raisins
1 tart cooking apple, peeled and chopped coarsely

1. Cover apricots with 5 cups cold water in a large saucepan. Let soak for 30 minutes.
2. Meanwhile, place prunes in a small saucepan and cover with 1 cup cold water. Bring to a boil and simmer covered for about 15 minutes.
3. Drain water into saucepan with apricots. Remove pits from prunes and chop coarsely.
4. Add prunes, cinnamon stick, lemon slices, sago and sugar. Stir, bringing to a boil. Reduce heat to low and simmer covered for about 10 minutes until sago becomes clear. Stir occasionally.
5. Add the raisins and chopped apples and continue to simmer another 10 minutes or until apples are tender.

The last time I made this I had a cup of blueberries to use up. I added them with the raisins and apples. It was delicious. You can serve this hot or chilled as a dessert soup, with cheese and breads if desired.

Judith Sigurdson's Hrísgrjónagrautur (Rice Pudding)

2 eggs, beaten
½ cup sugar
½ tsp. vanilla
¼ tsp. cinnamon
1 ½ cups cooked rice
⅓ cup raisins, optional
1 cup milk and 1 cup cream, scalded
or
2 cups 2% milk, scalded

Makes 6 servings.

1. Combine all ingredients, except the scalded milk and cream. Add in the milk and cream. Mix well.
2. Pour into greased 1½ -2 qt. casserole in pan filled 1 inch deep with hot water.
3. Bake at 350° F 45-60 minutes, until knife when inserted comes out clean. (For a better distribution of rice and raisins, stir after 30 minutes).
4. Serve warm or cold, with or without cream and additional cinnamon if desired.

I'm afraid my favourite recipe has become one of ease and also a little less fattening. We all love it and nobody misses the whole milk and cream called for – although when I feel deprived I may put some half and half on it with the cinnamon at serving time.   -Judith

This exquisitely sincere recipe, served steaming from the oven sprinkled with nutmeg and maple sugar, with a dash of real cream and a garnish of dried apricot, is a special offering to neighbours and friends at a bonfire inspired evening of laughter and carolling.   Or try packing as a scrumptious mid-day snack for a mid-week ode to simple comforts.

Jenivieve de Vries
Eden Mills, Ontario

Puddings and Desserts

Lillian Eyolfson's Hrísgrjónagrautur (Creamy Rice Pudding)

2 ½ cups boiling water
1 tsp. salt
½ cup rice
1 tin evaporated milk (385 ml)
⅓ cup sugar

1. Boil rice in water for about 20 minutes or until cooked. Water will have soaked in.
2. Add evaporated milk and sugar and cook in double boiler for ½ hour longer.
3. Serve hot or cold.

Jólahrísgrjónagrautur (Christmas Rice Pudding)

Prepare rice pudding (hrisgrjónagrauter), including a single almond. The lucky one who finds the almond in their serving receives a small gift.

Hrísgrjónagrautur (Rice Porridge/Pudding)

Original quantities followed conversions in ⅛ amounts:
6 litres, 3½ cups milk and water
700g, ½ cup rice
3-4 tsp., ½ tsp. salt
sugar and cinnamon
whole milk or fruit juice

The water and milk is set over the heat. The rice is washed, first with hot then with cold water until the water is clear, then added when the milk/water comes to a boil, stirred in until it comes to a boil again, and then let to simmer slowly for 1½ hours (about 45 minutes for the ⅛ conversion amounts) with the pot covered. The porridge is salted just before serving.
Served with sugar and cinnamon, milk or fruit juice.

"Fruit juice" refers to a fruit concentrate, raspberry or strawberry, blended with water (e.g. raspberry vinegar). As there is no sugar in the recipe, the "fruit juice" would add flavour and sweetness. Perhaps this practice originates from earlier days when berries were used when sugar was unavailable (as with skyr). This recipe and Lillian Eyolfson's are prepared on top of the stove. (The use of evaporated milk in Lillian's pudding dates her recipe to the days when evaporated milk was often used because of limited refrigeration.) Judith Sigurdson's baked version of Hrísgrjónagrautur is a later adaptation.

Kristin Thorvaldson's Cornstarch Pudding

1. In a heavy pot or double boiler, bring 4 cups milk and ¼ cup sugar to a boil.
2. Mix 4 tbsp. (level) cornstarch with ⅓ cup cold milk. Add to the milk and sugar, slowly, stirring all the while until the pudding is thickened.

Serve warm or cold with a dollop of jelly or preserves and milk or cream. Some prefer a sprinkling of sugar and cinnamon.
(It is important to be aware that when the milk shows bubbles all the way around the edge of the pot, it has almost reached the boiling point. It will overflow the pot very quickly if you are not prepared to stir it down and add the cornstarch liquid for thickening.)

Miss Emma Hannesson's Prune Whip and Boiled Custard

<u>Prune Whip</u>
⅓ lb. prunes
½ cup sugar
5 egg whites
½ tsp. lemon juice

<u>Boiled Custard</u>
2 cups milk (scalded)
3 egg yolks
¼ cup sugar
a little salt
½ tsp. vanilla

Prune Whip
Cook prunes in a little water until soft; stone. Put through a strainer, add sugar, and cook 5 minutes. Beat egg whites stiff, and add prune mixture gradually. Cool, add lemon juice. Put in a well-buttered dish and bake 20 minutes in a slow oven (300°-325° F). Serve cold with boiled custard.

Boiled Custard
Beat yolks, add sugar, stir, gradually adding hot milk. Cook in a double boiler, stirring constantly until mixture thickens.

I tried the Prune Whip and custard sauce expecting something totally different than the result; it was -surprise, surprise- very good. I took a sample of it to Tsang, the chef at the Scandinavian Centre and he was also impressed. It was very easy to make, and I suggest that if you have some prune purée left when you make vínarterta that you make this. One cup of prune purée was about right and I recommend using less sugar than the recipe. It is almost the consistency of a mousse. Tsang suggested that we drizzle a little raspberry sauce

over and add a few raspberries for a garnish. That did make a very elegant presentation -even the colour was appealing -the prune whip is about the colour of milk chocolate. This is definitely on my list for when I want something special.

Kendra Jonasson
Winnipeg, Manitoba

Flauelsgrautur (Velvet Pudding)

Original quantities followed by conversions in ¼ amounts:
425g, ½ cup butter
625g, 1¼ cup flour
4½ litres, 5 cups milk and water
2-3 tsp., 1 tsp. salt
sugar and cinnamon
milk or fruit juice

The butter is put into a cold pot which is set over heat and when the butter is melted, the flour is added and cooked well together. Then the mixture is thinned little by little with the hot milk which was previously scalded. The porridge (pudding) is salted and allowed to cook slowly for 6 to 8 minutes; stir all the while. Sugar and cinnamon is sprinkled on top with milk or fruit juice.

Flauelsgrautur was a childhood favourite of Guðrún Ágústsdóttir (Guðrún Jónsdóttir's granddaughter —the writer of this recipe). Velvet pudding is an example of a "basic" that is usually not recorded but simply considered common home-cooking knowledge. While a comparable "basic" might be cornstarch pudding (see Kristin Thorvaldson's), this recipe differs as there is no cornstarch, eggs, or sugar. However, if these ingredients are not on hand, with make-do substitutions, a homey, comforting pudding is still possible as in the following from **Cook Book** (1950): 'Substitutions: ...7. Substitute for eggs:...In custard mixtures... 2 level tablespoons of flour may be substituted for one egg... 12. Substitute for cornstarch: 2 level tablespoons flour= 1 level tablespoon cornstarch, in cream fillings, custards and sauces..." And as with Velvet Pudding, a sprinkling of sugar and cinnamon can compensate for the sugar omission. 'Fruit juice' refers to a fruit concentrate, raspberry or strawberry, blended with water (e.g. raspberry vinegar).

Mrs. T. Scambler's Citronsúpa (Lemon Pudding)

1½ cups milk
1 cup sugar
1 lemon
2 tbsp. butter
2 eggs, separated
2 tbsp. flour

1. Cream together sugar and butter. Stir in grated rind and juice of lemon, beaten egg yolks and flour. Add milk and fold in beaten egg whites.
2. Pour in buttered baking dish and set in a pan of water.
3. Bake for one hour in a moderate oven (350° F). Top should be brown. Serve cold with whipped cream if desired.

The pudding came out of the oven with a lovely golden brown crust and when we served it, there were two layers – a light puffy top with a creamy lemon sauce below. Tried it plain and warm., also with a garnish of strawberry preserves, and with whipped cream. Delectable every which way.

Marina (Jonasson) Wishnevetski and Kaitlin Wishnevetski
Kamsack, Saskatchewan

Brauðbúðingur (Bread Pudding)

2¼ cups milk
2 slightly beaten eggs
3-4 cups 1 inch day old bread cubes
½ cup brown sugar
½ tsp. cinnamon
1 tsp. vanilla
¼ tsp. salt
½ cup raisins

Butterscotch Sauce (makes 1 cup)
1 slightly beaten egg yolk
¼ cup butter
¼ cup water*
⅔ cup brown sugar
⅓ cup light corn syrup

1. Preheat oven to 350° F. Grease an 8 inch baking dish.
2. Whisk eggs and milk. Add remaining ingredients. Mix together and pour over bread cubes.
3. Put in baking dish. Place in pan filled 1 inch deep with hot water.
4. Bake about 45 minutes or until an inserted knife comes out clean.
5. Spoon butterscotch sauce over each serving as desired.

Butterscotch Sauce
1. Combine all ingredients in a double boiler; mix well.
2. Over hot water cook until thickened; stir frequently.
3. Stir before using (may be reheated).
   * Substitute whiskey or rum for water if desired.

Puddings and Desserts

> *This poor man's treat is perfect for a cold winter's night. Brown sugar, butter, and the comfort of home – what could be better than bread pudding.*
>
> Marno Olafson
> Winnipeg, Manitoba

Kristrun Sigurdson's Blueberry Crunch

1 cup quick cooking oatmeal
½ cup dry milk solids
½ cup flour
1 cup light brown sugar
½ tsp. salt
½ tsp. cinnamon
½ cup butter
2 cups blueberries

1. Combine all dry ingredients. Mix together. Cut in butter until mixture resembles coarse crumbs.
2. Press ⅔ of this mixture evenly in bottom of greased 8 inch pan. Top with berries. Cover evenly with remaining mixture.
3. Bake at 350° F for 40 minutes or until top is nicely browned. Serve warm with ice cream, whipped cream or sour cream as desired.

> *This was wonderful served warm with ice cream. I will omit the salt next time though because we are not big on salt here and the butter itself has enough for us. We made this twice and we thoroughly enjoyed it. It's quick and easy and so good too!*
>
> Sharon and Shelley Jonasson
> Winnipeg, Manitoba

Bogga Dalmann's Epla Kaka (Apple Cake-Pudding)

For a 2 qt. dish, boil about ½ dozen good-sized apples and sweeten to taste. Roll rusks for crumbs and then put alternate layers of crumbs and apples, having a layer of crumbs on the bottom and the last layer of crumbs. Toasted bread may be used instead of the rusks. Add a little butter and cinnamon. Bake about ½ hour in a moderate oven (350° F). Serve with whipped cream.

Búðingur(súpa) og Deserar

Apple or Rhubarb Crisp

6 cups apples or rhubarb, sliced
¼-½ cup sugar
(depending on tartness of fruit)
½-1 tsp. cinnamon

<u>Topping</u>
¾ cup flour
¾ cup brown sugar
⅓ cup butter, room temperature

1. Toss apples or rhubarb with sugar (and cinnamon if making apple crisp).
2. Layer in a 9 x 9 inch greased baking pan.
3. Sprinkle topping over and bake at 375° F 40-50 minutes or until apples or rhubarb are tender and topping is nicely browned.
4. Serve warm with cream, whipped cream or ice cream as desired.

<u>Topping</u>
Rub together into fine crumbs.

I baked the apple crisp and the results were: very well done, top was very crunchy (almost too much). I tried it warm with ice cream and cold with whipping cream. Both were good. I found the topping overwhelmed the apples. My suggestion would be perhaps more apples and a lower heat such as 350° F for 40 minutes. I am also a nutmeg lover and I will add it to the cinnamon in my next effort.

Grace Malm
Maple Ridge, British Columbia

Raspberry Supreme

1 pkg. (15oz., 425g) frozen sweetened raspberries (thawed)
or an equal quantity of fresh berries
1 envelope unflavoured gelatin
¼ cup sugar
1 tbsp. fresh lemon juice
1 cup whipping cream

Serves 4-6

1. Press berries and their juice through a sieve. Add water to make 1½ cups.
2. In a saucepan mix gelatin with sugar. Add raspberry juice. Stir over medium heat until gelatin is dissolved. Add lemon juice. Chill until slightly thickened. Beat until smooth.
3. Whip cream and fold in gently but thoroughly. Pour into a 3 cup mold, serving bowl or individual dessert dishes. Chill until set.
4. Serve with whip cream or Raspberry Strawberry sauce or both.

Raspberry Strawberry Sauce

Purée in a blender or food processor ½ cup strawberries, ½ cup raspberries and 1 tbsp. sugar. Add 3 tbsp. raspberry liqueur, kirsch, or créme de cassis and blend. Strain through a sieve and chill.

Pineapple Rice Cream

⅓ cup white rice, uncooked
2½ cups milk
⅓ cup sugar
½ tsp. salt
2 envelopes unflavored gelatine
19 oz., 540 mL crushed pineapple, undrained
⅓ cup flaked coconut
1 tsp. vanilla extract
½ tsp. almond extract
1 cup heavy cream, whipped
4 canned pineapple slices, halved
¼ cup apricot preserves

Makes 8 servings.

1. In top of double boiler, combine rice, milk, sugar and salt. Cook over boiling water, covered and stirring occasionally until rice is tender - about 1 hr. 15 min.
2. In small bowl sprinkle gelatine over pineapple. Let stand 5 minutes to soften. Turn into hot rice mixture, stirring to dissolve gelatin completely.
3. Stir in coconut, vanilla and almond extracts.
4. Refrigerate until cool (about 1 hr) or in freezer to cool more quickly. Mixture should be firm enough to mound.
5. With rubber spatula, fold whipped cream into cooled gelatine mixture. Mix thoroughly.
6. Turn into fancy 1½ quart mold. Refrigerate until firm enough to unmold - at least 3 hours or overnight.
7. To unmold: run a sharp knife around edge of mold to loosen. Invert on serving platter; shake to unmold. (If necessary, place a hot damp cloth on bottom of mold.)
8. Around base of mold arrange pineapple halves. Over low heat, melt preserves and brush over surface of mold. Decorate with rosettes of whipping cream if desired.
9. Refrigerate until serving.

Brauð - Bread

The 'old-fashioned' art of bread making is not as difficult as the uninitiated sometimes believe. Admittedly it does take some experience to get a 'feel' for when the dough is sufficiently kneaded but even first attempts can be very satisfying. Earlier generations of women had no choice but to bake the bread their families required. Luckily we can choose to bake bread for all kinds of wonderful rewards - the aroma of baking bread, the pride felt as the loaves cool on the racks, the enjoyment of that first slice of bread hot from the oven, and the nostalgia for the bread your Mother, Aunty or Amma (grandmother) baked. Explanations of bread-making terms as used in the recipes are provided to help ensure good results, especially for novice bakers.

Mixing and Kneading the Dough: After combining the yeast and other ingredients with enough of the flour to make a soft dough, turn dough out of the mixing bowl onto a floured surface. Knead in additional flour until the dough no longer sticks to your hands. Kneading is necessary to strengthen the gluten and is complete when the dough is elastic and has a sheen on the surface. Knead by pushing down with the heel of your palm. Give the dough a quarter turn; fold the dough over and continue kneading as you turn the dough clockwise.

Rising: Place the dough into a lightly greased bowl; turn over to grease surface; cover with a clean cloth to prevent a crust from forming and set in a warm place to rise. The rising time will depend on the type of yeast and the surrounding temperature.

Punching Down: Punch down by plunging your hand into the dough. Fold the dough into the centre. Knead briefly, let rise again or shape into loaves, according to the recipe.

Shaping into Loaves and Baking: Divide dough into portions according to the size of your pans and recipe guidelines as to yields. Flatten a dough portion with a rolling pin into a rectangle (as wide as the length of your pan and about three times the width long.) Roll up jelly roll style or fold in thirds. Tuck ends under firmly to give ends a smooth crust. Cover loaves and let rise in a warm place until double in bulk.

Loaves are baked when the top is nicely browned and when you tap the bottom it sounds hollow. Remove from pans and cool on wire racks.

For a soft shiny crust, brush the tops of loaves with butter while warm. Some like to glaze before baking by brushing with a beaten egg for a shiny crust, water for a crisp crust or milk for a soft crust.

See 'Notes on Ingredients' for information about flours, grains, and yeast.

BRAUÐGJÖRÐ (ON BAKING BREAD)

April 12, 1878

The baking of wholesome and tasty bread is among the most important aspects of the preparation of meals and every housewife should be familiar with it. It may therefore be essential for Framfari to give some pointers on this subject, since it is well known that most of the women in New Iceland have never had the opportunity to learn to bake bread in the manner customary in this country.

As is frequently the case in other matters, people have various recipes for baking bread, each of which can be good in itself, but it is always essential to follow certain basic rules. The first and most important of these is to knead the dough sufficiently, the second to use only the best yeast, and the third to take care that the dough has risen sufficiently before putting it in the oven, while the fourth is to ensure that the heat in the oven be maintained evenly and properly. In order to make an accurate determination of the baking time, the simplest method is to take into account the amount of water in the bread. Four to five pints (one pint is approximately half a Danish pint) is about sufficient for about one batch in a No. 8 oven. In the winter time it is best to let the flour to be used stand in a warm room for several hours so that it is warmed through, and it is best to sift it in a sieve made for that purpose. Salt is then added to the flour, water poured into it and stirred for a time. A porcelain bowl or tin container is best to use in baking bread. The heat of the water depends upon the season of the year; in summer it is sufficient that it be warm, but in cold weather it should be rather hot, although never so hot that one cannot put his hand into it. When the water and flour have been mixed together —and not before— the yeast is added and the dough kneaded vigorously for a few minutes. Enough flour is used so that the dough can be kneaded but does not become smooth, and then it is let to stand until the following morning to rise. In the winter time it is customary to cover the container so the dough does not become cold, for should that happen, such dough can never produce good bread, but in the summer it may not be covered, for then there would be a risk of it turning sour. When the dough has risen well, so that it is foamy and contains air bubbles, it is kneaded with flour until it will take no more and has become fine and dense. It is then let [to] stand covered to rise until large holes appear in it. Then it is taken, shaped into loaves and placed in the pan. In frying pans of the type sold with the stoves, it is best to have three to four loaves according to the size of the pan. If the dough has been properly prepared, little explosive sounds will be heard when it is being shaped into loaves, and then it must not be kneaded any more than is absolutely necessary, so that the air is not lost from the dough, and the dough should be hard enough to hold its shape when placed in the pan. Now the bread should be let [to] stand and rise again before it is baked. It is almost as bad to let bread rise too much as not enough before it is baked, for then it loses the savour it would otherwise have and soon dries out. If the bread has risen well before being placed in the oven, it is best to have the oven very hot, so that a crust forms on the bread at once. If it has been slow to rise, it may be set in a more moderate oven, covered with a thin sheet of paper, to hinder a crust from forming until it has been able to rise. Baking time for loaves of average size is considered to be one to one and a half hours. The loaves should be separated when they are removed from the oven, and as an indication they are thoroughly baked, the crust should rise again where pressure is exerted with a finger.

Another method of making bread is to knead it as hard as it ought to be before it has risen, and then nothing need be done the next morning but to form the loaves and let them rise until they are ready for baking. This method requires less effort, and the bread baked in this manner can be just as good. Each woman can use the method she finds best. The main consideration is, as mentioned earlier, that the dough be well kneaded. Good bread never has a sour taste and has evenly spaced small air pockets throughout, but that bread containing larger pockets, but which is dense and hard-packed between them, with dark edges, is not at all wholesome.

Up to now most women in New Iceland must have used sour dough in their bread. Although that can be very good, bread can be considerably better if good sweet yeast is used in its preparation, so we shall give some pointers here on the preparation of yeast.

A handful of unpressed hops should be boiled in two pints of water, or an appropriate amount of water if the hops are pressed. Place the hops in a loose bag and let them boil for fifteen to twenty minutes. Peel five or six good quality potatoes and boil them in that water. When they are tender, mash them with a potato masher after they have been drained, mix them together with three to four heaping tablespoons of flour and one of salt (some use a little sugar and ground ginger), pour the boiling hops water over that, a little at a time, and stir well, so it is of an even consistency. Some people use no hops at all in yeast, but it keeps better without turning sour when hops are used. In order to bring about fermentation, yeast cakes are used (Footnote: They can be obtained from Mr. Fr. Fridriksson at Gimli for 12-15 cents a package. One package is enough for three to four families.) and the procedure is as follows. Take two cakes and dissolve them in a large cup half filled with well warmed water. When they are completely dissolved, flour should be stirred in to make a rather thick gruel, which should be covered and let stand in a warm place until it begins to rise. After it has risen, it should be poured into the aforementioned hops broth, which should be quite warm, with fresh milk added to it, and let stand in a warm place until it has begun to ferment. Then it should be placed in a crock or bottle with a narrow neck and a tight cap, or with a sheet of paper bound over it. The yeast may be used the following day, and one average size cup should be sufficient for about four to five pints of water. The next time yeast is prepared, only one or two cups of old yeast is sufficient to cause fermentation in that which is being prepared, but it is not necessary to use yeast cakes in the preparation; it is, however, best to have on hand about one half more than is required if by any mishap the yeast should not rise. Pure yeast spores are also excellent to have on hand in case the prepared yeast will not rise. They will also bring about the required fermentation. In the winter time more yeast can be prepared than is recommended above, because it keeps well and survives a certain amount of freezing but in the summer it will not retain its freshness without turning sour in more than one or two weeks, unless preserved in an ice house or refrigerator. Yeast that has turned sour should be thrown out and a new batch prepared.

Brúnt Brauð (Brown Bread)

These brown bread recipes have always been unquestionably known as 'Icelandic', and yet it is stated in the preceding article, 'On Baking Bread', that 'most of the women in New Iceland have never had the opportunity to bake bread in the manner customary in this country' (in reference to their having had little or no experience baking bread with yeast). The closest comparison to a traditional bread in Iceland would probably be rúgbrauð, a very dark, dense rye bread. New Iceland Brown Bread was a very successful adaptation and with some admitted prejudice I would say that it is homemade bread at its best. It is richly flavoured and sweetened with molasses. Some prefer it very dense and others lighter-textured as is reflected in the recipes. Delicious with jellies, jams and preserves and traditionally served with fish and þorramatur (foods of the winter feast –see 'þorrablót' p. 93).

Sella Thorvardson's Brúnt Brauð

2 tbsp. or 2 pkg. traditional yeast
¾ cups warm water
1 tsp. sugar
1 cup milk
3 cups water
1 cup cooking molasses
2 eggs
1 tbsp. butter or shortening
½ cup brown sugar
2 tsp. salt
2 cups graham or whole wheat flour
10 cups white flour (approx.)

1. Add yeast to ¾ cup warm water with 1 tsp. sugar. Let set for 10 min.
2. In a large bowl, mix together all ingredients except white flour.
3. Add white flour, gradually kneading, until the dough no longer sticks to your hands. Knead well, about 15 minutes more.
4. Clean bowl; grease and place dough back into the bowl turning over so top is greased lightly. Cover and let rise in a warm place until double in bulk.
5. Punch down and knead again (10-15 minutes). Shape into 5 average sized loaves. Let rise until double in bulk.
6. Bake at 375° F for about 30 minutes.
7. Brush with butter while hot.

It was delicious-we each had two slices as soon as it came out of the oven. I have never made bread before that you have to knead. I bought the graham flour at a bulk food store so that was no problem. I'll bake it often now that I've done it.

Diane Kortesluoma
Sudbury, Ontario

Sylvia Sigurdson's Brúnt Brauð

2 tbsp. or 2 pkg. traditional yeast
1 cup warm water
1 tsp. sugar
1-16 oz. can evaporated milk
1-16 oz. can water
1 cup cooking molasses (light)
1 cup brown sugar
1 tbsp. salt
2 cups rye flour
9 cups white flour (approx.)

1. Add yeast to 1 cup warm water with 1 tsp. sugar. Let set for 10 minutes.
2. In a large bowl mix together all ingredients except white flour.
3. Add white flour gradually, kneading in just enough to handle dough (dough will be slightly sticky).
4. Clean bowl; grease and place dough back into the bowl turning over so top is greased lightly. Cover and let rise in a warm place overnight.
5. In the morning, punch down and shape into 5 average sized loaves.
6. Let rise until doubled in bulk.
7. Bake on bottom rack at 350° F for 50 minutes.
8. Brush with butter while hot.

I made bread yesterday-lots of it! With Sylvia's recipe - I added 2 tbsp. of margarine (melted). I made a batch earlier with 4 cups whole wheat and 4 plus cups of white. This made a very rich bread. I still think I'd go back to my Amma's Brown Bread. Maybe because I know it better - but I think it's lighter and it's a smaller batch and easier to handle.

Lorna Tergesen
Gimli, Manitoba

Brauð

Gudny Stefanson's (Lorna's Amma) Brúnt Brauð

2 cups milk (Lorna uses skim)
4 tbsp. shortening
½ cup sugar
¼ cup molasses
1 heaping tbsp. salt
2 tbsp. or 2 pkg. traditional yeast
¾ cup warm water
2 tsp. sugar
4 cups white flour
4 cups graham or whole wheat flour (approx.)

1. Scald milk. Add shortening, sugar, molasses and salt; stir together. Cool to lukewarm.
2. Add yeast to ¾ cup warm water with 2 tsp. sugar. Let set for 10 minutes. Add to lukewarm mixture.
3. Put 4 cups white flour in a large bowl and add liquid all at once. Beat until smooth. Add graham flour 1 cup at a time, kneading well until the dough is easy to handle.
4. Clean bowl; grease and place dough back into the bowl turning over so top is greased lightly. Cover and let rise in a warm place until double in bulk.
5. Punch down and shape into 3 small or 2 large loaves. Let rise until nearly double in bulk.
6. Place in 400° F oven; then reduce heat to 325° F. Bake for approximately 45 minutes.

A flavour treasure to be found only at home!

I decided to challenge myself and not the recipe. My instinct is to place the recipe on the counter and then try to change all the ingredients with whatever I have around the house at the time ... which never ... never works.

Out of respect for Gudny and Lorna I only broke the rules once. Now this is a first time for me ... I made sure I had everything I needed ... the only ingredient I had to seek out was the graham flour, which I found in a health food store.

Next challenge was to make sure I didn't take any short cuts ... which I did by trying to scald the milk in the microwave ... failed twice ... so the old fashioned on the stove method rendered me the success I so desired.

Success based on Gudny's wisdom and her tested and true recipe. I can now say, "Brown bread the way I remember it lives again on Willow Island." Thanks Gudny! Thanks Lorna! Thanks Kris! Anyone wishing to recreate the flavour of old times just add this to your weekly baking ... nowhere in any bakery will you find this treasure. There is magic in the aroma ... no person can resist falling in love with the baker ... be careful who you serve it to.

Recreated with love and patience.

Kathy Arnason
Willow Island, Manitoba

Johanna Wilson's Brúnt Brauð

2 cups lukewarm water
2 tbsp. sugar
2 tbsp. dry yeast (quick rise)
1 cup white flour
1 ½ cups lukewarm water
½ cup soft margarine
1 tbsp. salt
¾ cup molasses
1 cup brown sugar
6 cups whole wheat flour
2 cups white flour

Johanna won a prize for her Brown Bread recipe in the Side Dish category of a Winnipeg Free Press contest (December 1991). Recipes were judged on the basis of nutrition, economy, creativity, flavour and ease of preparation.

1. Mix yeast and sugar in the lukewarm water. Let set in a covered bowl for 20 minutes.
2. Add 1 cup white flour. Cover and leave another 20 minutes.
3. Mix in the remaining ingredients. Knead well and place in a greased bowl.
4. Let rise until double in bulk. (About 2 hours.)
5. Shape into 6 loaves ; place in well-greased pans. Allow to rise until double in size.
6. Bake at 350° F for 50-60 minutes.

I followed the recipe exactly. I used Fleishmann's Speedy Rise yeast - 3 individual packets made 2 tbsp. I used Gramma's molasses which might not be as thick as the molasses I remember. Consequently the dough ended up a little too sticky so I added about another cup of white flour. About ½ I added to the dough in the bowl and another ½ while kneading. Also my Pyrex loaf pans are slightly larger than metal ones (wider) so I made five loaves instead of six.

My husband Vin and I, my daughter her husband and grandson all pronounced the bread delicious. While warm it was especially crusty and nutty with a nice texture, not at all yeasty. Cooled it is most flavourful, especially with butter and toasted it is a treat.

I added raisins to one loaf. Vin and I enjoyed it very much but it didn't go over with family or friends. I remember having brown bread with raisins at one of my aunt's and thought it was great. I mentioned it to Johanna and she said her mother-in-law used to make a great raisin brown - so I tried it.

I remember from my youth that Icelandic Brown Bread was always dark brown. There was even a bakery in Selkirk that delivered the dark brown to my dad's store in Gimli. This bread is lighter in color - say a dark whole wheat.

Joyce (Thorkelson) Giedraitis
Vernon, Connecticut

Brauð

Laura Thorkelson's Brúnt Brauð
Adaptation for Bread Making Machines by Shirley Sigurdson

1¼ cups water
¼ cup molasses
2 tsp. oil
¼ cup brown sugar
1 tsp. salt
1¾ cups white flour
1 cup whole wheat flour
½ cup rye flour
3 tsp. yeast (as recommended for your machine)

Makes 1 loaf

1. Add ingredients to the pan in the order suggested by the directions for your machine.
2. Set machine for rapid loaf, light crust (or move after first rise to pan and bake traditionally.)

My mom says it should be sweet. This particular recipe, adapted for the bread machine, strikes her as great, but not magnificent. For that she advises a little more brown sugar and molasses. To you, according to your taste. For me, it's an epiphany. It is a return to summers long ago, the formica table and the ticking clock in Aunty Sella's kitchen - and the aroma! Sella's brown bread was legendary and an unfair advantage in establishing also the reputation of Arborg's butter, a necessary accessory. Those who came ate. And raved.

Clinical notes: outside sweetness, the other critical factor is density. Real Icelandic brown bread has to be solid, sturdy stuff. For this, you have to play around with salt, yeast, humidity and altitude. Salt prohibits rising and in this sense acts against the yeast. Altitude enhances the yeast's ability and humidity adjusts the flour's requirement for moisture, which plays into all of the above. Make a hundred loaves and find the right chemistry for your kitchen. Or make this recipe - it will probably work just fine. I also suggest that you add the wet first, then the dry, especially if you are going to delay the baking process to accommodate your return home later in the day. This stops the yeast from starting up - add it last.

Eric Olafson
Salt Lake City, Utah

I was not happy with the original recipe because it did not have the lightness of my mother-in-law Loa's brown bread so in trying various methods, I finally was pleased with the lightness of the following recipe and also found that it had a nice fine texture and a more moist quality that kept the bread fresher longer.

While I agree with Eric's comments about "Laura Thorkelson's Brúnt Brauð", Icelandic brown bread should have some substance but again I compare it to my mother-in-law Loa's wonderfully light and fine textured brúnt brauð and found that if I added an egg and 1 tblsp. lemon juice that I would get a loaf more like her bread. It is important to note that when you are using a 2 lb. bread machine that you add my suggestion of an egg and the lemon juice only with the 1½ lb. recipes. The egg and lemon juice make the bread rise to the size of a 2 lb. loaf. And as good as Auntie Sella's brown bread was, it was every bit as light as Loa's and both were famous for their superb breads.

Steini's 50% Whole Wheat Bread (for the bread machine)

<u>1.5 lb. loaf ingredients</u>
- 1 cup hot water
- 1 whole large egg (unbeaten)
- 1½ tbsp. extra virgin olive oil
- 1½ tsp. salt
- 1½ cups whole wheat flour
- 1½ cups all-purpose flour
- 2 tbsp. skim milk powder
- ¼ cup packed brown sugar
- 1½ tsp. quick-rise yeast
- 1 tbsp. lemon juice

1. Measure and add liquid ingredients to the pan.
2. Measure and add dry ingredients (except yeast) to the bread pan.
3. Use your finger to form a well (hole) in the flour where you will pour the yeast. (Yeast must NEVER come into contact with a liquid when you are adding ingredients.) Measure the yeast and carefully pour it into the well.
4. Snap the baking pan into the breadmaker and close the lid.
5. Press "Select" button to choose the Whole Wheat setting.
6. Press the "Crust Colour" button to choose light, medium or dark crust. (I use light).
7. Press the "Start/Stop" button.

Steini Jonasson,
Winnipeg, Manitoba

Brauð

Mrs. B. Guttormson's Raisin Brown Bread

3 cups graham flour
1 cup white flour
1¾ tsp. soda
1 tsp. salt
¾ cups raisins or walnuts or a combination
1 cup molasses
2½ cups sour milk or buttermilk

1. Mix all dry ingredients together.
2. Chop raisins small. Combine with molasses and milk. Add to dry ingredients; beat thoroughly.
3. Bake as for Boston Brown Bread. Fill buttered cans about ¾ full. Butter the lids before closing and tie or tape the lid on (from the original recipe: "This may be steamed in baking powder tins. It will require 4 or 5 tins." Today, baking powder is purchased in a cardboard container and so is unsuitable.)
4. Steam 1½ hours in one inch of water; then bake at 350° F uncovered until crusted and toothpick comes out clean.

Alternative Method
1. Fill two greased loaf pans with batter. Cover the tops with greased parchment paper and cover over with aluminum foil.
2. Set loaf pans in a larger pan. Add water to about 1 inch depth.
3. Bake at 350° F for approximately 1½ hours. Remove parchment paper and foil and continue baking until crusted and toothpick comes out clean.

It was good for breakfast-thinly sliced and toasted. The flavour mellows and I liked it better the second day.

Helga Bjornson
Wilmington, Delaware

Mrs. J.J. Vopni's Bran Bread

3 cups bran
2 cups flour
1 tbsp. baking powder
1 tsp. baking soda
½ cup brown sugar
1 tsp. salt
2 cups buttermilk
1 tbsp. molasses

1. Mix dry ingredients together.
2. Add buttermilk and molasses to the dry ingredients. Stir to combine well.
3. Smooth batter in one large greased loaf pan. Bake at 350° F for about 45 minutes (original recipe stated, 'turn top off, bottom on low').

The recipe was an easy one to follow – directions excellent and I followed it exactly. I used 1% buttermilk and cooking molasses. My loaf pan was 5 x 9 x 3 inches.

It made a very nice loaf-moist and I thought good tasting...It certainly is a healthy loaf and great for a high fibre diet. I feel raisins would improve the flavour. Or spread with butter (or margarine) and jelly.

Gladys Peterson
Surrey, B.C.

Brauð

Mrs. K. Thorsteinson's Anadama Bread

2 cups boiling water
½ cup cornmeal
2 tbsp. shortening
½ cup molasses
3 tsp. salt
1 tbsp. or 1 pkg. traditional yeast
½ cup lukewarm water
½ tsp. sugar
5 cups flour (approx.)
(original recipe: 1 cake fresh yeast)

1. Slowly add cornmeal to boiling water in large mixing bowl, stirring constantly.
2. Add shortening, molasses and salt. Stir to combine. Cool to lukewarm.
3. Meanwhile soften yeast in water with sugar. Let set about 10 minutes.
4. Add yeast to lukewarm cornmeal mixture; then add 4 cups flour, ½ cup at a time to make a stiff dough. Turn out and lightly knead in another ½ -1 cup more flour (dough will be slightly sticky).
5. Place dough in greased bowl and let rise until doubled in bulk.
6. Punch down, knead and form into 2 to 3 loaves. Let rise again.
7. Bake at 425° F for 15 minutes. Reduce heat to 375° F and bake for 30-45 minutes longer.

I saw the Anadama bread in my Icelandic cookbook but never made it before. Pam and I made it yesterday. Results- rather sweet, cakelike and chewy- a bit heavy. Liked it better as toast.

We beat in 4 cups flour, ½ cup at a time — and kneaded in 1 more cup. Dough very firm at that amount (omitted step 3). Rose very well — in 1 ½ hrs. was more than doubled. Made 1 long narrow loaf for the bread pans I have. Baked according to instructions. Results ... toast. Not a recipe I would particularly recommend. If I did I'd use ¼ or ⅛ cup of molasses and use part whole wheat flour.

Valgerdur Atkinson
Surrey, British Columbia

Pamela Atkinson
Mexico

Ingibjorg Olafson's Baking Powder Biscuits

2 cups flour
1 tbsp. baking powder
½ tsp. salt
¼ cup shortening
1 beaten egg plus milk to make one cup

1. Cut shortening into blended dry ingredients, add liquid and mix until just blended. This makes a very soft dough, handle as little as possible.
2. Turn out dough onto well floured pastry cloth, roll out to ½ inch thickness, cut into round or square or diamond shapes and place on a cookie sheet.
3. Bake at 450° F for about 12 minutes.

Serve hot with butter and jam or jelly.

Elva and Steini Jonasson's Biscuit Adaptations

Variation no. 1
To accommodate "heart-smart" diets substitute ¼ cup virgin olive oil for the shortening. Blend dry ingredients and add all liquids as above.

Variation no. 2
After dough is rolled out, spread with butter, sprinkle well with brown sugar and cinnamon. Roll up the dough as you would a jelly roll and slice into 1 inch slices. Place cut side down in muffin tins and bake at 450° F. To cut the soft dough, use a doubled up length of sewing thread and place under the rolled up dough. Bring thread up over the roll so that it crosses and pull the thread across the top so that it cuts neatly through the dough.

Variation no. 3
As with no. 1, instead of spreading the dough with butter, brush on extra virgin olive oil before adding the sugar and cinnamon.

Variation no. 4
Roll out dough to ½ inch thickness and spread with one of the following: Ground up leftover chicken or turkey with onions, salt and pepper to

Brauð

taste, leftover gravy if you wish or some thickened chicken broth. Roll like jelly roll and slice. Bake in muffin tins at 450° F.

Flaked salmon or tuna, with peas if desired, with onions, salt and pepper to taste, add white sauce for moistening and roll as before. Bake in same manner.

Ground ham with green relish and onions, if desired, salt and pepper to taste, white sauce or home made cooked salad dressing for moistening. Roll and bake as above.

The above all freeze very well and make a quick snack or light lunch when served with a green salad. My mother used to put this in lunches for us when we had to take lunch to school and I used this a lot for our children's lunches. The biscuit recipe came from Amma Ingibjorg. We usually double the recipe.

> *I enjoyed making the biscuits; the recipe is pretty much fool-proof if you follow the instructions. I'd never used a pastry cloth before, but will from now on. It made working with the dough so much easier and you don't handle it as much, which is so important.*
>
> *When I made the basic recipe, I used 3% milk. This recipe made 10 large biscuits. I brushed 5 of the biscuits with milk before I baked them and left the other 5 dry. I preferred the shiny golden brown biscuit as opposed to the dry, slightly floured biscuit after they'd been baked. Both rose beautifully and tasted delicious, especially warm out of the oven with a bit of butter and jam.*
>
> *Light and flaky –Excellent!*
>
> *I made the heart-smart variation, substituting the shortening with virgin olive oil. The dough was a bit stickier and required a little more flour. They rose beautifully, had the same light and flaky texture, but I found the flavour of the olive oil to be quite overwhelming and didn't really care for them. (Perhaps with a bit of butter and home-made jam, they'd be better tasting –ha! ha!)*
>
> *I made the biscuits with the butter (1/4 cup), brown sugar (1/2 cup) and cinnamon (2 tblsp.) and used the thread as suggested in the recipe to cut them. Worked like a charm!! You need to be sure the roll is pinched to keep the*

sugary filling from spilling out while baking.

Didn't try the meat or vegetable variations as they didn't appeal to me —but I did try a variation of my own (if you'd like to give it a try). I spread butter (¼ cup) on the dough, covered the buttered surface with grated aged cheddar (about ½ cup), 2 tbsp. parmesan, and some chives. Excellent!!

Joanne O'Hara
Gimli, Manitoba

Kristrun Sigurdson's Air Buns

½ cup warm water
1 tsp. sugar
1 tbsp. or 1 pkg. traditional yeast
½ cup shortening or butter
½ cup white sugar
2 tsp. salt
3 tbsp. vinegar
3 ½ cups warm water
8-10 cups flour

Makes approximately 4 dozen buns.

1. Soften yeast in ½ cup warm water with sugar. Let set about 10 minutes.
2. In a large bowl combine the remaining ingredients except the flour. Add the softened yeast to this mixture.
3. Stir in about 6 cups of flour, adding gradually until the dough begins to leave the sides of the bowl. Turn out on counter and knead in remaining flour until dough is smooth and elastic.
4. Set in a lightly greased bowl and cover with cloth. Let rise in a warm place until doubled in size (about 2 hours). Punch down. Knead lightly and let rise once more, another 2 hours.
5. Punch down and form into buns the size of an egg. Set slightly apart (farther apart for a crustier bun) on a greased baking sheet. Let rise until doubled in size (about 1 hour).
6. Bake at 375° F for 20-25 minutes. Remove and glaze with milk and sugar (2 tbsp. milk, 2 tbsp. sugar).

Brauð

Cinnamon buns:
This dough also makes great cinnamon buns. My children will gladly testify to this. I use half the dough for buns and then roll out the other half into a large rectangle. Spread it with softened butter; sprinkle with brown sugar, cinnamon and raisins if you like. Roll up, jelly roll style and seal edge. Cut into 1¼-1½ inch slices. Place cut side down into greased cake pans prepared with melted butter covering the bottom-sprinkled over with brown sugar. Let rise and bake as for air buns. Turn out upside down after baking. TIP: Ground cardamom may be added when you make the dough for "New Iceland" flavour. The whole recipe would have to be used for cinnamon buns. More to enjoy!

I made the recipe twice and found it easy to follow. Although it would have been nice to have watched Kristrun do it a couple of times. The buns were a hit with the kids(aged 29 to 39). The cinnamon buns didn't have time to cool off.

Eleanor Schellenberg
Winnipeg, Manitoba

Flatbrauð (Flat Bread)

Flatbrauð are thin round breads about the size of a dessert plate. They are good served with butter, cheese, smoked fish, meats such as hangikjöt, lifrarpylsa or other þorramatur.

Betty Jane Wylie's Laufabrauð (Leaf Bread)

4 cups flour
2 tbsp. sugar
1 tbsp. salt
1 tsp. baking powder
3 cups milk
¼ cup butter
oil (or lard) for frying

Laufabrauð is traditionally served at Christmas with hangikjöt.

1. Combine the flour, sugar, salt and baking powder in a large bowl.
2. Heat the milk and butter together until the butter melts. Blend into the dry ingredients and stir well.
3. Flour a board or countertop generously; dump the dough on it and roll out very, very thin. Cut the dough into rounds about the size of a salad plate (8 inches in diameter).
4. Hand out circles to people to take their turns at decorating. Roll the cutter (described below) over the dough (some people use a knife or scissors if they're impatient) and create interesting effects.
5. Deep-fry in hot oil (my Icelandic relatives used lard) until golden brown on both sides, turning once, or not, depending on how it looks.

It's a lovely family activity and there's no such thing as a failure. They all get eaten -or hung up.

This recipe and the following quotation were taken from **Letters to Icelanders -Exploring the Northern Soul** by Betty Jane Wylie. In chapter six, "Food", Betty Jane is addressing her amma (grandmother):

    Do you know, Amma, I had never heard of laufabrauð before I went to Iceland at Christmas time? Then it's impossible to avoid it. Every household I went into served it, and at Brekka, where I stayed to visit the Glaumbær Museum, I was allowed to help. After that, when I went into Akureyri, I bought a laufabrauð cutter at a bakery. A laufabrauð cutter is like a pie or pizza-cutter, a little cutting wheel on a handle, but this wheel is brass and three-dimensional, shaped like a barrel with a deep relief design on it in a chevron pattern. When it's rolled over a circle of dough it cuts impressions in it which, when the dough is fried, puff up into various designs, depending on which way it is cut. A finished laufabrauð looks like a fried doily. Some people instead of eating them hang 'doilies' in their windows as a Christmas decoration. They're fun to make and fun to eat. I've made a batch with my grandchildren since that trip. I have to keep doing it because the laufabrauð cutter cost so much! Maybe that's why you didn't own one, Amma; it's not the most

Brauð

necessary item to take with one across the ocean at the age of 17.

Betty Jane Wylie
MacTier, Ontario

Katrin Brynjolfsson's Flatbrauð #1

½ tsp. baking soda
½ tsp. salt
1 cup rye flour
1 cup white flour
½ cup cracked wheat

1. Mix ingredients together in a bowl.
2. Make a well, pour in boiling water for a fairly stiff dough, stirring rapidly. Knead together.
3. Roll flat (about ¼ to ½ inch thick).
4. Fry on a very hot griddle (or just on top of burner*) using just a small amount of grease.

*As original recipe: See Shirley Sigurdson's comment for Thura Thorsteinson's Flatbrauð.

Runa Gislason's Flatbrauð #2

1 cup whole wheat flour
½ cup white flour
3-4 tsp. bacon drippings (margarine or butter if you prefer)
¼ tsp. salt
2 tsp. brown sugar

1. Mix together in a bowl.
2. Add enough water until it is easy to knead.
3. Roll flat (about ¼ to ½ inch thick), prick with fork.
4. Fry on a medium to hot griddle. After well fried on both sides, take off pan and dip into milk (to soften) and place between dinner plates.

It is delicious eaten hot with butter and served with coffee.

Thura Thorsteinson's Flatbrauð #3

1 cup white flour
1 cup whole wheat flour
½ cup graham flour
(use rye flour if not available)
½ tsp. salt
1 tsp. baking soda
1 tsp. sugar
1 cup sour cream (approx.)

1. Mix the dry ingredients together. Add the sour cream to make a stiff dough.
2. Divide dough into 12 equal parts and roll each on a lightly floured board to pastry thickness. Prick several times with a fork.
3. Place on hot ungreased frying pan. Bake until brown on bottom and puffy on top. Turn and brown on the other side.

Serve hot with plenty of butter.

A cast iron pan was all we had; or the cleaned stove lid on the wood-stove! but electric works just fine.

Shirley Sigurdson (Thura was Shirley's step-grandmother)
Edmonton, Alberta

Very easy to make - Flatbrauð #1: used 1 - 1 ½ cups of boiling water, if rolled very thin not as doughy in texture - crisper is better, 2-3 minutes till browned, has a nutty taste, best with butter and jam. Flatbrauð #2: used bacon drippings - butter would be better, dipping into milk makes the bread rather slippery. Flatbrauð #3: best one, baked 1 ½ - 2 minutes each side, 4 to 5 inches in diameter, has a better texture, tastes sort of like pita bread.

Doreen Sigurdson
Winnipeg, Manitoba

Brauð

Flatkökur (Flat Cookies)

Ingibjorg Sigurgeirson McKillop's Flatkökur

1 cup flour
½ tsp. salt
boiling water

1. Stir boiling water into flour and salt until a firm ball is formed and comes away from the bowl. Roll out with flour about ¼ inch thick.
2. This makes two pan sized cookies.
3. Fry in pan in 1 tbsp. melted butter.

Flatkökur

½ cup white flour
¾ cup graham flour
½ tsp. salt
3 tbsp. brown sugar
1½ tsp. baking powder
¾ cup boiling water (approx.)

1. Mix all dry ingredients together in a bowl.
2. Add enough boiling water to make a soft dough.
3. Roll dough on a floured surface into a flat circle to cover bottom of heavy fry pan. Prick with a fork all over. Fry at medium heat with a little butter for 15 minutes on each side.

I rolled out one ¼ inch thick cookie with the dough. Cooked in an 11 inch cast iron skillet. ¼ inch thickness works with the suggested cooking time. It would be easier to turn in a smaller pan (6-7 inch). The flatkökur reminds me of a very firm pancake with a slightly sweet flavour and grainy consistency. This would be a great treat for someone who doesn't enjoy really sweet cakes with coffee. We ate it at the cottage with the Mysuostur that Shirley prepared. It was received well. Another serving suggestion would be herb flavoured butter.

Shelley Munro
Winnipeg, Manitoba

Mrs. S.W. Reid's Oat Cakes

1 cup oatmeal
¼ tsp. baking soda
1 tbsp. beef drippings or bacon fat
½ cup warm water
¼ tsp. salt

1. Put oatmeal in a bowl.
2. Mix in a cup the drippings, soda and warm water. Stir this into the oatmeal and knead to a soft paste. Add more water if needed.
3. Knead this again into a ball.
4. Put dry oatmeal on your rolling surface. Roll out into a round cake, quite thin, and cut, not breaking the edges.
5. Bake in a hot oven, 375° F until edges curl up.

Maybe if you had been working out in the field all day and came home to find oat cakes were your only food, you might just eat them.

Dora Olafson
Riverton, Manitoba

Kaffibrauð
Sweet Breads and Fried Cakes

Pönnukökur - Thin Pancakes (Crêpes)

Pönnukökur are a well-loved traditional favourite. They are made from a thin batter like a crêpe. Spices and flavourings added to the batter vary according to preference; cinnamon and vanilla are the most prevalent although nutmeg, cardamom and lemon juice are also customary. You cannot make too many. They are irresistible when rolled with sugar, especially for children -or for the child in all of us. They are equally tempting folded with jam (preserves), fruit or berries and whipped cream. Prepared without sugar, spices and flavourings, they may also be served as an hors d'oeuvre or main dish with a savoury filling (see 'Fiskimatur -Lake Winnipeg Fish').

Sylvia Sigurdson's Pönnukökur

2 eggs
⅓ cup sugar
¼ tsp. salt
½ tsp. vanilla
½ tsp. cinnamon
½ tsp. soda
½ cup sour cream
1½ cups flour
1 tsp. baking powder
2 cups milk

1. Beat eggs lightly. Mix in sugar, salt, vanilla and cinnamon.
2. Dissolve baking soda in a little boiling water and mix with sour cream. Add to the first mixture.
3. Stir in flour and baking powder sifted together. Beat well, gradually stirring in milk.

To bake:

Use fairly heavy griddle pan. Rub bottom of pan with butter tied in a small cloth. Lift pan off heat while you pour about ⅕ or ¼ cup batter on it. Tip griddle around until the entire bottom is covered. Set back on the heat as quickly as possible. Then turn and bake on other side. Sprinkle with brown sugar and roll.

Additional information, I have found helpful- ideal pan is an 8" diameter pönnukökur pan with a ½-inch lip, found or made in Iceland. I place the pönnukökur as I bake them on a pizza pan that I have placed aluminum foil on, large enough to cover over top to keep them warm until they are ready for rolling. Also with some pans it is necessary to place a little butter on top of each pönnukökur before turning. I also find that when bubbles have appeared

Kaffibrauð

on the first side it is a good time to turn them.

This recipe first appeared in a cookbook published in the 1930's by the Dorcas Society of the First Lutheran Church in Winnipeg. The contributor was Mrs. B. B. Jonsson, the wife of a long time minister there. So it is truly an old recipe. I have used it for some 35 years.

Sylvia Sigurdson
Surrey, B.C. (previously resided in Riverton, Manitoba)

Pönnukökur are my favourite. The first few didn't work. I used my pan that I bought on my trip to Iceland. We put brown sugar and white sugar inside just like my Aunty Ruthie first showed me. It is the same recipe as the one I usually make.

Alexandra Eyolfson, age 15
Winnipeg, Manitoba

Kathy Arnason's Pönnukökur

3 eggs, lightly beaten
1 tsp. sugar
1 tsp. salt
2 tsp. cinnamon
2 tsp. vanilla
¼ cup melted butter
3 cups flour
½ tsp. baking soda
½ tsp. baking powder
5-6 cups milk

1. Stir all ingredients together until well combined.
2. Bake on a fairly heavy griddle pan. Rub bottom of pan lightly with butter tied in a small cloth-only if necessary to prevent sticking. Some pans are well seasoned and would not require butter as included in the batter.

It was not as rich a batter as the recipe I'm used to with sour cream and more sugar so was easier to fry. The butter in the batter helps too. I'm so used to buttering the pan before every pancake, I found myself doing that without thinking-did try a few without and it worked. As for ways of serving-I have never done anything but with brown sugar or whipped cream and fruit.

Alma Sigurdson
Gimli, Manitoba

Pönnukökur

500g, 3¾ cups flour
6 eggs
about 1¼ litres, 5½ cups milk
⅛ litre, ½ cup light ale
50g, ¼ cup butter, melted
3-4 tbsp. sugar
pinch of salt
butter for frying, castor sugar, jelly

Make a hole in the flour and add the egg yolks, some of the milk and light ale. Blend the sugar and melted butter and thin down with some of the milk; mix all together. Thin to the right consistency with milk, add a pinch of salt. If desired, you may add some vanilla or cardamom or rum. Let the batter stand for ½ hour; then the beaten egg whites are folded in. Bake the pönnukökur. Sugar, jelly or preserves and whipped cream are served with the pönnukökur.

This recipe most closely resembles Kathy Arnason's Pönnukökur. The differences are that while Kathy's has baking powder and soda, this recipe has more eggs (yolks and beaten egg whites added in separately would balance out the difference) and the light ale would also serve as a replacement rising agent. The omission of baking powder should not suggest that it is not typical in Icelandic recipes. Ale and soda water are used by some to produce an airier, lacier pönnukökur.

Kathy's recipe includes cinnamon which along with nutmeg are the usual spice preferences in New Iceland. Vanilla and lemon flavourings would be considered common in Iceland and New Iceland.

Castor sugar is another difference. In New Iceland brown sugar, granulated sugar or a combination is most common. (Castor sugar is close to our superfine or berry sugar). Pönnukökur are traditionally served rolled with sugar or folded with fruit, berries or jam (preserves) and whipped cream in Iceland and this was maintained in New Iceland.

Kaffibrauð

Johanna Wilson's Pönnukökur

2 eggs
1 tbsp. sugar
¼ tsp. salt
1 tsp. vanilla
1½ cups sifted all purpose flour
1 tsp. baking powder
½ tsp. baking soda
¼ cup sour cream or buttermilk
2-3 cups whole milk

They may also be served with whipped cream and jam, jelly or preserves (Johanna likes peach jam). When serving this way, spread a little jam and cream on the pönnukökur, fold in half and fold again (forming a triangle). Serve individually on a plate as a dessert.

1. Beat eggs. Add sugar, salt and vanilla.
2. Combine and sift the flour, baking powder and soda.
3. Add the sour cream or buttermilk and the sifted ingredients to the egg mixture and mix together until smooth.
4. Gradually stir in milk until of consistency that will spread over the hot griddle pan when baking.
5. Use a hot griddle lightly greased with butter. Pour about ⅕ of a cup of batter on the pan; lifting and tilting the pan to distribute the batter evenly. Loosen edges of the pönnukökur with lifter, then loosen entire pönnukökur and flip over to brown the other side.
6. Layer the cooked pönnukökur on a platter and when finished cooking the batch sprinkle each with brown sugar mixed with some cinnamon. Roll and when ready to serve, cut each one in half and arrange on a plate.

Making these pönnukökur took me back to making them with my little Amma. The recipe is very similar - only difference is much less sugar. My recipe (Amma's) calls for ⅓ cup. They were lovely, easy to handle in the pan and browned nicely. I put the cinnamon into the batter as my Amma did. My opinion of this recipe is "GREAT!" Great to taste and great to bring to bring back those fond memories of loved ones.

Pat McKetchen
Selkirk, Manitoba

Sweet Breads and Fried Cakes

Pönnukökur with Mandarin Oranges

Cream Filling:
1 8oz. pkg. of cream cheese
1 cup skyr or sour cream
⅔ cup sugar (less sugar may be used)
1 tsp. vanilla
¼ tsp. cinnamon
1 cup whipping cream

Reduce or increase the amount of cream filling that you make according to the number of servings required.

1. Pönnukökur: Prepare as directed in preceding pönnukökur recipes.
2. Cream filling: Combine cream cheese, skyr or sour cream, sugar, vanilla and cinnamon. Beat until smooth.
3. Whip cream until thick. Fold whipped cream into cream cheese mixture.
4. Chill.

To Serve:

1. Warm prepared pönnukökur in oven wrapped in foil.
2. Lay pönnukökur on serving plate. Spoon cream on one half of pönnukökur. Arrange mandarin orange slices across. Fold pönnukökur in half.
3. Put another dollop of cream on top, a few more orange slices.
4. Sprinkle with toasted slivered almonds. Lastly pour over top a small amount of orange liqueur. (Optional.)

Ingibjorg Olafson's Lummur (Pancakes)

¼ cup shortening
¼ cup sugar
1 tsp. vanilla
4 large eggs
1 tsp. nutmeg
½ tsp. salt
2 tbsp. baking powder
1½ cups flour
1 - 1½ cups milk (approx.)

1. Beat shortening and sugar together until light and fluffy. Beat in the eggs one at a time and add vanilla.
2. Combine the nutmeg, salt, baking powder and flour. Add milk a little at a time alternately with the flour mixture. Exact amounts for the milk are difficult because the flour varies from brand to brand. For lummur, the batter will be the right thickness when a spoonful of the batter spreads out to about twice its size on a hot pan.
3. Pour out 3 pancakes (4-5 inches across) at a time on a hot 10" cast iron or teflon pan (grease pan the first time only). Turn once when bubbles form across the entire surface. Serve with butter and syrup or with fruit and whipped cream.

Kaffibrauð

> *They were very good and made approximately 18-20 pancakes. The recipe was easy to follow and turned out as expected. Our children really love pancakes so will definitely make these again!*
>
> *Lynne Stefanson*
> *Winnipeg, Manitoba*

> *To use this batter for pönnukökur add ½ cup whole milk or milk and light cream. Batter should be thin enough to flow over pan when it is tilted so that you get a thin pönnukökur. You can add milk gradually to get the correct consistency. Ladle a portion of the batter on the pan; tilt and swirl the batter over the pan. Bake until bubbles form on the surface and bake on the other side. To serve: spread brown sugar lightly over the surface and roll up into a cigar shape. Cut in half. Alternate serving method: On each pönnukökur, place a spoonful of fruit of your choice (strawberries or lingönberries are nice), then add a spoonful of whipped cream. Fold the pönnukökur in half and then in half again to make it into quarters, then spoon some more whipped cream over and a garnish of the same fruit. In Iceland, this is called Rjóma Pönnukökur.*
>
> *Elva Jonasson*
> *Winnipeg, Manitoba*

Hrísgrjónalummur (Rice Pancakes)

1 cup rice
1 cup water
3¾ cups whole milk
1 tsp. salt
1 egg beaten
¼ cup flour
1 tsp. cinnamon
1 tbsp. sugar
⅓ cup of chopped almonds and currants, optional
1 tsp. lemon rind, optional

1. Bring rice and water to a boil. Drain well.
2. In another pan bring milk to a boil. Add rice gradually, stirring, until it reaches the boiling point. Add salt and cover pan. Simmer over low heat for about 45 minutes. Remove from heat and cool for 15 minutes.
3. Mix in the beaten egg and then the flour. Stir in the remaining ingredients.
4. Melt butter in a griddle pan and drop 1 tbsp. of the rice mixture into the pan for each pancake. (If it is too runny, add a little more flour.) Serve hot with jelly.

I froze this batch after Stefan proclaimed them good with raspberry jelly. I am going to try them on my grandchildren next weekend for breakfast with maple syrup and bacon.

Sylvia Sigurdson
White Rock, British Columbia

Hrísgrjónalummur (Rice Pancakes)

2 full plates rice porridge (flat style soup bowls)
4-6 rounded tbsp. flour
2 tsp. sugar
lemon rind, grated
4 eggs
approx. ⅛ litre, ½ cup milk
pinch of salt
approx. 250g, 1 cup margarine for cooking
castor sugar or preserves, jelly or jam

The porridge is stirred carefully so that it does not separate, then the eggs are mixed in, one at a time, then the flour and milk and lastly the sugar, pinch of salt and grated lemon rind if desired. Fry in the fat. Served with castor sugar and preserves as desired.

There is an overall similarity to the New Iceland recipe even though there are more eggs and less milk. The cinnamon and option of almonds and currants in the New Iceland Hrísgrjónalummur could be considered variations to enhance a basic recipe. Lummur in Iceland refer to pancakes made from a thick batter as opposed to pönnukökur made from a thin batter. They are sometimes made with left over porridges and raisins may be added. They would be considered a coffee time treat. In New Iceland lummur came to refer to the more typical pancake served with syrup for breakfast and even dinner. (See also Ingibjorg Olafson's Lummur).

Kaffibrauð

Kleinur (Doughnut Bows)

Kleinur are deep-fried bowtie-shaped twisted doughnuts which may be rolled in sugar or a cinnamon-sugar mixture. They are a traditional coffee time favourite for New Icelanders.

Runa Gislason's Kleinur

3 eggs
1 cup sugar
4 cups flour
2 tsp. baking powder
1 tsp. soda
½ tsp. salt
¼ tsp. nutmeg
1 cup milk
½ cup sour cream
1 tsp. vanilla
2 tbsp. soft butter

1. Beat eggs and add sugar gradually.
2. Sift dry ingredients together. Combine milk, sour cream and vanilla.
3. Add the dry ingredients alternately with the milk mixture, beating well with each addition. Lastly, add butter.
4. Roll the dough on a lightly floured surface to ⅛ inches thick. (Suggestion: divide the dough in half. Roll out ½ at a time.) Dough will be a little sticky. Cut into strips, 1-1½ inches wide in a slantwise direction. Cut these 3 inches long on a angle to make diamonds. Cut slit in centre. Pull one end through this slit forming a knot. Deep-fry at 370° F in vegetable oil. When golden brown on one side, turn over to brown the other side. Remove to brown paper to drain.
Optional: Sprinkle with icing sugar or roll in a cinnamon-sugar mixture.

This recipe is good but practice is required. I liked the diagonal cutting style.

Joyce Benedictson
Gimli, Manitoba

Ingibjorg Olafson's Kleinur

2 eggs
½ cup sugar
1 tbsp. melted butter
½ cup milk
2 tsp. baking powder
½ tsp. nutmeg
¼ tsp. salt
2 cups flour
(additional flour to make a soft dough for rolling)

1. Beat eggs until light, adding sugar gradually.
2. Sift together salt, nutmeg, baking powder and flour. Add to eggs and sugar alternately with milk. Add more flour as required.
3. Roll out to ⅓ inch thickness and cut into strips about 1 inch wide. Cut the strips into 2-3 inch lengths. Cut a slit in the centre and twist one end of each piece through the slit in the middle.
4. Fry in hot fat at 375°-400° F until golden brown; turning once.

These may be rolled in either icing sugar or fine granulated sugar after cooling.

Good recipe, as not a huge amount at one time. We found that you have to add flour gradually until you achieve the right texture for rolling. We used 3-3 ¾ cups flour.

Debbie Johannson and Arlene Robins
Rivers, Manitoba

Bergthora Einarson Morrison's Kleinur

1 cup brown sugar
1 cup white sugar
3 eggs, beaten
1 cup buttermilk
½ cup cream
2 tsp. ground cardamom seeds
1 tsp. baking soda
2 tsp. baking powder
1 tsp. salt
5-6 cups flour

1. Mix the first 5 ingredients together.
2. Stir in the remaining ingredients sifted together, adding enough flour to make a soft dough.
3. On a floured surface, roll out to about ¼ inch thick. With a pastry wheel, cut into 1 inch strips length-wise. Next, cut across to make strips 3 inches long. Cut a slit in the centre. Twist one end through the hole.
4. Deep fry at 350° F on both sides (as for doughnuts-turning when golden brown on one side). Drain on brown paper. After cooling, roll in icing sugar, granulated sugar or cinnamon-sugar mixture if desired.

Kaffibrauð

Well, I made Aunt Becky's Kleinur recipe this weekend. Have to admit that I never made Kleinur before. I do believe it is one of those things that would get better each time you made it-seems you need to develop the certain 'touch'. I think this recipe would be very hard to follow if you had never made these before and had no idea how they should look. It would be a great help if there could be a picture of how to cut the dough and how to twist them properly.

Karen Carlson
Minot, North Dakota

DeeDee Westdal's Kleinur

6 tbsp. melted butter
2 cups sugar
5 eggs
2 cups whole milk
3 tsp. baking powder
1 tsp. ground nutmeg
½ tsp. salt
7 cups flour

This batch makes about 8-10 dozen, depending on size. They freeze well and thaw quickly. Heating them in the oven and dipping them in icing sugar is a nice way to serve Kleinur.

1. Cream butter and sugar. Add eggs, one at a time, and beat together. Stir in milk.
2. Mix baking powder, nutmeg and salt with the first cup of flour. Add this mixture and the remaining flour. (The dough will be quite soft and will require extra flour for rolling out.)
3. Work with about one third of the dough each time and roll or pat it out to less than ½ inch thickness. Cut strips of dough about 1 ½ inches wide and 3 inches in length. Make a slit in the centre of each and pull one end through the slit to form the Kleinur.
4. Deep fry the Kleinur. Canola oil is the best frying oil to use and should be about 325° F. Make about 7 or 8 at a time and drop them into the hot oil. As soon as they rise to the top turn them over - and then later turn them again to brown evenly on each side. Lift out of oil and drain on brown paper.

This is good but we found it to be a very large recipe. I'm not a great kleinur maker, so thank goodness for Arlene's experience.

Debbie Johannson and Arlene Robins
Rivers, Manitoba

Kleinur

1 kg, 7½ cups flour.
250 g, 1¼ cups butter or margarine
7½ tbsp. cream
2 tsp. baking powder
250 g, 1¼ cups sugar
5 eggs
5 tbsp. cognac
vanilla or cardamom
tallow (fat or oil for cooking)

The butter is cut into the flour, sugar, cardamom and baking powder which has been blended together. A hole is made and the beaten eggs, cream and cognac which are mixed together in a bowl are poured in and are blended well together and kneaded well, rolled out and shaped into 'kleinur'; cooked until light brown. Remove from fat with a spatula and drain on a drain tray, paper or 'hefilspæni'.

Dough for the bowlike shaped doughnuts varies from recipe to recipe in richness, sweetness and flavourings. This dough is quite rich and not as sweet as some of the New Iceland recipes. While cardamom and cognac are used in New Iceland, it is nutmeg that finds more overall favour. Cognac, while not recorded in cookbooks, would be added only sometimes for a special occasion such as Christmas.

    Of the four kleinur recipes in this collection only Bergthora Einarson Morrison's includes cardamom. I found another example **Cook Book** (1930). Contributed by Mrs. N.S. Thorlaksson this recipe interestingly was titled 'Fattigmand' which is Norwegian and means 'poor man'. Kleinur, known variously in their respective languages are made in other Scandinavian and European countries. She includes cardamom and also cinnamon and gives the directions 'cut in diamond shape, slit and twist and fry in hot lard.' The specification for lard is of interest as over time we have become accustomed to using vegetable oils for frying. Earlier in New Iceland as in Iceland tallow (suet or drippings collected from the cooking of meats) as specified in this recipe was used. On the same page of **Cook Book** a recipe for Rosettes contributed by Mrs. S. Johnson includes the instructions – 'Fry in deep tallow.' 'Hefilspæni' refers to hefilspònn (noun) —clean wood shavings which could be used to absorb the excess fat if paper was unavailable.

Kaffibrauð

Thorunn Johnson's Sour Cream Doughnuts

2 eggs
¾ cup sugar
½ cup thick sour cream (if using dairy sour cream-14%-add extra shortening or use soured whipping cream-32%)
½ cup milk
1 tsp. vanilla
⅔ tsp. salt
½ tsp. soda
1¼ tsp. baking powder
3¾ cups sifted flour

1. Beat eggs until very light. Add sugar and beat until sugar is dissolved.
2. Add sour cream, milk and vanilla. Combine well.
3. Add dry ingredients, sifted together.
4. Roll and cut with a doughnut cutter (handle as lightly as possible).
5. Deep-fry, turning once.

These doughnuts are delicious -light and of good consistency. They are easy to make. A few tips -I used 14% sour cream and no extra shortening and deep-fried the donuts at 400° F for about 30 seconds each side (as soon as you see that they are golden brown, flip them). Good plain or rolled in sugar or a sugar and cinnamon mixture. Great reviews in the neighbourhood!

Catherine Filmon
Winnipeg, Manitoba

A double recipe makes about 6 dozen.

Sella Thorvardson's Ástrabollur (Drop Doughnuts) -(also known as "Love Balls")

2 eggs
1 cup sugar
heaping tbsp. softened butter
1 tsp. vanilla
1 cup milk
3-4 cups flour
4½ tsp. baking powder
¼ tsp. nutmeg
1 tsp. salt

1. Beat eggs and sugar.
2. Add butter, vanilla and milk. Combine the remaining dry ingredients. Stir into the egg mixture, blending well.
3. Deep fry by dropping rounded teaspoonfuls into the hot oil (360° F). Drain on absorbent paper when golden brown on all sides.
4. Optional: While warm roll in cinnamon-sugar, sprinkle with icing sugar or drizzle glaze over; add currants to the batter if desired.

Sweet Breads and Fried Cakes

> *I made these with my class at school and they liked them. We used the smaller amount of flour. The name 'Love Balls' made for a few giggles. I used a fryer and that kept the temperature constant.*
>
> Diane Keighley
> Newark, Delaware

Elva Jonasson's Steiktir Partar (Fried Parts or Boats)

2 tbsp. butter
1½ cups sugar
1½ cups boiling water
1 tsp. soda
1 tsp. nutmeg
1 tsp. salt
1 cup flour

1. Cream butter and sugar well.
2. Add boiling water and soda.
3. When sugar has melted, add salt, nutmeg and flour. Knead a little, adding more flour if necessary. Chill dough slightly to make it easier to work with.
4. Take a small quantity of dough, roll out thin and cut in diamond shaped pieces with two large slits in the middle of each piece.
5. Deep-fry at 350° F on both sides.
6. Serve plain, sprinkle with icing sugar or filled with whipped cream.

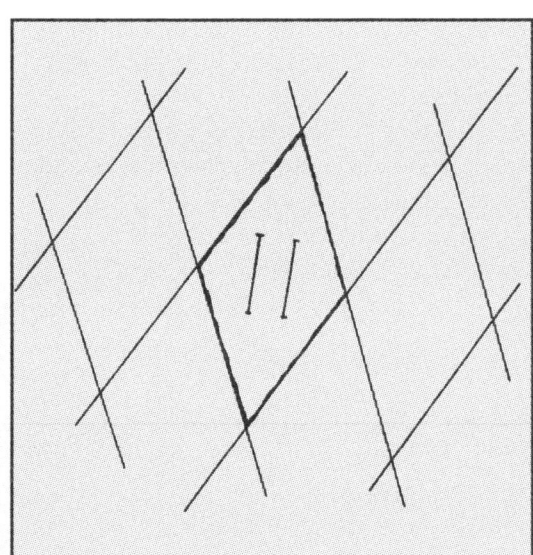

Additional cutting instructions: From another recipe -"cut in oblongs 2 x 3 inches". After reading varying instructions I experimented and the following is my method. Roll out as thin as possible on a lightly floured surface. Cut into strips 2 inches wide in a slantwise direction. Cut these 2½ inches long on an angle to make diamonds. In the middle of each diamond cut two slits lengthwise.

Kaffibrauð

Rosettes

2 eggs
1 cup milk
1 tsp. sugar
¼ tsp. salt
1 cup flour

Rosettes may be frozen. Re-crisp to serve by placing upside down on a baking sheet. Heat in 400° F oven for 2-4 minutes depending on how many you are serving.

1. Beat eggs. Add milk, sugar and salt. Beat together.
2. Gradually add flour, beating until it is the consistency of thick cream.
3. Deep-fry in hot oil at 365-375° F. Method: Dip rosette mold into hot oil to heat (10-15 seconds). Shake off excess oil and dip into batter (no batter should go over the top of the rim of the mold). Dip batter covered mold into the hot oil. When the rosette has formed and is a light golden brown, remove from the oil (you may need to loosen the rosette from the mold gently with a tap or with a knife if the mold is not hot enough).

To serve: Top with a spoonful of whipped cream. Garnish with a dab of jam or jelly in the centre or fruit such as mandarin orange segment, berries, or kiwi slices.

I heated the oil to 375° F in a teflon pot. The element setting I used was '6' - 10 being high. You can double this recipe -but I wouldn't recommend it due to the oil dripping in and out of the batter. As this recipe has so few ingredients it's easy to whip up a second batch.

I have served rosettes with whip cream and fresh fruit, sprinkled with icing sugar, and with whip cream, chopped onions and smoked fish. It's always a hit -light and crispy for a special breakfast or for dessert.

It's hard for me to tell you the yield as I usually do this with my girls and they start out sampling and the rosettes all seem to disappear! However, I did get two dozen into the freezer and everyone else seemed quite happy with their snacks!!

Laurie Olafson-Jervis
Selkirk, Manitoba

Sweet Breads and Fried Cakes

Mrs. Finnur Johnson's Vatnsdeigsbollur (Cream Puffs)

1 cup water
1 cup flour
5 tbsp. shortening
4 eggs
¼ tsp. salt

Suggestion for baking today: 400° F for 10 min then 350° F for 25. Do not remove from oven until firm or they will fall.

1. Put shortening and water into saucepan and bring to boiling point, add the flour and salt quickly, stir well with a wooden spoon until mixture leaves sides of pan, remove from fire (heat), allow mixture to become cool, but not cold.
2. Add eggs one at a time, and beat each one thoroughly in. Set in cool place one hour.
3. Take and put a spoonful about 3 inches apart on a greased pan and bake 40 minutes. Be sure to bake very slowly and for a full 40 minutes, for if you don't they will fall. If the oven gets too hot it would be advisable to open it for a few minutes and cool it.
4. Then, when baked, cut with scissors and fill with whipped cream.

*This recipe comes from **Cook Book** (1930). There were two recipes for cream puffs included in that edition which were omitted in the 1950 edition. As is the case with the other recipes in this early edition, the baking temperature is not given (see Victoria's comment for baking temperatures). Butter could be substituted for the shortening.*

While not observed in New Iceland, Bolludagur (Bun Day) has been celebrated in Iceland for over a hundred years. It falls on the Monday at the beginning of Lent and came to include the eating of buns (derived originally from the eating of white food during Lent). There is another custom associated with this. A decorated stick or bolludagsvöndur is used to spank people –children make sticks at school and decorate them with coloured paper. A prize of a rjomabolla (cream bun) is to be had if one can manage to spank someone before they get out of bed. The buns have been mostly of two kinds in Iceland: vatnsdeigsbollur (cream puffs) and gerbollur, which are made of yeast.

My amma, Kristrun Sigurdson, made cream puffs, and whether or not she was aware of Bolludagur, I am grateful for the happy memories of eating them.

For further indulgence, place some jam in the bottom of the puff before filling with whipped cream and some melted chocolate on top.

Kaffibrauð

1. I used butter instead of shortening. 2. Turn off the elements and add the flour/salt while still on the heat source. Then remove to cool. 3. Add eggs. For the last egg I added I used a fork instead of a wooden spoon- up until that point I was worried it looked lumpy but the fork worked. I didn't do the 'cool for one hour' as I found that by the time you finished beating the eggs and turned on the oven to heat up -between the time I removed the pan from the element and finished beating the eggs and waited for the oven -was roughly 1 hour. 4. <u>Cooking Times</u>: First round (size of half an orange): 400° F for 10 minutes and 350° F for 12 minutes. Second round (same size): 375° F for 12 minutes, turn tray around and then another 12 minutes. (Turning the tray around allows the build up of steam to escape. Third round (golf ball size): 400° F for 20 minutes. (Wherever it was set -left the oven door open 4-5 inches for the last 5 minutes). 5. Yield: I think you can expect 12 medium biscuit-sized puffs or 2 dozen appetizer size.

Victoria (Olafson) Sparks
Selkirk, MB

Smjörkringla (Butter Kringle)

2 tbsp. or 2 pkgs. traditional yeast
2 tbsp. sugar
½ cup lukewarm water
3 cups flour
2 tbsp. (rounded) shortening or lard
1 cup milk
½ lb. butter (softened)
½ cup each of brown sugar, chopped nuts and raisins

1. Soften yeast in warm water with sugar. Let set about 10 minutes.
2. In large mixing bowl cut shortening into flour as for making pie pastry.
3. Add milk and yeast mixture. Combine thoroughly. Chill in covered buttered bowl about 3 hours.
4. Turn out on to lightly floured pastry board or cloth and roll out to ¼ inches thick. Spread ¼ of the butter over ½ the dough. Cover with the other half and roll and pound gently with rolling pin. Fold up dough in thirds or quarters and return to bowl. Chill 20-30 minutes.
5. Repeat #4 three more times until all the butter is used.
6. Roll out thin (the width should be the length of your baking sheet). Divide into 3 sections.
7. Combine brown sugar, nuts and raisins in a small bowl. Sprinkle this mixture down the centre of each strip. Fold over the edges to meet. Lay length-wise on lightly greased baking sheets.
8. Chill covered for at least 12 hours longer.
9. Preheat oven to 375° F. When ready to bake, brush with egg beaten with a little water and sugar. Bake for 20-25 minutes. Slice to serve.

Sweet Breads and Fried Cakes

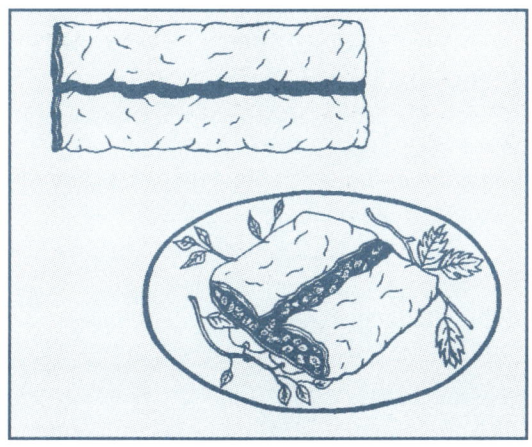

This is a real test. I will use parchment paper in the future – burns a bit with the grease on the bottom. 20 minutes at 350° F worked for me. Delicious with sock coffee and great company! As with all things practice makes perfect and I'll be making it again soon.

Sharon Jonasson
Winnipeg, Manitoba

Jólabrauð (Christmas Bread)

1 tbsp. or 1 pkg. traditional yeast
¾ cup warm water
1 tsp. sugar
½ cup shortening*
¾ cup milk
¾ cup water
¾ cup sugar
1½ tsp. salt
6 cups flour (approx.)
1 egg
½ tsp. finely grated lemon peel
(and/or a little lemon extract)
1 cup raisins
1 tsp. cardamom seeds, ground
(softened butter, sugar, cinnamon)

*Shortening is as the original recipe; butter or margarine may be substituted.

1. Soften yeast in warm water with sugar. Let set about 10 minutes.
2. Cut up shortening in chunks and place in large mixing bowl. Heat milk and water in small saucepan and pour over shortening. Stir to melt shortening.
3. Using a whisk, stir in sugar and salt, then ½ cup flour, softened yeast, egg, lemon peel and/or extract, raisins and ground cardamom seeds.
4. Stir in 5 cups flour to make a stiff dough. Turn out on lightly floured surface and knead in lightly about another ½ cup flour.
5. Put dough in a large buttered bowl and let rise until doubled in a warm draft-free place. (1-1½ hours)
6. Divide dough into 3 or 4 sections. Roll out each one into a rectangle (slightly longer than loaf pan). Spread with butter and sprinkle with sugar and cinnamon. Roll up and twist each loaf. Tuck ends under, patting to form a nice shape. Place in greased loaf pans and let rise about 1 hour.
7. Bake at 350° F for 30-45 minutes. Remove from pan. Optional: While warm drizzle with lemon glaze (juice of lemon, icing sugar) or plain glaze (2 tbsp. milk, icing sugar).

Kaffibrauð

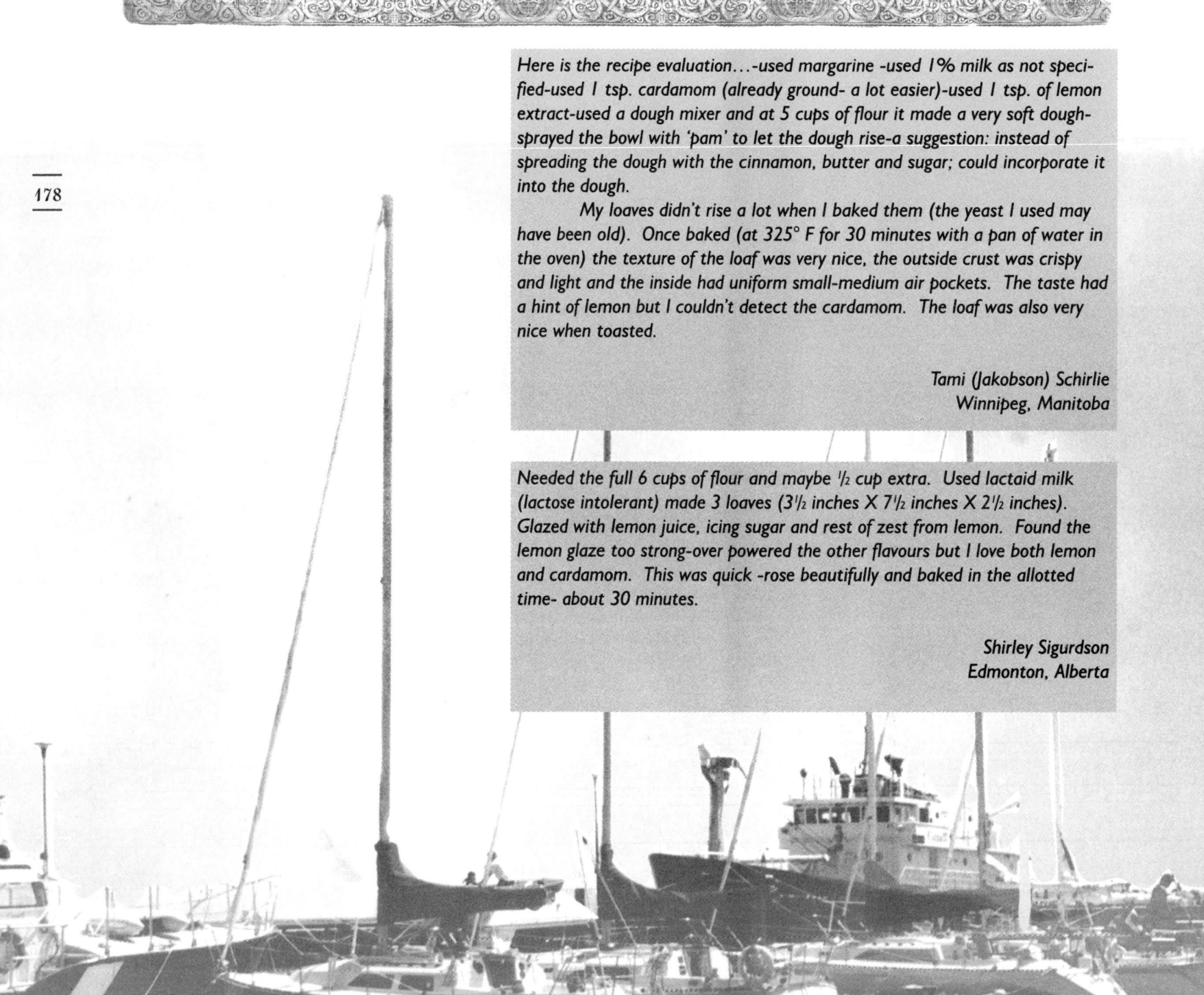

Here is the recipe evaluation...-used margarine -used 1% milk as not specified-used 1 tsp. cardamom (already ground- a lot easier)-used 1 tsp. of lemon extract-used a dough mixer and at 5 cups of flour it made a very soft dough-sprayed the bowl with 'pam' to let the dough rise-a suggestion: instead of spreading the dough with the cinnamon, butter and sugar; could incorporate it into the dough.

My loaves didn't rise a lot when I baked them (the yeast I used may have been old). Once baked (at 325° F for 30 minutes with a pan of water in the oven) the texture of the loaf was very nice, the outside crust was crispy and light and the inside had uniform small-medium air pockets. The taste had a hint of lemon but I couldn't detect the cardamom. The loaf was also very nice when toasted.

Tami (Jakobson) Schirlie
Winnipeg, Manitoba

Needed the full 6 cups of flour and maybe ½ cup extra. Used lactaid milk (lactose intolerant) made 3 loaves (3½ inches X 7½ inches X 2½ inches). Glazed with lemon juice, icing sugar and rest of zest from lemon. Found the lemon glaze too strong-over powered the other flavours but I love both lemon and cardamom. This was quick -rose beautifully and baked in the allotted time- about 30 minutes.

Shirley Sigurdson
Edmonton, Alberta

Helga Einarson Almquist's Jólabrauð

2 cups scalded milk
½ cup shortening
⅔ cup sugar
2 tsp. salt
1 tsp. cinnamon
¼-½ tsp. ground cardamom seeds,
2 tbsp. or 2 pkg. traditional yeast
¼ cup lukewarm water
2 eggs, beaten
8 cups flour
1 cup raisins
1 cup citron or fruit mix
1 cup candied cherries

1. Scald the milk. Stir in shortening, sugar, salt and spices. Cool to lukewarm.
2. Add yeast to lukewarm water. Add softened yeast to milk mixture.
3. Add beaten eggs and mix well.
4. Toss fruit in 2 cups of the flour.
5. Combine the milk mixture, the fruit and the remaining flour. Mix together.
6. Let rise in warm place until doubled in size. Punch down and knead lightly. Let stand for 10 minutes. Form into loaves. Let rise until doubled.
7. Bake at 350° F for approximately 35-45 minutes. Glaze while warm if desired. (See the preceding Jólabrauð recipe for glazes).

This recipe seemed really large; so I halved it. The water for yeast was sufficient (⅛ cup). Worked very well: rose beautifully. I got 2 small loaves (3½ inches X 7½ inches X 2½ inches)

Notes:
-used Fleishmann's traditional yeast, lactaid milk (I'm lactose intolerant) and Crisco shortening-used the milk, vanilla and icing sugar glaze.
-I read my 'Bread Cookbook' and as they recommended -hiked up the ambient temperature in the house, warmed the flour in a warm oven! And warmed the ceramic mixing bowl with hot water!! I've never had better success with any bread project!!!
Learned something too-these breads are almost cake-so kneading isn't really necessary for the 'bread' texture. I hardly kneaded at all and it was fine and smooth.
A Jólabrauð taste test panel consisting of Shirley, Solli (husband), and sons Ryan, Grant and Grant's girlfriend Kerri: The verdict is in-We all liked both breads very well but all but Solli liked the first recipe (lemon and cardamom) best. We four agreed it is a little richer (butter!!) and the aroma and texture and general appearance were very appealing. Both recipes had nice fragrance and texture and sliced easily.
Solli's humble opinion: 'I vote for the second one (Helga's)-very tasty and also isn't as rich.'

Shirley Sigurdson
Edmonton, Alberta

Vínarterta (Vienna Torte)

Vínarterta, in New Iceland, consists of six to eight cookie type layers with prune filling spread between each layer and usually coated overall with almond flavoured icing. 'Cooking for Today' published by the Ladies Aid of the Unitarian Church circa 1970, provided the following information regarding the origins of vínarterta: 'The recipe for this torte is one of the recipes brought to Iceland by Icelandic members of the Constantinople guard who passed through Vienna as they crossed Europe going between Iceland and Constantinople.' As the name implies vínarterta or Vienna torte has its origins in Vienna being an adaptation of a torte with layers of cake (sometimes with ground hazelnuts or almonds in the batter) filled with apricot jam and glazed with chocolate (e.g. Sachertorte – chocolate cake layers, some recipes containing ground nuts, apricot jam filling, chocolate glaze; Doboschtorte – vanilla cake layers, chocolate icing filling, sugar glaze). Like many other baked goods, vínarterta came to Iceland via Denmark in the 1800's becoming popular coinciding with the increase of the import of flour.

Confusion surrounds the differences and similarities between traditional vínarterta as it is known in New Iceland and vínarterta in Iceland. Vínarterta in New Iceland has remained the same through the years enjoying a rather reverential treatment as an established traditional favourite. The differences between the New Iceland recipes are slight overall even though from one family to another will come proclamations that their mother bakes the best vínarterta. It may be more or less cardamom in the dough or in the prune filling, the inclusion of almond flavouring in the dough or in the icing or even whether there should be an icing. These differences do not compare to the many variations of vínarterta in Iceland. Depending on the region in Iceland various fillings were predominantly used and today other innovative fillings as well (South and West – Rhubarb, North and Northeast- Prune, East and Southeast- Apricot). Prunes probably became the filling for vínarterta in New Iceland because large numbers of emigrants originated from the North and Northeast and also for practical reasons. Prunes were more readily available and less expensive than apricots. I have wondered why rhubarb never found favour as it certainly flourishes in the New Iceland area.

Other variations in Icelandic vínarterta that differentiate it from the New Icelandic version are that the layers are sometimes lighter and cake textured; there may be less layers than the New Icelandic counterpart and may also sometimes be coated with a chocolate buttercream icing. It is somewhat surprising given all the variations in Icelandic vínarterta that vínarterta in New Iceland came to be baked in one standard way and that it is prominently identified in North America as being 'Icelandic.' Many Icelanders now call this kind of cake 'Landalín' which means 'something that is striped'.

Kökur og Smákökur

The Icelandic Millennial Celebration in Milwaukee on August 2, 1874, was held to commemorate a thousand years of settlement in Iceland. By this time, the number of Icelanders who had emigrated with Milwaukee as their first destination had grown to approximately 200. The following is an excerpt from Bödvar Gudmundsson's book 'Where the Winds Dwell' in which he writes about preparations for the celebration:

...[T]he Icelanders in Milwaukee were preparing a celebration to commemorate 1000 years of settlement in the Old Country. Those who were employed chipped in a few cents to cover the cost. Gerd Wickmann got together the Icelandic women along the shores of Lake Michigan who could be expected to do their bit, baking the twisted doughnuts called kleinur and raisin pound cakes. Gerd herself had learned from the merchant's wife in Eyrarbakki how to bake vínarterta, the cake which for a hundred and twenty years has done the most to unite the hearts of all those people in Canada and the U.S. with Icelandic blood in their veins. Even though this cake is held in anything but high regard in Iceland, where it is usually called a striped tart, it has warmed the cockles of so many North American Icelandic hearts that it deserves to be placed with a crown atop it on the Icelandic coat of arms, no less than split codfish that King Jorund used on his national flag (230).

Following Bödvar Gudmundsson's impassioned endorsement, I would only add that vínarterta continues to be firmly ensconced as an accompaniment to all special occasions in New Iceland.

To serve: Cut round or square-shaped vínarterta into strips (about ½ inch) and then into serving size pieces (1-2½ inches).

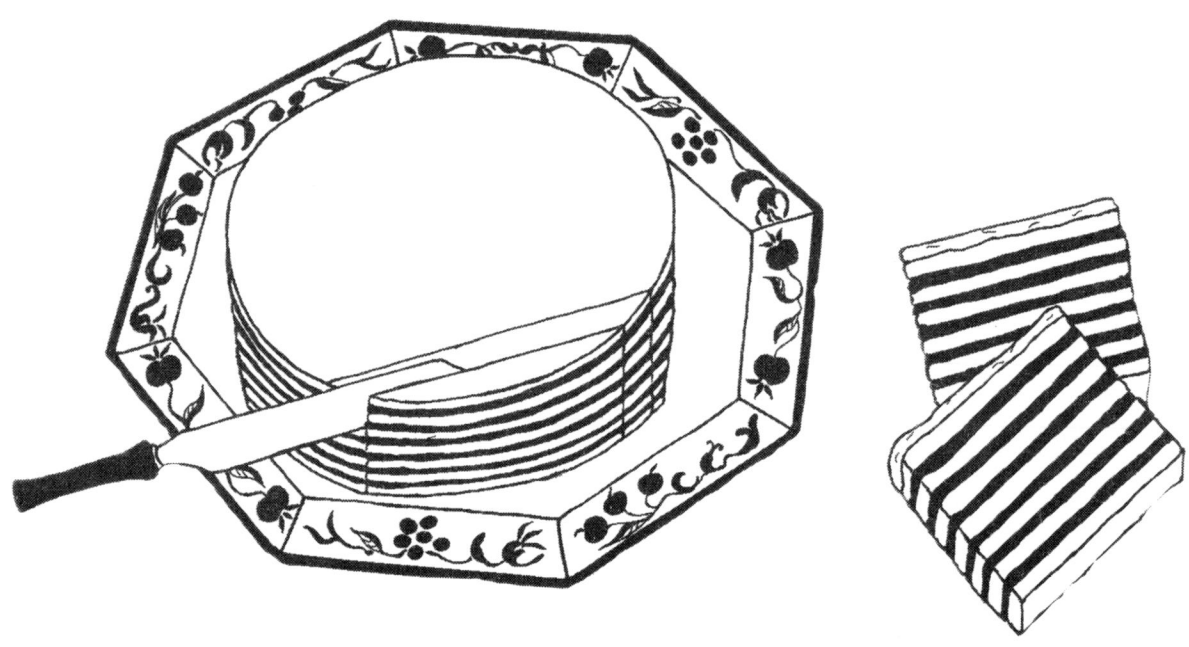

Lois Olafson's Vínarterta

1½ cups sugar
1 cup butter
3 eggs
½ cup milk
1 tsp. vanilla
1½ tsp. ground cardamom seeds
3½ cups flour(more if required)
3 tsp. baking powder
pinch of salt

Layers
1. Cream butter. Add sugar gradually beating until mixture is light and fluffy. Add eggs one at at time, beating well after each one.
2. Mix in milk, vanilla and cardamom.
3. Add dry ingredients and combine well. Knead in enough flour to make a soft cookie dough.
4. Chill the dough for about 1 hour (the dough will be easier to roll).
5. Roll out the dough thin on the counter with a little flour, one layer at a time. Arrange on greased and floured pan and trim edges. There are variations for pans used. Some recipes suggest using cake layer pans, the inside or outside bottoms. (For inside the pan you would have to pat the dough in place.) Loose bottoms of cake pans are another alternative. Lois uses the loose bottom of a Christmas cake tin. The loose bottom of a spring-form pan would also be good, providing it does not have a ridged edge.
6. Bake each layer at 350° F for about 8-10 minutes or until golden brown. Continue until you have baked all your layers. Lois's vínarterta is usually 6-8 layers.
7. Meanwhile prepare the prune filling. When filling and layers have cooled, assemble cake by spreading the filling between each layer.
8. Ice top and sides with a butter icing flavoured with almond extract.

2 lb. pitted prunes
½ cup sugar
½ tsp. ground cardamom seeds

Filling
1. Cover prunes with water and boil until soft. Drain and cool. Chop fine.
2. Return to pot and add sugar and cardamom. Heat until the sugar dissolves, being careful not to burn.
3. Cool.

Kökur og Smákökur

The recipe for the layers is very similar to the recipe I normally use so found it very easy to pull together. The only thing I didn't do was to chill the dough before rolling out. I have always had trouble working with chilled dough so I added more flour (1/2-3/4 cup approximately) to make a stiff cookie dough.

A trick that I learned to make the rolling of the layers easier is to do it on waxed paper. (I still flour the surface.) When the layer is at the desired thickness you just flip the paper onto the baking pan and pull it away.

The filling recipe is also similar to the one I normally use. I found it easier to put the cooked prunes through a meat grinder. It grinds the skin of the prune very fine and I find the vínarterta easier to cut when the prunes are done that way. One thing we add to the prunes when they are cooking is a good shot of whiskey. You will never find that in any cookbook though.

I have a recipe for an icing I use every year for my vínarterta. I usually end up freezing some of the vínarterta (wrap it very tightly in saran wrap.) This icing never sticks to the wrap.

4 tbsp. butter
1 1/4 cup sifted icing sugar
1-2 tbsp. lemon juice
1/4 tsp. vanilla
Cream butter. Gradually add icing sugar; beating well after each addition. Beat in lemon juice and vanilla. Spread evenly over top and sides of the cake.

I normally let my vínarterta sit out on the counter for 3-6 days before serving. This gives the time for the moisture from the prune filling to be absorbed into the layers and it holds together better.

Freezes very well!

Susie Erickson-Jakobson
Winnipeg, Manitoba

Ingibjorg Olafson's Vínarterta (adapted by Elva Jonasson)

¾ cup butter (I use ½ butter and ½ shortening)
2 cups sugar (I use 1½ cups sugar)
5 eggs
4½ cups flour (plus some for handling)
½ tsp. salt
1 tsp. ground cardamom seeds
3 tsp. baking powder
2 tbsp. cold water
1 tsp. vanilla

Layers
1. Beat together the butter and sugar. Add eggs one at a time, beating well.
2. Combine 2 cups of the flour, cardamom, baking powder and salt. Add to the butter, sugar and eggs.
3. Add the water and vanilla. Beat well.
4. Add the remaining flour and mix until smooth (this will be a very soft dough and I will usually let it rest for about an hour before rolling it out).
5. On a well floured pastry board place a portion of the dough and gently roll out until it is the right size for your pan and in the shape of your pan (I generally use enough flour so that there is too much on both sides of the layers-so I use a soft hake which is a flat oriental watercolour brush-a regular pastry brush is too stiff-and brush off the excess flour). Now take a piece of wax paper with about an inch of it folded over. Lay this on top of your layer and carefully start rolling the wax paper and dough towards yourself, brushing off the excess flour as you go. Then unroll on the bottom of your cake pan. Trim excess with a sharp knife. Use a fork to indent the surface but do not put the fork right through the dough (I use either 8" round or square cake tins, 2 or 3, and turn them upside down, dusted lightly with flour. I will mark the dough out into 12 sections so that I have even layers).
6. Bake for 8-10 minutes at 375° F Cool on rack. (Note: I do not put the trim in with the dough in the bowl. Instead I set it aside and re-roll this dough to use for the top and bottom layers. This recipe will general make 14-16 layers so you get 2- for all the work you may as well have lots to enjoy. If you do not want to make up all the layers you can simply wrap the cooled layers in double or triple layers in plastic bags and store in a dry area. The layers will keep in the cupboard up to 3 months without becoming stale. It is not necessary to freeze the layers when they are not filled.

2 lb. pitted prunes
½ cup sugar
1 tsp. vanilla

Filling
1. Put prunes into heavy large saucepan and almost cover with water.
2. With heat at medium bring to a boil. Reduce heat and simmer until prunes are very soft. Add sugar and vanilla and remove from heat.
3. Mash well with a fork or a potato masher.

To assemble
Place layer on serving plate and spread a smooth even layer of the prune puree (about ⅛ inch thick). Top with another layer and continue until you have 7 or 8 (7 is traditional) layers with the top layer plain. Let stand 2-3 days before icing and serving. The filled layers must sit at least overnight to soften and will slice more easily if left for 2-3 days.

Icing
I use a plain butter icing with a few drops of almond flavouring (icing sugar, butter, milk or cream and flavouring).

Thora Orr's Vínarterta

1 cup soft butter
1½ cups sugar
2 eggs
2 tbsp. light cream
1 tsp. almond extract
4 cups sifted flour
1 tsp. baking powder
pinch of salt
1 tsp. ground cardamom seeds
½ cup ground almonds

Layers
1. Cream butter until fluffy. Add sugar gradually, beating thoroughly. Add eggs one at a time, beating well after each one. Mix in cream and almond extract.
2. Sift dry ingredients together. Mix into creamed mixture. Add ground almonds. Blend well.
3. Turn onto unfloured pastry board and knead gently 10-15 times to smooth up. Refrigerate dough for at least 20 minutes.
4. Divide dough into 6 equal parts. Pat 1 part into 9 inch round layer cake pan. Bake 2 at a time at 350° F for 15-20 minutes, until golden. Turn out on rack to cool. Continue with the remaining dough.

Cakes and Cookies

2 lb. prunes
1 cup sugar
2 tsp. cinnamon
1 tsp. vanilla

Filling
1. Cover prunes with boiling water in saucepan. Bring to a boil. Reduce heat; cover and simmer 20 minutes or until tender. Drain, saving ½ cup of the cooking water.
2. When cool, pit if necessary and put through a food chopper (fine).
3. Return to saucepan with the reserved water, sugar and cinnamon. Cook gently until just thick enough to spread. Add vanilla. Cool.

6 tbsp. soft butter
1½ cup sifted icing sugar
1 egg yolk
½ cup ground almonds
¼ tsp. almond extract

Rich Butter Icing
1. Cream butter and sugar well. Add egg yolk and beat until fluffy.
2. Stir in almonds and almond extract. Add a little more icing sugar if necessary to spread.

To assemble
1. Spread prunes between layers of cake.
2. Wrap and allow to ripen for a few days before icing.

Here's the 'very special' vínarterta recipe I told you about. I got her recipe from my cousin, Alice, Thora's niece, who said 'you'll never want to make vínarterta any other way!!' I remember thinking it was marvelous.

Shirley Sigurdson
Edmonton, Alberta

The cake part of this recipe is pretty well the same as the one I use although the ½ cup of ground almonds is a very nice addition. Re: the prune filling - this is a very rich cake. I would cut back on the sugar to ½ cup. The icing is very good and freezes well.

Lois Olafson
Gimli, Manitoba

Vínerterta No.1

250g, 1¼ cups butter
250g, 1¼ cups sugar
5 eggs
250g, 2 cups flour
2 tsp. baking powder
jam preserves or purée

The egg yolks and sugar are beaten until they are thick and white. The butter is melted, froth removed (clarified) and stirred until it is cold and then added to the egg and sugar mixture, with the flour and baking powder added; lastly the well beaten egg whites are folded in. An alternate method for mixing the cake would be to first mix together the sugar and the butter, then the egg yolks, one at a time, then the flour and baking powder and lastly the beaten egg whites. From the dough you bake 4-5 layers in well greased pans until light brown in a medium to hot oven. When the layers are cold, the preserves or purée is put in between the layers and set aside with 'létt farg' (something not too heavy on top to press it down) until the next day before serving.

This recipe's ingredients are comparable to Ingibjorg Olafson's with the exception of less flour but that is where the similarity ends. The methods vary considerably. In this recipe the eggs are separated; the yolks and whites (which are well beaten) are added separately resulting in more cakelike textured layers, and there are fewer layers. 'Vínerterta' is as in the original. In Iceland now the spelling is 'Vínarterta'.

Vínerterta No.2

500g, 4 cups flour
500g, 2½ cups sugar
500g, 2½ cups butter
250g, 1¼ cups almonds
2 eggs
jam preserves or purée

The almonds are peeled, washed, dried and ground very fine. The butter is cut into the flour; the sugar, almonds and eggs are added and all are kneaded well together. The dough is divided into 6-7 layers (cut around a plate for round shape). Bake on well-greased baking paper until light brown at medium heat. When the layers are cold, they are spread with the jam preserves or purée between the layers and then set aside with 'létt farg' (something not too heavy on top to press it down) for 4-5 days before serving

This recipe while richer with more butter and sugar compares most closely with Thora Orr's vínarterta which also includes ground almonds and has a similar number of layers.

*The earliest edition of **Cook Book** (1930) included five vínarterta recipes. The 1950 edition has only two. The earlier recipes favoured some interesting variations to note. The recipe contributed by Mrs. Finnur Johnson included finely ground almonds in the dough as does this one from Guðrún Jónsdóttir and the one from Thora Orr. Mrs. Bjorg Johnson's specifies lemon flavouring in the dough and allspice in the prune filling. Mrs. F.J. Bergman's recipe states 'spread well with raspberry jam'. Of the last two, Mrs. A. Blondal's recipe is repeated in the 1950 edition and has almond flavouring in the dough and cardamom in the prune filling. Mrs. S.F. Olafson's has cardamom in the dough and includes the instruction to flavour the prune filling as desired. These two recipes are as vínarterta came to be commonly known in New Iceland.*

Fillings for Vínerterta

Rabarbarmauk (Rhubarb Purée)

Original quantities followed by conversions in ¼ amounts:
5 kg, 2¾ lb. rhubarb stalks
4 kg, 5 cups sugar
¼ litre, ¼ cup water
¼ litre, ¼ cup vinegar
whole cinnamon sticks, reduce to taste
1 tsp., ¼ tsp. vanilla
some whole cloves, reduce to taste

The rhubarb stalks are washed and broken up into 1 inch pieces. The sugar is melted in the water and vinegar over low heat. The rhubarb pieces are added and boiled (simmered) with the spices and cooked until the pieces fall apart. Put in jars, cover with paper soaked in rum or spirits. Parchment paper is tied over immediately. The jars are kept in a dry, cool and preferably dark place. Rhubarb is best for "sulta" (jam) in July.

Sveskjumauk or Aprikósumauk (Prune or Apricot Purée)

1 kg, 2¼ lb. prunes or apricots
water
slice of lemon
500g, 2½ cups sugar

Wash the prunes (apricots) and soak them for 24 hours. Cook in the same water until the stones are easily removed (or the apricots are very soft). Put through the meat grinder 1-2 times. Then they are again put into the same water and cooked until of a thick consistency. Put in jars, cover with paper soaked in rum or spirits. Parchment paper is tied over immediately. The jars are kept in a dry, cool and preferably dark place.

Kökur og Smákökur

Joyce Benedictson's Vínarterta

Layers
- 1 cup butter or margarine
- 1½ cups sugar
- 3 eggs
- ½ cup milk
- 1 tsp. vanilla
- 1 tsp. almond flavouring
- 4-5 cups flour
- 2 tsp. baking powder

Layers
1. Cream butter; add sugar gradually and then eggs one at a time.
2. Add milk and flavourings. Mix together.
3. Sift flour and baking powder and add to the first mixture. Knead in enough flour to make a soft cookie dough.
4. Refrigerate the dough for about 1 hour. This will make the dough easier to roll.
5. Invert layer cake tins and roll out dough thin.
6. Bake at 375° F for 5-6 minutes or until the edges start to turn brown. Continue to roll out and bake layers (Joyce usually makes each cake with seven layers and states you should get 17-18 layers per recipe).
7. Meanwhile prepare the prune filling. When filling and layers have cooled, assemble cake by spreading the filling between each layer.
8. Ice top and sides using a butter icing with almond flavouring.

Filling
- 2lb. pitted prunes
- 1½ cups water
- 2 cups sugar
- 1 tsp. ground cardamom seeds or more if desired

Filling
1. Boil prunes until soft and prunes have absorbed most of the water. Cool.
2. Put through the meat grinder.
3. Add sugar and cardamom. Heat mixture until sugar has dissolved being careful not to burn.

Kanelterta (Cinnamon Torte)

These two kanelterta recipes are completely different. The first one has two cake layers assembled with a lemon filling and enclosed with a meringue topping. The second is multi-layered, assembled with jam and whipped cream and covered with a chocolate glaze.

Mrs. M. J. Matthiasson's Kanelterta

Cake

½ cup butter
½ cup sugar
4 egg yolks
6 tbsp. milk
1 tsp. baking powder
1 cup flour
pinch of salt

Cake

1. Cream butter and sugar together.
2. Beat egg yolks lightly. Add yolks and milk to butter and sugar. Beat well.
3. Sift baking powder, flour and salt together and add to batter. Combine well.
4. Smooth batter in a greased 8 inch round cake pan. Bake at 350° F for about 25 minutes. Cool and split cake into two layers.

Lemon Filling

3 tbsp. flour
1 cup sugar
1 cup hot water
1 egg
1 tbsp. butter
juice of 1 lemon
finely grated rind of ½ lemon (less if preferred)

Lemon Filling

1. Combine the flour, sugar and water in double boiler over simmering water.
2. Cook, stirring until slightly thickened.
3. Beat egg slightly. Beat about ¼ of the sauce into it. Return to pan, and add the butter, lemon juice and grated rind. Continue cooking and stirring until thickened.
4. Cool to lukewarm.

Meringue Topping

4 egg whites
1/8 tsp. cream of tartar
1 tsp. vanilla
1 cup sugar
1/3 cup chopped nuts, ie. sliced almonds
1/4-1/2 tsp. cinnamon
(cream of tartar and vanilla are not in the original recipe and may be omitted)

Meringue Topping

1. Beat egg whites until foamy. Add cream of tartar and vanilla if desired.
2. Gradually add sugar until stiff peaks form.
3. Reserve nuts and cinnamon.

Cake Assembly

1. Place bottom layer on baking sheet or attractive ovenproof serving plate.
2. Spread lemon filling over and replace the top layer. Spread a thin layer of filling on the top layer.
3. Swirl the meringue over the cake to enclose it completely. Sprinkle with the reserved nuts and cinnamon.
4. Bake in a slow oven (250°-300° F) for approximately 45-60 minutes or until lightly browned. Cool and transfer with wide spatula to serving plate if you used a baking sheet.

I tried the cake and it was good -will definitely make it again.

Clarice Demers
Edmonton, Alberta

GunnÞóra Gisladóttir's Kanelterta (adapted by Elva Jonasson)

3/4 cup margarine
3/4 cup sugar
1 1/8 cup flour
1 tsp. cinnamon
2 1/4 cup whipped cream

1. Half melt the margarine and mix well with sugar.
2. Add the flour and cinnamon to the sugar and butter mixture and blend well together.
3. Divide the dough into eight layers and spread on waxed paper in 8 inch rounds. (I turn layer cake tins upside down and spread the dough on the wax paper.)
4. Bake the layers at 350° F. Watch carefully because the batter burns

Cakes and Cookies

very easily.

5. Shortly before the cake is to be served, spread whipped cream between each layer. It is nice to have a little raspberry or apricot jam between some of the layers in addition to the whipped cream. The top layer may be covered with a chocolate glaze or icing with a fancy garnish of the whipped cream as well. (For chocolate glaze or icing: Melt milk chocolate bar with a little cream or milk.)

I tried out the recipe and it seems to be the same as the one she gave me. I never quite get eight rounds out of the dough but that is neither here nor there. Something she told me initially was to use a little cocoa in the whipping cream - just enough to make it a pale tan brown and a hint of chocolate taste. I think it is quite pretty - try it - she did do this herself when I once tasted her creation.

Dee Dee Westdal
Winnipeg, Manitoba

Jólakaka (Christmas Cake)

½ cup butter
1 cup sugar
2 eggs
1 cup milk
½-1 tsp. ground cardamom seeds
1 tbsp. finely grated lemon peel
½ tsp. salt
2 tsp. baking powder
2½ cups flour
1 cup raisins

1. Cream the butter and sugar until light.
2. Beat in the eggs. Add the milk and mix well.
3. Add the cardamom, peel, salt and baking powder. Mix together. Add the flour gradually, combining well. Stir in the raisins.
4. Spoon batter into a lightly greased loaf pan. Smooth top. Bake at 325° F for one hour and 15 minutes or until done.

Kökur og Smákökur

> *First of all, I was delighted to be included in this project. My oven took one hour, 30 minutes to bake the cake. I invited Johanna Sigson over to taste the finished product. It is a very nice cake. Jo mentioned that her mother, Amma's (Margaret Sigmundson, Gimli) back door neighbour for years, used the clean upper straws from a corn broom to test for doneness!*
>
> Fiona Sigmundson
> Sidney, British Columbia

Jólakaka No.1 (Christmas Cake)

500g, 3¾ cups flour
200g, 1 cup butter
1 tsp. cardamom
¼ litre, 1 cup milk
6 level tsp. baking powder
200g, 1 cup sugar
3-4 eggs
100g, ½ cup raisins
50g, ¼ cup mixed glacé peel

Melt the butter. The baking powder and cardamom are blended together with the flour. The sugar is added. A hole is made in the middle and the butter, egg and milk mixture is poured in and all is mixed well together. Then the raisins and the peel are added. The cake is put into a loaf pan and baked in good heat for approximately 1 hour. (Suggestion for good heat : 325°-350° F).

This Jólakaka recipe is richer than the New Iceland one preceding. The mixed glacé peel would not be considered a usual addition. The New Iceland recipe flavoured with cardamom and lemon peel including only raisins would be considered more traditional. (Mrs. H.M. Sveinson contributed a recipe for 'Jóla Kaka' to **Cook Book** (1930). It is almost identical to the New Iceland recipe preceding. It includes ¼ lb. citron peel. Jólakaka is omitted in the 1950 edition.) Jólabrauð is a yeast dough variation. (Recipes for Jólabrauð in *Kaffibrauð* – Sweet Breads and Fried Cakes). Helga Einarson Almquist's Jólabrauð- includes citron or fruit mix as well.

Ingibjorg Olafson's Rúlluterta (Jelly Roll)

3 large eggs
1¼ cup white sugar
2 tbsp. cream
2 tbsp. cold water
1 cup flour
2 tsp. baking powder
1 tsp. vanilla
¼ tsp. salt

Any kind of jam that you may prefer (e.g. strawberry, raspberry, lingönberry, cherry or lemon filling) may be used as fillings. Serve in slices and may also be garnished with whipped cream or ice cream as desired. See Mrs. M. J. Matthiasson's Kanelterta (Cinnamon Torte) for Lemon Filling recipe.

1. Preheat oven to 325° F Prepare cookie sheet, 11 x 17 x 1 inches, by lining with wax paper.
2. Beat eggs until foamy and add 1 cup of the white sugar a little at a time and beat until thick and creamy.
3. Blend flour and baking powder with the salt and stir half into the egg mixture. Add the cream, water and vanilla and stir well (do not beat). Add remaining flour mixture and stir until well blended.
4. Pour into lined cookie sheet and bake in preheated oven for approximately 20-25 minutes or until the cake begins to pull away from the edge of the pan.
5. Immediately turn out onto a tea towel which has been sprinkled with ¼ cup white sugar. Allow to cool slightly, no more than 5 to 10 minutes. Spread with strawberry jam and gently roll using the tea towel to help in rolling. Then continue to roll the tea towel around the filled cake and let cool completely.

I made it twice and my daughter Christine also made it. MY GRANDSONS LOVED IT! The first one I baked for 25 minutes and it was a deep golden colour. I filled it with raspberry jam and served it with whipped cream. The roll had a 'chewy' quality to it. It is not as light as the jelly rolls one finds today because the consistency of the dough is thicker.

The second one I baked for only 20 minutes and it was a light golden color. We liked the texture of this one better than the first. I used a blackberry jam spread with whipped cream. Christy spread hers with strawberry jam and served half with whipped cream and half with ice cream. Either can be used.
I froze one of mine and when I served it later it was delicious!

Sigrid Johannesson Woltzen
Christy Woltzen Ehrenreich
St. Louis, Missouri

Rúlluterta (Jelly Roll)

100g, ½ cup butter or margarine
100g, ½ cup sugar
2 eggs
100g, ¾ cup flour
2 tbsp. milk
1½ tsp. baking powder
jelly or jam

The butter is softened and creamed with the sugar, then the eggs are beaten in one at a time. It is better to beat the eggs well in a cup before adding. Then the flour and baking powder and lastly the milk. Bake in a well-greased paper lined pan until light brown with a medium to high heat. Use a 42 x 36 cm pan. Sugar is spread on white paper (waxed paper); the cake is turned out on the sugar; spread with the jelly or jam and rolled up with the paper, immediately.

This recipe is richer than Ingibjorg Olafson's Rúlluterta as it is prepared with butter. Ingibjorg's roll has a lighter more sponge cake-like texture. Otherwise the two recipes are quite similar.

Kúrenu Smákökur (Currant Cookies/Bar)

⅔ cup softened butter
1½ cup sugar
3 eggs
1 tbsp. grated lemon rind
2 tbsp. lemon juice
½ tsp. salt
1 tsp. baking powder
1 cup flour
½ cup currants or raisins
½ cup sliced almonds

1. Cream butter and sugar. Beat in eggs, lemon rind and juice.
2. Add salt, baking powder and flour. Combine well.
3. Spread in lightly greased and floured 9 x 13 inch pan. Sprinkle with currants and almonds.
4. Bake at 350° F for 25-30 minutes or until golden brown. Cool and cut into bars.

An excellent slice with a chewy texture and subtle balance of lemon and almond flavours. The perfect foil for a good cup of Icelandic coffee.

Elaine Sigurdson
Oakville, Ontario

Featherweight Cake, Hurry-up Cake and Lazy Daisy Topping

These cakes were standard in our house. My mother made Featherweight if eggs and time were freely available and Hurry-up cake if they weren't. Both made a 9 inch square cake and both were covered with 'Lazy Daisy' topping. Or used for shortcake or...

Shirley Sigurdson
Edmonton, Alberta
(Shirley grew up in Husavik, Manitoba)

Featherweight Cake

1 cup sugar
3 eggs
1 cup flour
1½ tsp. baking powder
pinch of salt
½ cup milk
"butter the size of an egg" (about 3 tbsp.)
1 tsp. vanilla

1. Beat sugar and eggs together until light and fluffy.
2. Combine flour with baking powder and salt. Sift together three times.
3. Heat milk with butter until butter melts and mixture is nearly at the boiling point.
4. Add flour mixture to the sugar and eggs. Combine, then add hot milk. Mix together, adding vanilla. Spread batter smoothly into lightly greased and floured 9 inch square pan.
5. Bake at 325° F for 35-45 minutes. While hot, top with Lazy Daisy topping if desired.

Hurry-Up Cake

2 eggs
1 cup sugar
1 cup flour
1 tsp. baking powder
½ tsp. salt
½ cup milk
1 tbsp. butter
1 tsp. vanilla

1. Beat eggs.
2. Combine sugar, flour, baking powder and salt. Add to the eggs and mix together.
3. Heat the milk and butter until the butter melts.
4. Combine both mixtures and stir in vanilla. Spread batter smoothly into lightly greased and floured 9 inch square pan.
5. Bake at 325° F for 30 minutes. While hot, top with Lazy Daisy topping if desired.

Kökur og Smákökur

Lazy Daisy Topping

1. While cake is still hot spread with a mixture of ½ cup coconut, 5 tbsp. brown sugar, 3 tbsp. melted butter and 2 tbsp. cream.
2. Return to oven until mixture bubbles. Watch to prevent burning. Cool cake before cutting.

These are great cakes to whip up if you're getting unexpected company - as is typical of us Icelanders, especially growing up in a small town. We all love to drop in for coffee! They are light and moist and especially good warm!

Janice Benedictson
Winnipeg, Manitoba

Judith Sigurdson's Matrimonial Cake

1½ cups flour
1½ cups brown sugar
3 cups rolled oats
1 tsp. baking powder
1 tsp. soda
1 cup butter

Filling
500g, 1 lb. dates
1 cup sugar
1 cup water
1 tsp. vanilla

1. Mix flour, brown sugar, rolled oats, soda and baking powder. Add butter. Rub and crumb together.
2. Pat about ½ into greased 13 X 9 inch pan, spread with filling, pat on remainder of crumbs.
3. Bake at 350° F for 25-30 minutes or until top is nicely browned.

Filling
Cook until dates are well broken up and thickened.

Delicious and very substantial!

Penny Olafson
Winnipeg, Manitoba

Cakes and Cookies

Sigga Eyolfson's Calla Lilies

3 eggs
1 tbsp. hot water
1 cup white sugar
1 tsp. vanilla
1 tsp. baking powder
pinch of salt
1 cup flour

May be frozen; if freezing in layers, place wax paper between.

1. Preheat oven to 375° F.
2. Beat eggs with hot water at high speed of mixer until foamy.
3. Still beating on high speed, add sugar gradually until the batter is thick and ivory coloured.
4. On low speed, add vanilla, baking powder and salt. Then gradually add flour, beating only until all is combined well.
5. Drop tablespoons of batter on a greased baking sheet.
6. Bake only 6 at a time, until lightly browned for about 8 minutes.
7. While hot from the oven: quickly loosen from pan and pinch together at one end to form a cone shape.

To serve: Fill with a spoonful of whipped cream (sweetened with a little sugar and vanilla). Garnish with a canned mandarin orange section (well drained) in the centre.

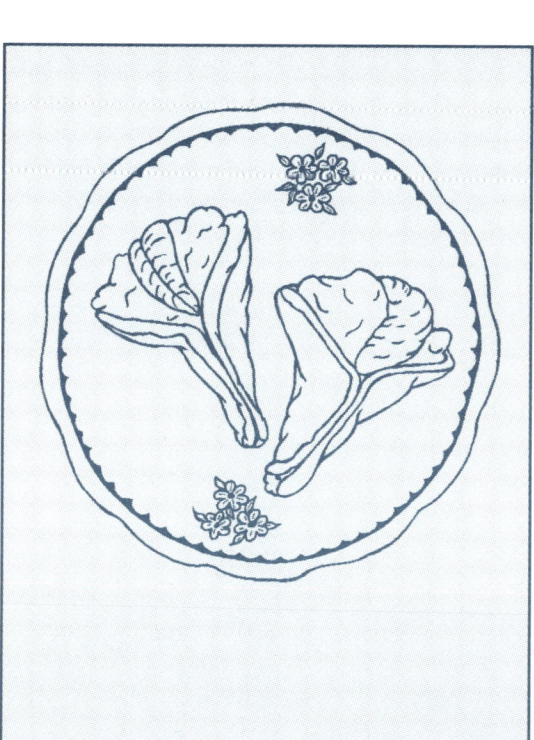

I find baking at 425° F better than 375° F for 6-7 minutes. Each oven is different — also my best calla lilies were at the west coast. (Oven temperature may vary at different altitudes.) Calla lilies are ready when edges start to brown ... with time and practice each baker learns.

My first experience in making calla lilies was when Aunty Lois asked if I could make a few hundred for a function on the Blackhawk. I said "Sure, no problem" whoa what a surprise!

When I started Second Helpings catering in Vancouver calla lilies were on the menu- perfect bite sized sweets — they were a huge hit. Nobody was able to eat 'just one' after they ate one. Word spread about how wonderful they were and it was an item often requested both for work and by friends for dinner parties, mine and theirs.

Traditionally I'd fill them with whipped cream and cold drained mandarin slices but also with ice cream and nuts; whipped cream, pecans, shaved chocolate, ½ cherry; ice cream and strawberry pieces dipped in Swiss chocolate.

Ingrid Sigurdson
Riverton, Manitoba

*The following recipe is from **Cook Book** (1930). While the ingredients are basically the same as Sigga Eyolfson's, the instructions for presentation in Mrs. Frederickson's showcase the elegance of this delectable pastry.*

Mrs. F. S. Frederickson's Calla Lily Sponge Cake

Three fresh eggs beaten together, then add 1 tbsp. of hot water. To this, beating in slowly add one scant cup of granulated sugar. Add to the mixture, one cup of sifted flour, 1 tsp. of baking powder and 1 tsp. of vanilla —also a pinch of salt. Drop the batter by scant teaspoon onto buttered tin, forming round flat cakes, not touching one another. Bake quickly, but not brown, as they must be soft and pliable. Press together from the outside while hot, into the form of a lily. Fill the cavity of these forms just before serving with sweetened cream, place a small piece of orange between the centre of the cream for the stem (stamen), and use a strip of Angelica for stem.

This recipe will make 48 cakes and, served on a dessert plate to each guest with a cup of cocoa or coffee, makes a delicious and artistic refreshment for an afternoon party.

Elva Jonasson's Almond Cookies

<u>Single recipe</u>
1 cup lard
1 cup sugar
2 eggs
1 tsp. almond flavouring
2½ cups flour
toasted almonds

<u>Double recipe</u>
1 lb. lard
2⅓ cups sugar
3 eggs
2 tsp. almond flavouring
5½ cups flour
toasted almonds

1. Lightly toast almonds in 350° F oven for 15-20 minutes. Stir once or twice to prevent burning. Set aside.
2. Beat lard and sugar until light and fluffy. Reserve 1 egg yolk for topping. Beat in eggs and almond flavouring. Add flour and mix thoroughly.
3. Take a teaspoon of dough and form into a ball. Place on an ungreased cookie sheet and flatten with a glass to ¼ inch thickness. Dip glass lightly into flour before pressing down dough.
4. Beat egg yolk and add an equal amount of milk. Brush on the top of each cookie. Press a toasted almond into each centre.
5. Bake at 350° F for about 8 minutes until lightly golden brown.

My cookies were good. I used butter not lard and instead of toasted almonds placed several pignoli nuts on top of each one - Italian influence!

*Christine Cerasoli
Nanuet, New York*

Kransar (Wreaths)

1 large egg
½ cup sugar
1½ tsp. vanilla
¼ tsp. almond extract
½ cup finely chopped almonds
1 cup butter
2 cups flour

1. Beat eggs. Add the sugar, vanilla, almond extract, almonds and 1 cup flour. Combine well.
2. Knead in the butter and remaining cup of flour.
3. Wrap in wax paper and chill dough thoroughly (at least 1 hour).
4. Pinch off small bits of dough. Roll with hands to make ropes 3 inches long and ⅜ inches diameter. Join ends to form a circle.
5. Bake on ungreased baking sheets at 325° F for about 12 minutes or until lightly golden brown. Watch carefully.

Quite tasty for a basic recipe – would be great with a cup of coffee.

Janice Robidoux
Cypress River, Manitoba

Vanillekransar (Vanilla Wreaths)

500g, 3¾ cups flour
250g, 1¼ cups sugar
125g, ⅔ cup (4 oz.) almonds
1 tsp. baking powder
1 egg
350g, 1¾ cups butter
½ vanilla bean

The almonds are peeled and crushed fine. The vanilla bean is heated with the sugar. The baking powder is blended together with the flour, vanilla flavoured sugar, butter, almonds, and egg added in. All are well kneaded together, shaped into cookies with the cookie maker (or cookie press or spritzer) and baked until light brown with medium heat. (Suggestion for medium heat: 350° F.)

This recipe would yield a larger quantity but is very similar to the preceding New Iceland Kransar recipe. The difference is mainly in the method for shaping the cookies. The traditional wreath or ring shape is not specified but probably just assumed. (Certainly, 'kransar' in the name translates as 'wreath'.) Without a cookie press through which the dough is squeezed out (like a pastry bag) rolling bits of the dough into lengths and joining to form the wreath shape is simply an alternate method. The following recipe contributed by Mrs. K.K. Olafson of Gardar, North Dakota, also uses this shaping method.

Vanilla Rings

One c. sugar, 1¼ c. butter, 1 egg, 2 tbsp. milk, 1 lb blanched almonds, finely chopped. Flavour with vanilla. After mixing ingredients, roll into lengths about 3 inches long, form into rings and bake in quick oven. (This recipe has considerably more almonds and probably not a suitable texture for the cookie press).

Mrs. N.S. Thorlaksson contributed the recipe 'Berliner kranser' to **Cook Book** (1930). While her recipe has no almonds, it employs the same shaping method – 'Roll into rolls not quite ½ inch thick. Shape into wreaths (Kransar) and dip each in beaten white egg and again dip into coarse white sugar and bake until a delicate brown on buttered and floured pans in a moderate oven'.

Cookie presses were also used in New Iceland. I inherited one from a great aunty; included were a number of Christmas motifs -shapes such as Christmas trees and snowflakes (and from this I would assume that these spritz-type cookies were popular at Christmas).

Gyðingakökur (Jewish Cookies)

2½ cups flour
½ tsp. salt
1 tsp. ground cardamom seeds
¾ cup butter
1 egg

Topping
1 cup cold strong coffee
1 cup blanched slivered almonds, coarsely chopped
1 cup crushed sugar lumps (coarse bits not fine)

1. Stir flour, salt and cardamom together.
2. Cut in butter as for pie pastry.
3. Beat egg with a fork and add to dough. Combine well.
4. Wrap in wax paper. Chill thoroughly (at least 1 hour) until firm.
5. Roll out dough on wax paper ⅛ inch thick. Cut in 1½ inch rounds with a cutter. Brush tops with coffee; sprinkle generously with almonds and sugar (mixed together). Press down gently with your hand to help the almond sugar mixture stick. Place on greased baking sheets and bake at 350° F for about 12 minutes or until lightly golden brown.

I took a dozen to the reception we were attending where they were very positively received. Bouquets re cookies: 1) Everyone enjoyed the light flaky pastry of the cookies. 2) Comments that the cookie was enjoyable but 'not too sweet' (Two people at the party are diabetic. One could crush only almonds for a topping if necessary.)

Maureen Sigurdson
Vancouver, British Columbia

Ingibjorg Sigurgeirson McKillop's Gyðingakökur (Jewish Cookies)

3 eggs
1 cup sugar
2 tbsp. water
1 tsp. ground cardamom seeds
1 lb. butter
4 cups flour
1 tsp. baking powder

1. Beat eggs well; add sugar and beat again.
2. Add water and cardamom and one cup flour.
3. Turn out on board and knead in butter, remaining flour, into which baking powder has been sifted. The flour should be worked in very gradually.
4. Roll and cut into cookies. Now beat one egg and 1 tbsp. water. Put a dab on each cookie, then fine sugar and finally chopped almonds.
5. Bake at 350° F until golden brown.

Gyðingakökur No.2 (Jewish Cookies)

500g, 3¾ cups flour
300g, 1½ cups butter or margarine
200g, 1 cup sugar
4 tsp. baking powder
2 eggs
egg, almonds, sugar

The butter is cut into the flour; sugar and baking powder is added, then the eggs and all is well kneaded together and rolled out a little thinner that in the No. 1 recipe. (¼ inch thickness in the No.1 recipe.) The beaten egg is brushed on top and the cookies are spread with the almonds and sugar, then baked at medium heat until light brown. (Suggestion for medium heat: 350° F; the almonds would be coarsely ground.)

This recipe's list of ingredients compares closely to Ingibjorg Sigurgeirson McKillop's Gyðingakökur. The differences to note are that Ingibjorg's includes cardamom and this recipe has much more baking powder which would produce a very different cookie. The name Gyðingakökur implies that these cookies have their origins with the Jewish people, coming to be baked in Iceland through Danish influence as did many other recipes.

Hálfmánar (Half-moons)

1⅓ cups butter
⅔ cup sugar
1 egg
½ tsp. salt
½ tsp. baking powder
1 tsp. ground cardamom seeds
2½ cups flour

1. Cream butter and sugar. Add egg and beat well.
2. Add the dry ingredients and combine well.
3. Chill dough thoroughly (about 2-3 hours).
4. In the meantime, prepare Prune Filling: Cover 375g pkg. of prunes with water in a saucepan. Simmer about 1 hour. Drain. Remove pits. Cut up with knife and fork. Return prunes to saucepan with 2 tbsp. sugar and ¼ tsp. ground cardamom seeds. Cook until sugar is dissolved and the prunes are a nice clear colour (about 15 minutes).
5. **To bake cookies:** Roll out dough on lightly floured surface. Cut in 3 inch rounds with a cutter. Put ½ tsp. prune filling in the centre. Fold over and press edges firmly with fork. Bake at 350° F, on greased baking sheets for 10-15 minutes or until lightly golden brown.

Cakes and Cookies

I had fun making -though fussy- hálfmánar and the family and neighbourhood enjoyed the eating! Make sure the dough is kept well chilled to work with. Once it gets soft working with it becomes impossible. Tried to pack more prunes for your punch into each pocket but that did not work either. By the time I had the technique down pat the dough was used up.

Once made I delivered a few to four of my neighbours. Everyone thought they were great-Yummy little morsels! Would be a nice treat for Christmas baking.

Lynne Welock
Revelstoke, British Columbia

I tried this recipe. Followed it to the letter and received many compliments. Even the younger kids liked them!

Joyce Benedictson
Gimli, Manitoba

After a four hour choir rehearsal these cookies were very popular.

Lyn Sigson
Discovery Bay, Hong Kong

Sykur Smákökur (Sugar Cookies)

½ cup butter
1 cup sugar
2 eggs
1 tbsp. cream
½ tsp. vanilla
pinch of salt
1 tsp. baking powder
2½ - 3 cups flour

Icing
1 egg white
¾ cup icing sugar
½ tsp. vanilla

Variations: Omit icing and bake sprinkled with a cinnamon-sugar mixture, candy decorettes or coloured sugar. Or bake plain and decorate with a frosting and sprinkles if desired when cooled.

1. Cream butter. Add sugar gradually, creaming until light and fluffy.
2. Add eggs, beating after each one. Stir in cream and vanilla.
3. Add dry ingredients gradually to make a soft cookie dough.
4. Chill the dough thoroughly at least one hour.
5. Roll out dough on floured surface to ⅛-¼ inch thickness. Cut in shapes and place on ungreased baking sheet. Drizzle a small amount of icing on each cookie.
6. Bake at 350° F, 6-8 minutes or until lightly golden brown on edges.

Icing
Beat egg white. Add vanilla and icing sugar. Beat well.

Our children really enjoyed decorating them. So much so that I will probably invite the neighbourhood children to help at Easter time.

Lyn Sigson
Discovery Bay, Hong Kong

Johanna Wilson's Date-Filled Oatmeal Cookies

½ cup margarine
½ cup butter
1 cup brown sugar
1 cup flour
1 tsp. vanilla
1 scant tsp. baking soda
3 cups rolled oats
(put oats through a blender or food processor for a finer textured cookie)

1. Mix all ingredients together.
2. Roll thin (between sheets of waxed paper) and cut into rounds with a cookie cutter.
3. Bake at 350° F for about 8-10 minutes.

Filling
Cook over low heat; stirring until thickened. Spread between cooled cookies just before serving.

Filling
1 cup chopped dates
½ cup brown sugar
1 cup water

Cookies are also very good without filling.

> Ava and I really enjoyed making the Date Filled Oatmeal cookies. Not only did they taste great, it was fun having my 7-year-old daughter get a tiny taste of her Icelandic heritage by helping. They were so easy to make. Ava did most of the work herself, cutting out the circles was the most fun for her, well, maybe second only to eating them. They went so fast we found ourselves making a second batch very soon.
>
> Brenda and Ava Cerasoli
> Healdsburg, California

Elva Jonasson's Engifer Smákökur (Ginger Cookies)

1 cup butter (or ½ butter and ½ shortening)
1½ cups sugar
1 beaten egg
2 tbsp. molasses
1½ cups flour
2 tsp. baking soda
2 tsp. cinnamon
1 tsp. ginger
1 tsp. ground cardamom seeds
¾ tsp. cloves

Traditionally, these cookies were thin and crisp and were used to makes wishes come true. It was thought that if you placed a cookie in the palm of your hand and snapped it with gentle pressure from the heel of your other hand, you would know that your wish would come true if the cookie broke into no more than three pieces.

1. Cream the butter and sugar together until light and fluffy. Mix in the beaten egg and molasses.
2. Combine the remaining dry ingredients. Add to the butter mixture and blend together.
3. Form into rolls and refrigerate until the dough is chilled through (at least 2 hours).
4. Slice thinly and bake at 375° F (Be careful as the cookies bake quickly and can burn easily.) If you prefer the dough can be rolled out and cut into shapes.

> I've just finished baking Elva's cookies. It's a lovely recipe. I found it simple to follow. The cookies are mildly spicy and very buttery. They are wafer thin and crispy. They are a sinful treat, which is what a cookie should be.
>
> I formed the dough into two logs and sliced them thinly as the recipe suggested. They more than double in size when baked. I used insulated cookie tins which helps a lot when baking cookies that burn easily. I found the baking time to be just over 10 minutes. The yield from the recipe was about 9 dozen. I will definitely bake this recipe again. The cookies are elegant.
>
> Steinunn Bessason
> Winnipeg, Manitoba

Augusta Jonasson's Lemonade

2 cups sugar
2½ cups water
juice of 6 lemons
juice of 2 oranges
grated rind of 1 orange
1 cup mint leaves

Serves 10-12.

1. Cook sugar and water 5 minutes. Cool. Add fruit juices and rind.
2. Pour over mint leaves, cover and let stand one hour.
3. Strain into jar and keep in refrigerator.
4. Use ⅓ cup syrup for each glass, fill with crushed ice and water.

Here's lemonade with a twist — of mint and orange. With a touch of mint and a taste of orange, this adaptation of an old standard lets you travel the world from Morocco to L.A. Lemonade with flair! And if appropriate or required, your favourite vodka, say Icy (there has to be something Icelandic about this), will offer another dimension altogether.

Jaye Olafson
Salt Lake City, Utah

Lemon Syrup

2 oz. citric acid
1 oz. tartaric acid
1½ oz. epsom salts
5 lb. white sugar (or 10 cups)
3½ pints boiling water
6 lemons, grated rinds and juices

Mix altogether and strain through cheesecloth and put in glass jars. This makes 4 quarts. Keep in refrigerator. Dilute with water or ginger ale, as strong or as weak as you wish.

I remember my mother making this syrup every summer. It was so refreshing on a hot day.

D. Johanna Sigson
Saanichton, BC

Hressandi Drykkur

Cranberry Juice Cocktail

5 cups cranberries
5 cups water
2/3 cup sugar
4 cups ginger ale
juice of 1 lemon

Cook cranberries in water, bringing to a boil and then simmering until skins pop. Squeeze through a cheesecloth bag. Bring juice to a boil and add sugar. Stir until all sugar is dissolved. This makes 4 cups cranberry juice.

For cocktails, chill the prepared juice and serve in punch glasses, filling them half full of cranberry juice and half full of cold gingerale. More sugar may be added if a sweeter drink is desired.

> I made the cranberry juice cocktails at a get-together with relatives. As a cranberry lover, I enjoyed the real taste of the fruit, and my cousin who thought she didn't even like cranberries also complimented the recipe! Overall the drink was a hit and I intend to make it again.
>
> Reyna Jenkyns
> Waterloo, Ontario

Ingibjorg Sigurgeirson McKillop's Raspberry Vinegar

4 qts. raspberries
1 qt. vinegar
sugar

1. Pour vinegar over berries and set aside until following day.
2. Mash berries and set aside for 24 hours.
   Strain and measure juice, allow 1 lb. sugar to 1 pt. liquid. Heat slowly and skim. Boil gently for 25 minutes, then pour into bottles.
3. Use with cold water, according to taste.

Diane Kortesluoma's Raspberry Vinegar

2-15 oz. packages of frozen sweetened raspberries
¾ cup white vinegar
1 cup sugar
Brandy (optional)

This is the recipe I have used and everyone has liked it. In the summer at Amma Stina's we would have raspberry vinegar or lemonade.
-Diane

1. Empty raspberries into a bowl and break apart with a fork. Stir in the vinegar and refrigerate.
2. Next day, stir in half the sugar and return to the refrigerator.
3. Repeat on the second day.
4. On the third day strain through a cheesecloth or a fine enough sieve to remove berry seeds. Measure the juice and for each cup stir in 2 oz. of brandy, if desired.
5. Bottle the syrup and keep refrigerated.
6. **To serve:** Pour ⅓ cup of syrup over ice cubes and fill with soda water or water.

Elin made the Raspberry Vinegar as she was on March break. We tried it with soda water and it is very good. We would like to try it in the summer with the raspberries that Elin's Afi grows at our cottage.

Wendy and Elin Sigurdson
St. Louis, Missouri

Sukkulaði (Creamy Hot Chocolate)

3 squares semi-sweet chocolate
½ cup sugar
1 cup water
4 cups milk, scalded

Hot chocolate or cocoa was always served as a treat for the children, especially at Christmas.

1. Flake the chocolate. Add the sugar and water and cook gently over boiling water for 20 minutes.
2. Stir until smooth, gradually adding a little of the hot milk. Then stir in the remaining milk. Serve immediately.

I would use unsweetened or semisweet chocolate if you like cappuccino and I'd use milk chocolate for a sweeter taste. I put it in the blender and that made it frothy. Made at least 8 mugs.

Olivia (Olafson) Sparks -age 15
Selkirk, Manitoba

Kaffi (Coffee) Traditions

In earlier days there were many chores to be done and harsh weather to endure but interspersed throughout these long pioneer days were reviving cups of strongly brewed kaffi. An inflexible kaffi schedule consisting of all meal times and also mid-morning, mid-afternoon and evening breaks. At home around the kitchen table, out on the lake or in the fields, the opportunity for sociability was as rejuvenating as the kaffi.

At the turn of the century coffee technology in North America was such that upon boiling the ground coffee in a pot one would pour off the infusion and, hopefully, leave most of the grinds behind. The New Icelandic settlers were early advocates of the manual drip method. The filter for this advanced and unique early drip method was a closely woven unbleached cotton or muslin bag. (Thrifty Icelanders made coffee bags from flour or sugar sacks.) These filters were also known as kaffi póki, which translates as "coffee bags" although in later years came to be referred to as "coffee socks". The bag filter, once made, was cured by leaving it to simmer in a pot of boiled water and coffee grounds. The bag was then sewn onto a ring with a handle sized to fit over the top of the coffee pot. These rings were fashioned from copper since it was soft, malleable and available and the kaffi pot itself was cast aluminum or enamelware.

To make the kaffi the pot was placed at the back of the warm wood stove, or, in later years on low heat on a stove element. For kaffi purists it was important to leave the used kaffi grinds in the bag after making kaffi until just before the next pot, at which time the bag would

be rinsed out with cold water. Cold well water was no doubt the reason for the superior flavour of the kaffi in earlier days.

Coffee was always ground very finely. It is a memory for many of being allowed to stand on a chair as a child to grind the coffee beans. The coffee grinder often being wall mounted at a height safely out of the reach of small children. The brands of ground coffee, when they became available that seemed to find the most longtime favour were Blue Ribbon (pulverized, now extra fine) and Nabob (extra fine). The contemporary amount of finely ground coffee to cold water is a matter of household preference but I would suggest a level tablespoon per cup or 3-4 heaping tablespoons for a ten cup pot (and possibly more!).

Mention must be made of a peculiarity amongst New Icelandic kaffi drinkers for a sugared kaffi, kaffi og mólaskyur (literally, coffee with sugar cubes). Whilst most pride themselves on a love of strong, black kaffi, others enjoy their coffee with sugar cubes dipped in or -more peculiarly- with sugar cubes placed between their teeth whilst the kaffi is sipped!

Another peculiarity (or, rather, preference) of older gentlement was 'kaffi á skál' ('coffee in the saucer'). Kaffi was poured into the saucer and sipped. The intent was that the kaffi drinker could then blow on the kaffi to cool it and if he boasted a moustache (usually full and untrimmed) the moustache would not be drenched in kaffi.

In my early married years I made my coffee with a bag but inevitably I have succumbed to the convenience of the automatic drip brewer. However, there are some New Icelanders who still use and favour the coffee bag. I respect them for holding out against convenience; after all, to be a New Icelander is to know the pleasure of a good cup of kaffi.

New Icelandic Holidays

Other holidays observed (although somewhat intermittently through the years) include: **Sumardagurinn Fyrsti** —the first day of summer, usually held on the third Thursday in April; **Drottningardagur** —Victoria Day on May 24; and although not official holidays, ice break up and the first swim on the Icelandic River and Lake Winnipeg were occasions for excitement and fun.

Viðbætir
Appendix

Notes on Ingredients

Flours and Grains

There are many types of flours and grains. Described here are only those that are included in the recipes found in this book. When flour is called for in a recipe all purpose white flour is what is meant.

In earlier times, white flour was not in everyday use. It was not until the 1840's when a new method of milling flour was introduced in Hungary whereby the coating of the kernel and the germ was left behind. This flour was expensive to mill and few could afford it. In the 1870's porcelain rollers replaced iron rollers in the milling process resulting in a more affordable flour. Unfortunately discarding the germ also meant nutritional loss, but as this flour had a longer shelf life everyone was pleased.

Bread was baked almost exclusively at home particularly in rural areas until the early 1900's. By the 1950's, bread came to be purchased regularly at bakeries and stores. I enjoyed the slogan in the Lundar Bakery's advertisement found in **Cook Book** (1950): 'The Home of the Bread that Mother Quit Baking'. Convenience aside, many continued by preference to bake their own bread.

Wheat

Simply put, there are hard and soft wheats. These are milled into flours for particular uses:

Bread Flour: milled from hard wheats as they are high in gluten which produces a more elastic dough;
Cake and Pastry: milled from soft wheats which are low gluten to achieve a finer texture;
All Purpose Flour: a blend of hard and soft wheat flours;
Cracked Wheat: the whole wheat grains are called berries; cracked wheat is the whole berry, uncooked or processed, but cut into coarse pieces;
Bran: the outer coating of the berry which is scraped off in the refining process;
Whole Wheat Flour: the entire wheat berry is ground into the flour. Whole wheat flours vary depending on the variety of wheat, the method of grinding, the proportion of the berry that remains in the flour and if they are enriched with additives;
Graham Flour: there is some confusion regarding graham flour. Sylvester Graham, a nineteenth century nutritionist objected to the practice of milling out the bran. He developed a flour that had the bran and germ separated out, finely ground, then returned to be mixed back into the flour. From a number of cookbooks the following conflicting descriptions of graham flour - stone-milled

whole wheat flour, very finely milled whole grain flour, finer brown flour with the coarsest bran sifted out, whole grain flour having a coarser grind. I would conclude that graham flour today depends entirely on where you purchase it and the brand or miller. For the purpose of recreating the recipes herein as originally intended the graham flour used was a finer grind of whole wheat flour;

White Flour: there are variations in white flour - unbleached (refined but not treated further to make it whiter, enriched, pre-sifted, cake or pastry and all-purpose). White flours used in combination with whole grain flours produce a lighter bread.

Oats

Oats can be purchased in many forms. Oat flour while not used in any recipes in this cookbook is available for purchase. The recipes have been left for the most part as they were written. Oats as called for are oatmeal, rolled oats and quick cooking oatmeal. Rolled oats and oatmeal are synonymous terms. For the recipes it is a question of the desired texture as to what is specified. When we think of porridge we generally assume oatmeal is what is meant. In early days in Iceland, porridge was made with barley, buckwheat, ryemeal or whatever else was available.

Whole Oats: with the hulls still on;
Oat Groats: with the hulls removed;
Rolled Oats: groats that have been steamed and run through rollers to flatten them, generally referred to as oatmeal;
Quick Oats: thinner than regular rolled oats because the groats have been cut into pieces before rolling;
Instant Rolled Oats: made from partly cooked groat pieces and rolled even thinner than quick oats.

Rye

Rye Meal: a coarser grind of whole rye flour, used in Iceland for flatbrauð and porridge;
Rye Flour: generally labelled as light, medium or dark, depending on how much bran was sifted out in the processing; interchangeable in recipes and fairly similar in taste.

Other

Potato Flour: usually used in combination with other flours for baking or as a thickener for soups, gravies, sauces and puddings;
'Shorts' and 'Vita b' Flour: 'shorts' refers to crushed or ground whole grains (barley, oats and sometimes flax) which was fed to cattle especially in the winter to supplement hay. It was used with or instead of white flour mainly because it was the whole grain including the bran. "Vita b" flour refers to vitamin enriched flour which today is very common.

Buying Tip: Flours and grains unavailable in supermarkets can usually be found in health food or natural food stores.

Yeast

Recipes in this book call for Active Dry Yeast - Traditional and Rapid or Quick Rise Yeast because they are more readily available today. Compressed yeast may be substituted and is what would have originally been used. (1 cake of compressed yeast equals 1 package or 1 tbsp of dry yeast.)

Sugar is added to the yeast with the warm water for proofing because it activates the yeast enabling it to produce a leavening gas. Salt is added to the dough to strengthen the gluten, making it more elastic, and to control the fermentation. Too much salt however, could actually inhibit rising. Salt also adds flavour.

Dairy Products and Fats

'Sweet' Milk: Older recipes often call for 'sweet' milk, and in this book, all listings for 'sweet' milk were changed simply to 'milk' in order to avoid confusion. 'Sweet' milk in recipes meant fresh milk, not condensed or evaporated milk.

Buttermilk, 'Sour' Milk, Sour Cream: Buttermilk or 'sour' milk were considered interchangeable in older recipes as were buttermilk or sour cream. 'Sour' milk referred to unpasteurized milk allowed to sour, contrastingly, pasteurized milk does not sour, but it will spoil. To substitute for 'sour' milk, place 1 tbsp. lemon jiuce or vinegar in a measuring cup, fill with milk, stir and let stand for about ten minutes.

Whey Powder: Whey is the liquid part of the milk that remains when the curd or solid part of the milk is separated out. Whey powder is dehydrated whey. Available at health or natural food stores.

Rennet: Rennet is an enzymatic material extracted from a calf's stomach and certain plants that will curdle milk. The process is also used for junket, ice cream and cheese making. Liquid rennet is called for in a Skyr and Mysuostur recipe. Check health or natural food stores for availability.

Lard: Lard was a very important fat in cooking and baking. Cooks for centuries rendered their own lard. It gives a flaky texture because of its crystalline structure which while good for pastry and biscuits is not good for cakes.

Butter and Margarine: For many there is no substitute for butter as they prefer the flavour. Margarine is a modern highly refined product that has improved in flavour over the years. Margarine (if not low fat) can be used for baking and substituted for butter cup for cup but will differ from butter somewhat in texture and of course flavour.

Shortening: Shortening is a bland vegetable oil-based product which produces a somewhat different texture from butter which, depending on the desired result, may in some recipes be preferable. It may be substituted for butter cup for cup.

Miscellaneous

Sago: Sago is sold in stores labeled as seed tapioca. Sago is processed from certain Indian palms and tapioca from the Brazilian cassava root. Pearl tapioca and sago are used in similar ways.

Cardamom: It is recommended that you grind cardamom seeds in amounts only as needed to prevent loss of the aromatic flavour. I prefer grinding the seeds as not

only is there a difference in flavour, but I find the texture of commercially ground cardamom to be too fine. This is a personal preference and the following directions for grinding are as I watched my mother do countless times. As children my siblings and I were quite amused to witness mom, hammer in hand, pounding away at a little packet of seeds.
~Remove the seeds from pods, wrap in wax paper and crush with a hammer.
Nutmeg: The following imperative is for the numerous times New Iceland cooks have zealously impressed upon me their preference for freshly grated nutmeg. For them commercially ground nutmeg in simply unthinkable.
~Grate whole nutmeg as required for its best aromatic flavour.

Hvernin Búa Skal Til Edik (How Vinegar Should Be Prepared)

One should take 4 pottar (1 pottur = 0.965 litre) of rain water and pour it into a vessel or crock, cold. Add ½ pela (1 pela = ¼ pottur) of syrup and a small amount of the film that grows in vinegar when it is let stand (vinegar plant); let it stand in a warm place, and it can even be heated a little occasionally so it sours more quickly. After six to eight weeks it should be sour enough to use and have a very good flavour.

Another method is to take 4 pottar of rain water, ½ pela of syrup and a small amount of yeast —no more than one ounce- and let that stand in a warm place until it has become sufficiently sour.[1]

(Framfari March 28, 1878)

Geymzla á Rotar-ávöxtum (Storing Root Vegetables) Pt. 1

We want to explain to our countrymen in a few words the most suitable way to store root vegetables over the winter so they do not spoil. Where we cannot speak from our own experience we are passing on the advice of agronomists from this country who have written on the subject.

Turnips, carrots, beets, etc. must be taken up before severe cold sets in, and care must be taken that they are not damaged in handling. The leaves are cut off about half an inch from the root, then the vegetables are spread out for several hours to dry. For this purpose one should select a dry spot in a sheltered area, place a layer of sand two inches thick, set a layer of roots on it and cover that with sand that has been thoroughly dried, continuing until all the roots intended for storage are heaped together and covered. The roots should be heaped evenly into a conical mound, or if into an oblong mound, it should resemble a house ridge with gable-ends attached. The heap is then covered with a thick layer of sand, which is covered with straw or hay in the same manner as a house is thatched, so that no rain water can penetrate into the heap. Next, a ditch is dug around the heap and the earth tossed up on it and this layer of earth must be thick enough so that frost does not reach the roots. Here three to four feet would hardly suffice. There can be an opening on the south side of the mound, through which roots can be taken out when they are needed, but this opening must be well protected with straw or hay leavings. Some people heap roots with leaves attached to the outside of the mound, the leaves directed towards the outside to protect the roots from frost and dampness, but on the inside of the mound store roots from which the leaves have been removed. Whether or not this is done,

the mound must be prepared in the manner described above.

It is considered more convenient to store roots in cellars, either in heaps or containers, for then it is easier to have access to them when they are needed. It is always necessary, however, to keep them in order and have sand between the layers or, if sand is not available, sandy earth well dried, if it is at hand. To be sure, some people use hay instead of sand, but then there is danger of it becoming mildewed, thereby damaging the roots and spoiling their flavour.

Potatoes may be stored in cellars that do not freeze or in pits. If they are stored in pits, the pits must be dug on rises or heights of land so that water does not seep into them and the potatoes covered with hay or earth to prevent them from freezing. In cellars they keep best, however, in containers, covered with some slightly moist sand or earth that they have been grown in, for its best they be exposed to as little air as possible. It is not only unnecessary to dry potatoes before storing them; one should always mix a little earth with them, both to keep them moist (not wet) and to prevent air from reaching them. They must also be kept cool, or only warm enough to prevent them from freezing. Care should also be taken not to subject potatoes to very much sunlight, for although it will not turn them into stone as is the case with night trolls, it will give them a greenish colour, in which case they are not safe to eat.[2]

(Framfari September 30, 1877)

STORING ROOT VEGETABLES PT. 2

In conjuction with our article under this rubric in the previous issue of Framfari, we would point out that in burying potatoes or the like outdoors it is a good idea to cover the mound with a heap of brushwood which, when it snows, will fill up with snow and hold it in place. This provides good protection from frost, for one foot of snow gives almost as good protection as a foot of earth if the snow is not allowed to be trodden. To prevent this it is necessary to fence in the mound.[3]

(Framfari November 17, 1877)

UM ÍS-GEYMSLU (STORING ICE)

It would appear that very few Icelanders have yet become fully aware of the advantage and utility to be derived from having sufficient ice here in the summertime. We would therefore first devote a few words to that subject and then make some suggestions on the storage of ice. If sufficient ice is available, fresh fish can be preserved in it for days, even weeks, without spoilage. Thus, for example, fish could be shipped to Winnipeg, packed in ice, so that it arrived there as though it were freshly caught. In our opinion that is the best, simplest and cheapest method of turning our spring and summer fish into a viable commodity farther south. We have no doubt that a steamboat could be engaged to transport fish, packed in ice, from various localities in the colony to Winnipeg once a week or once a fortnight.

Over and above the advantages to be gained from having ice in several localities for this purpose, it is truly an advantage for each home to be able to preserve a catch fresh and unspoiled for several days, so men would have to set their nets less frequently in order to have fresh fish, and that would save both wear and tear on the nets as well as a great deal of time devoted to inspecting them. Just as people can preserve fish, they can also preserve all kinds of meat. Furthermore, it is very convenient to have ice to keep milk and cream sufficiently cold to prevent it from turning sour. This is accomplished in the following manner: water is placed in a large but shallow vessel, and enough ice in the water to chill it, then the container of milk, which has to be of tin, earthenware or iron, is set in the water in order to chill the milk. Butter can be kept firm and fresh by storing it in icewater or an appropriate container in one's ice cellar or ice house. In addition one can make warm and flat drinking water potable and refreshing by adding a lump of ice to it. More might be cited to demonstrate how convenient and desirable it is to have sufficient ice in the summertime, but we hope this will suffice to convince people of that.

Now we shall discuss the harvesting of ice and its preservation. In order to facilitate the work of cutting ice, it should not be allowed to get thicker than 1½ - 2 feet. Then a hole is cut in the ice so that one can get a saw through it. The ice is sawn into rectangular blocks, two to three feet on each side, which are taken up as soon as they are severed. For this work a day with only a few degrees of frost should be chosen, so that men can move the ice at their own convenience to where they intend to have their icehouses. It is best to have this in a shady spot or on a slope. The ice can then be stacked and it is best to have the stack 8 to 12 feet on each side and about 6 feet high. The stack should be as dense as possible, with the blocks fitted together as tightly as can be. Ice can, of course, be stored in the stable in the early spring, but it is necessary to construct an icehouse before it begins to melt. The house can be constructed like an ordinary log cabin, but there is no need to fit the logs together except at the corners, but the stack of ice can be no closer than 1½ - 2 feet to the walls. Dry hay is stuffed into the space between the stack and the walls, as tightly as possible, and it is best that the space be as small as possible. Then the ice is covered with a layer of hay one to two feet thick and that must be as dense as possible. It is also best to have sawdust around the ice and on top of it. This needs to be only one foot thick. The roof of the icehouse should be made of thin strips of wood and bark, or something else which doesn't leak, and the space between the covering of hay and the roof can well be as large as possible. It is necessary to have gravel, sand or some other substance through which water can drain, on the floor of the icehouse. This layer should be from six inches to one foot thick.

When ice is broken out of the stack in summer it is best to take it from the top. The best way of storing fish and meat is to place it on top of the stack of ice, then cover it with chopped ice and cover it with hay as before, or to place it in a box or barrel with chopped ice all around it, replacing the ice as soon as it melts and letting the water run off through a hole in the bottom.

If desired, one can lower the floor of an icehouse a little by excavating, but we consider that unnecessary if the ice is covered with hay or sawdust. If the floor of the icehouse is excavated, it becomes necessary to dig a trench around the house, as deep as the excavation, in order to drain away the water produced by the melting of the ice. In conclusion we would mention that the larger

the stack of ice, the more intense the cold in the icehouse, and therefore less risk of the ice melting.[4]

(Framfari January 4, 1878)

Matsuda Með Gufu
(Cooking With Steam)

In a number of cities in the United States, Lockport, N.Y., and Springfield, Mass., for instance, houses are heated in winter by steam, delivered into them by pipes from large steam boilers in one or a few places in the cities, just as gas and water is delivered into dwellings from gas works and water works. It was therefore conceived that steam might also be utilized to cook or fry food, eliminating the necessity for cookstoves in the houses. This was tried, and actually succeeded to some extent, but not entirely, since really suitable stoves for the exploitation of steam did not exist. Now, however, a man in New York is said to have invented such a stove. It was recently tested in Lockport with excellent results. All kinds of meat were cooked in it, pork roasted, potatoes boiled, bread baked, coffee heated, and everything accomplished remarkably quickly. The meat, roasts, potatoes etc. became so wonderfully tender and tasty that they were considered to be remarkable, and even though all this was let stand in the oven half as much longer than necessary, the food became neither hard nor dry, but was just as good and tasty as it would have been otherwise. The bread was baked in forty minutes and the coffee made in ten. Another advantage of this stove is that the food can never burn in it.

The time is coming when to have enough light and heat in one's room, to have his food cooked and drinks heated when required, it will be necessary only to turn switches here and there in one's home. It must be remembered, however, that this will be the case only in densely populated cities.[5]

(Framfari October 23, 1879)

Smjörgjörð
(On Making Butter)

As people know, it is often difficult to get milk to thicken in the winter time, especially when it is very cold, and then churning is slow work. The method of butter-making described here helps solve this difficulty and is both easy and quick. When strict cleanliness is observed, the first essential in all butter-making, the product is excellent as well.

Fresh milk should be taken, warm from the cow, and strained, then placed in a wide, shallow tin vessel which is set on the stove inside another pan containing water and let stand until a film forms on the milk and it is just below the boiling point. The water in the lower container serves two purposes: it prevents the milk from scorching and also prevents it from boiling up too quickly, for if that happens the cream cannot be seen on top. At this point the container should be taken up without disturbing the film on top and let stand without being moved for at least twenty-four hours, after which the cream is skimmed off and placed in a crock. The cream can be collected for three days without spoiling if it is let stand in a place where it is not affected by any unpleasant odours, for few substances are more susceptible than milk to absorb the taste of whatever is close to them and gives off an odour. While the cream is being collected, it is essential to stir it gently every day and it must not be permitted to freeze. The implement used for churning is nothing more than a wooden bowl, moistened on the inside with hot salt-water, and a butter paddle, rather broad. The cream is stirred briskly with the paddle and butter forms within a few minutes. Now the lumps should be pressed out with the paddle, the butter placed in cold water, washed well and then salted. The salt should be spread evenly with the paddle. One ounce of salt is considered sufficient for one pound of butter. Finally the butter is stored in a crock or formed into cakes (with the paddle), which may, if desired, be embellished with raised edges or ridges...

One of the many things to which colonists here must direct their attention and make a reality when they have sufficient supply of milk is to build a little storehouse to be used only for milk and butter; such milk-houses are considered an absolute necessity here and the next most important necessity is ice, to keep the milk and butter cold and sweet. It would be desirable if several capable Icelandic girls going into service in Manitoba would devote their efforts especially to learning the process of making butter, so they could later teach it to others in New Iceland.[6]

(Framfari March 6, 1878)

Icelandic Food and Drink
By Nelson S. Gerrard

ICELANDIC EATING HABITS WERE TRADITIONALLY VERY SIMPLE AND PRACTICAL, REFLECTING THE FUNDAMENTAL NATURE OF THE COUNTRY'S FARMING AND FISHING ECONOMY WHICH WAS IN MANY WAYS AT A SUBSISTENCE LEVEL. PEOPLE THROUGHOUT THE COUNTRY ATE THREE MEALS A DAY IN NORMAL TIMES: BREAKFAST AT 7 IN THE MORNING, A MIDDAY MEAL AT 2 IN THE AFTERNOON, AND AN EVENING MEAL AT 9 P.M. EATING UTENSILS WERE FEW AND SIMPLE, CONSISTING FOR THE MOST PART OF A KNIFE, SPOON, AND A WOODEN EATING BOWL (ASKUR) WITH A LID, WHILE COOKING FACILITIES WERE LITTLE MORE THAN AN OPEN FIRE IN A STONE HEARTH, THE SMOKE FROM WHICH ESCAPED THROUGH AN OPENING IN THE ROOF.

While the food eaten varied somewhat depending on the season and location, the standard was much the same throughout Iceland. Both breakfast and the evening meal, for example, consisted primarily of skyr (yogurt) and fresh milk during the summer months, while in winter hot gruel with a little skyr and milk stirred in was served. In some areas, blueberries or krækiberries were mixed with the skyr to add a little flavour, and often a little ryemeal porridge or grasagrautur (grass gruel made from lichen) accompanied the skyr. The midday meal then consisted of a little meat, porridge, and bread the year round –the meat being either harðfiskur (hardfish), chewed with butter; fresh fish in the case of those who lived near the sea or a good river or lake; or a little mutton. Gruels and porridges were made from whatever was available; rye meal, meat stock, and always soured whey; and the breads, for those who could afford to purchase imported meal, were of two kinds: flatbrauð (flatbread) and súrbrauð (sourdough). The flatbrauð consisted of round slabs of ryemeal and whey cooked on hot stones by the fire, while the súrbrauð was a thicker, denser, and more tasty cake.

Special days, however, were occasions for a little variety. On Sundays, for example, barley or buckwheat porridge, or milk pudding made with ryemeal, were served together with a little meat of some kind, and a special smoked meat known as hangikjöt (hung meat) was eaten on special holidays such as Christmas –boiled the night before. Pressed and dried before it was hung among the kitchen rafters to cure, this meat could be kept indefinitely until the fall slaughter, and it generally constituted the best cuts, not unlike a ham. In the South of Iceland the old custom of wind drying meat without smoking it was prevalent, and in some areas meat was salted. When an animal was butchered for a special occasion, as at the end of haying when each adult member of the household was given a lamb (slægnalamb), the meat was boiled into a stew known as spað, also containing grain

and whey, but frying meat in steaks was unknown. Other occasions for feasting were the eve of Shrove Tuesday, known as "Bursting Eve" (Sprengikvöld) because the hired help were allowed to eat as much hangikjöt as they could hold, and Sumardaginn Fyrsta (the First Day of Summer, the Thursday between April 18th and 25th), when the head of the house gave each member of his household a special treat, such as smoked brisket, a length of cured haddock or catfish, or a choice piece of meat with butter.

Garden vegetables, including potatoes, were rare, but were being introduced during the mid-1700's. In 1750, for example, the King of Denmark decreed that all farmers in Iceland should prepare ground for gardens, and in some districts attempts at gardening met with immediate success. The Icelandic people were very conservative in their likes and dislikes, as well as being inexperienced in working the land, however, so that this excellent means of supplementing their food supply was largely resisted, ignored, or unsuccessful until well into the 20th Century.

Butter held a special importance, both in the Icelandic diet and economy. Eaten universally with various kinds of food, as a source of heat and energy which was especially important for men working long hours in the cold, butter was also used as a trade item and in lieu of currency for the payment of tithes and taxes, so that both merchants and officials stockpiled it like gold. It was both salted and unsalted, and while the upper class preferred salted butter because of its fresher taste, the majority of people favoured the unsalted or "sour" butter, which had a distinct flavour of its own. Salted butter had the disadvantage of being more perishable, its storage life only extending to about one year, while "sour" butter kept up to 20 years or more. This unsalted butter underwent a natural transformation during its first year of storage, becoming denser and gradually whiter in colour, as well as somewhat "sour" to the taste. People acquired a taste for it, however, and as it was considered more nutritious and energy giving than fresh butter, it was valued at twice the worth. Icelandic butter was generally churned from a blend of cows' and sheeps' milk, but sheeps' milk produced both faster aging and whiter butter than pure cows' milk.

Various other milk products were eaten occasionally as well, including mysuostur, made by boiling skim milk down to a thick, caramel coloured substance; ábreystur, a custard made from new milk, and ostur, or cheese. Cheesemaking, ironically, had become almost a lost art in most parts of Iceland by the 18th Century, despite the traditional importance of this food in Iceland's history.

The most common drink of Icelanders was sýra (soured whey) or mysa (buttermilk), also known as áfar, which was blended together with water, usually 1 to 11 parts, to make a drink called blanda. Occasionally berry juice or a plant called blóðberg (literally "blood rock" = Arctic thyme), was mixed with this to add flavour, and fully soured whey was also collected in barrels for pickling meats, which kept indefinitely and took on a certain flavour if kept submerged in sýra. Skim milk, on the other hand, was usually served to guests and on special occasions, and whole milk was given to infants and those in poor health.

Large fish, such as cod (þorskur), haddock (ýsa), skate (skata), and shark (hákarl), were also eaten somewhat "soured" (úldinn), rather than fresh like smaller fish with more finely textured meat. This was done both for practical reasons, such as large fish providing more than could be eaten all at once, and as a result of the belief that both the texture and digestibility of such fish improved with aging. Shark, for example, was not only difficult to digest when eaten new, but it could produce such symptoms as bleeding, fainting, swelling, and even death. Most fish were simply hung raw in a shaded place where the air could circulate freely, until after 2 or 3 weeks they had become sufficiently "úldinn", while shark had to be cut into chunks and hung for an entire year before being eaten. Shark also produced oil which was very much in demand, and the belly, which took on an orange colour, was considered much like smoked salmon. The cured meat was also believed to be conducive to sound sleep, and fishermen believed it generated an exceptional amount of heat if eaten before long spells of cold outdoor work.

The ocean around Iceland was also exceptionally rich in shellfish of various kinds, but only in the Breiðafjörður Isles did people utilize these for food, the common attitude being that they were inedible and repulsive. Two varieties in particular were collected and eaten on Breiðafjörður; kræklingar or mussels, and sniglar (snails, likely shrimp). Either fried or boiled into chowders, these shellfish were to be gathered when the moon was full, or caught by leaving lines baited with strips of hardfish skin, to which these creatures would then attach themselves.

Seals were likewise plentiful along the coast at certain times of the year, and while their meat was not considered good or strength giving by many people, they were widely hunted and butchered for food, especially by the poor and during hard times. The blubber from seals was also useful, providing oil for lighting and being eaten both salted and smoked.

Whales were not generally hunted, but it was not an uncommon occurrence for one to wash up on the beach, and these were readily butchered both for their meat and blubber. Whale meat was considered, choice food, very much like beef though coarser in texture, and soured blubber was also eaten.

People in coastal districts also hunted certain seabirds, such as the lundi or puffin, as well as collecting their eggs, and while larger birds, especially the eider duck, were protected, their eggs were also eaten. Eider down was likewise collected from the nests of the eider duck, and many farmers whose lands included nesting grounds built special stone shelters for these birds in order to protect their nests and encourage their return. Among the most commonly hunted land birds was the rjúpa, or ptarmigan.

The only alternate source of food, especially in times of famine, were wild plants. Fjallagrös (literally "mountain grasses" = lichens) in particular were gathered on the mountain slopes in many districts, and after being dried were pulverized into a type of meal which could be made into both porridges and dough when combined with rye meal. Many subsisted on this food when nothing else was available, and dried seaweed, especially the variety known as söl (dulse), was likewise eaten in some regions, most notably the South and West. Dried söl, which was enjoyed raw with hardfish and butter, or stewed into a porridge, was collected by fisherfolk and sold to farmers from inland throughout Southern Iceland, the price for 80 pounds being 70 fish or 40 skildingar. Dandelion roots were roasted and eaten with butter by some, and one of the best known natural foods was hvannarót, the root of the angelica plant. This plant grew wild on cliffs and along the seashore, but it was also transplanted into gardens and cultivated domestically. Finally, throughout parts of Southern Iceland, a natural wild grain called melkorn was harvested. A coarse grass which grew in clumps on the open sands of kaftafellssýsla

and elsewhere, melgras was cut and transported home in bundles in late summer, following which it was dried and threshed. The kernels which were generally still soft, were then fire baked in a special shed, and eventually they were ground into a fine meal which was well suited to the making of breads and porridges. Farmers who harvested melkorn were happy to glean a barrel full, even if it meant a great deal of effort, as with this they could get by without buying imported grain from the merchants.

It was not until the 1700's that these simple, age-old eating customs began to show foreign influence and depend more heavily on imported foodstuffs. By 1750, for example, tea and sugar brought all the way from the Tropics, had become so popular in Iceland, that the wives of most good farmers had all the necessary paraphernalia for brewing and serving tea, if only on special occasions. Coffee, ironically, was slower to catch on and was less commonly drunk at that time, though it has since become almost synonymous with Icelandic hospitality. All sorts of foreign spices, such as pepper and cinnamon, were also becoming popular amongst the upper class during this era, and officials were beginning to import increasing quantities of white and red French wines, cognacs, and brandies —only white wine having been commonplace previously, as communion wine and a treat for special occasions in the homes of officials. Brennivín, the distilled hard liquor now considered the Icelandic national drink, was also being imported in greater and greater quantities, and it was becoming available to virtually anyone with a few goods to trade at the local merchant's. Such innovations in food and drink were welcomed by the upper class, as a relief from the monotonous diet of the landspeople, and they were also considered a sign of culture and refinement, especially on such occasions as the national assembly (Althing). Those concerned with the country's welfare, however, saw the impractability and extravagance of such habits and viewed such changes as detrimental to the overall well being of the nation.

(Originally appeared in *The Icelandic Heritage* by Nelson S. Gerrard.)

Icelandic National Costume

The national costume for women in Iceland is usually perceived as being of three types: the 'upphlutur', 'peysuföt', and 'skautbuningur'. Normally the 'upphlutur' is worn by young girls and younger women, though not restricted to any age category. It is by far the most commonly worn of the costume styles.

The 'upphlutur' consists of a pleated black skirt with a simple white long-sleeved blouse or shirt, a sleeveless vest or bodice in matching black fabric which is often embellished with embroidered panels at the front closure. The closure is accomplished with a silver chain threaded through the eyelets of the 'millur', which are decorative filigree paired ornaments of either silver, silver-gilt or gold using a 'nál' (a blunt needle to thread through the eyelets). An apron, which is often of a striped woven fabric or a lace fabric for dressier occasions or more colourful plaids for young girls is worn over the skirt, the self-belt held in place by a button. The costume is enhanced with an elastic or velvet belt decorated with filigree ornamentation and fastened with a filigree buckle. The final touch would be the 'skotthúfa' (a small skull cap) either knitted or of velvet with a long silk tassel suspended below the 'skúfhólkar' (a decorative tube) of silver or silver-gilt. Black hose would be appropriate with either a closed black oxford type shoe or the softer 'sauðskinn skór' (shoes made from sheep skin).

'Peysuföt' translated literally refers to 'sweater clothing'. Originally the jacket of the costume was fashioned from a length of knit material, cut as if it were fabric and sewn together to fit the wearer. The fabric used in both the skirt and jacket is fashioned with long sleeves usually with velvet cuffs adorned with tatted lace at the edges. The front of the jacket does not have any closures other than a concealed hook at the top and at the waist front. The jacket is worn over a white 'peysubjróst' (dickey-type insert) which sometimes has fine pin-tucking, lace or tatted detail. Occasionally there may be velvet panels on either side of the jacket front opening. The 'peysuföt' is further enhanced by a broad scarf of brocade or similar material sometimes with decorative fringe at either end and is fastened with a filigree pin or brooch to form a decorative bow over the jacket. Again worn with either a brocade or woven fabric apron and the 'skothúfa' completes the ensemble.

The most elaborate of the women's costume is the 'skautbuningur' which is often worn by more mature women. The cost of the more elaborate silver or gold 'baldýring' which is stylized floral embroidery of the women's costume, usually meant that only the more affluent would have worn this style of costume. The 'skautbuningur' was often the choice of the wealthy for bridal finery and in that event may have been decorated with

'blómstursaumur', a very colourful form of embroidery featuring a split-thread type of stitch which has been associated primarily with Icelandic needlework. The skirt is designed with a flat front panel with deep folds on either side to give the illusion of a wide panel more reminiscent of an apron. When 'blómstursaumur' was the choice of embroidery, the panel may have been embellished with a brightly coloured satin-stitched edging over the folds. The skirt has fine pleating at the waist and was usually made of finely woven woollen fabric. The jacket would be a similar shape as in the 'peysuföt', again worn over a 'peysubjróst', but narrow panels of silver or silver-gilt would be on either side of the front opening. As well, a circular stiffened collar, which is not attached to the jacket, embellished with elaborate silver or silver-gilt embroidery is also worn. The headdress is unique – a tiara style featuring a curved white satin horn (similar to a curved ram's horn) with lace bordered veiling pleated to form a 'pouffe' above the cone (somewhat like a Spanish mantilla). There can be very elaborate filigree jewellery in either silver, silver-gilt or gold worn over the jacket area and a linked form of belt, buckled in front and often with several links hanging down over the front panel. The black shoes often had a silver or gold buckle ornament.

Generally the women's costumes were black although dark blue was often chosen. Young girls' costumes often had either bright red or blue vests or decorative panels of red or blue on these vests. For the young girls the tassels of the 'skotthúfa' were often red or blue. Variations were very prevalent in the costumes worn by dancers, especially if the basic design was what is commonly referred to as a 'kyrtil', a flowing-type gown belted with a link-type belt and buckle.

There is also a very elaborate cloaked costume which is worn by the 'Fjallkonan' (the 'Maid of the Mountains'). A forest green velvet cape edged with white fur to represent the mountains and ice is worn over an ivory 'kyrtil' belted with a gold link belt and enhanced with gold braid. The tiara-style cone headdress with a lace-bordered veil completes the ensemble. The 'Fjallkonan' title is an honour bestowed on a woman, chosen for her contribution to the community, who reigns over the 'Íslendingadagurinn' in Gimli and throughout the New Icelandic community for a period of one year.

Over the centuries there have been minor variations in the national costume but it has remained consistent over the years.

-Elva Jónasson

Note: In 1924, the tradition of selecting a Fjallkonan (Maid of the Mountain) for the Icelandic Celebration of Manitoba began. She became the reverential emblem of the festival – the Fjallkonan representing Iceland and the Icelanders, her children. Her address has always been the focal point of the program. Her attire for the occasion is a white gown, green robe and a high-crowned headdress with a long white veil. She is accompanied by two maids of honour, who formerly wore Icelandic Upphlutur (costume) but now are dressed in white.

Icelandic Alphabet and Phonetics

Aa Áá Bb Dd Ðð Ee Éé Ff Gg Hh Ii Íí Jj Kk Ll Mm Nn
Oo Óó Pp Rr Ss Tt Uu Úú Vv Xx Yy Ýý Þþ Ææ Öö

'ð' is pronounced like the 'th' in father	bað	[ba:ð]	bath
'þ' is pronounced like the 'th' in cathedral	þing	[þing]	parliament
'æ' is pronounced like the 'i' in life	bær	[bai:r]	farm
'ö' is pronounced like the 'u' in pun	pönnur	[pun:nur]	pans

The accent over the vowels represents different sounds:

'á' is pronounced like 'ow' in how	mál	[mau:l]	language
'é' is pronounced like 'ye' in yes	bréf	[brje:f]	letter
'í' and 'ý' are pronounced like 'ee' in tree, while i and y sound like 'i' in this			
'ó' is pronounced like 'o' in no	sól	[sou:l]	sun
'ú' is pronounced like 'ou' in you	hús	[hu:s]	house
but 'u' is pronounced like the 'e' in father	sandur	[sandør]	sand

Some dipthongs and sound combinations have special pronunciations:

'au' is pronounced like 'eu' in the French "feuille"	hraun	[hroey:n]	lava
'ei' is pronounced like 'a' as in clay	kleinur	[klan:ur]	kleinur
'll' is pronounced like 'dl'	jökull	[jö:kødl]	glacier
'fn' is pronounced like 'bn'	höfn	[höbn]	harbour
'fl' is pronounced like 'bl'	Keflavík	[Keblaví:k]	

It is also important to note the 'j' is treated more like a vowel and pronounced very much like 'ý' as 'ee'. The emphasis or stress is on the first syllable in almost all spoken words.

Endnotes

Notes on Matreiðslubók (Recipe Book)
1. 'News From Iceland'. **Framfari**, Vol. 1, No. 33. Lundur: July 31, 1878. P. 323.

New World Settlements and the Founding of New Iceland
1. Briem, Jóhann. 'A Few Hints to Icelandic Emigrants'. **Framfari**, Vol. 1, No. 7. Lundur: January 4, 1878. P. 64.
2. Lindal, J. 'From the Icelanders in Muskoka, Ontario'. **Framfari**, Vol. 1, No. 7. Lundur: January 1, 1878. Pp. 66-67.
3. Johannesson, Sigurdur. 'Hljeskógar, Icelandic Settlement, Halifax County, Nova Scotia'. **Framfari**, Vol. 1, No. 8. Lundur: January 14, 1878. P. 76.
4. 'The Icelandic Settlement in Nova Scotia' (Translated from **The Toronto Globe**. **Framfari**, Vol. 1, No. 8. Lundur: January 14, 1878. Pp. 81-82.
5. Högnason, S(norri). 'A Few Words About the Icelandic Settlement in Minnesota'. **Framfari**, Vol. 1, No. 13. Lundur: February 27, 1878. P. 129.
6. 'The Icelandic Settlement in Nebraska. Extract of a Letter from Jón Halldórson'. **Framfari**, Vol. 1, No. 25. Lundur: May 31, 1878. P. 245.
7. 'Journey of Lord Dufferin, Governor-General of Canada to Manitoba and Keewatin'. **Framfari**, Vol. 1, No. 3. Lundur: November 17, 1877. P. 27.
8. Ibid.
9. 'About the Icelanders in Dakota'. **Framfari**, Vol. 2, No. 32. Lundur: September 23, 1879. P. 678.

New Icelanders and the Lake Winnipeg Fisheries
1. 'From the Diary of Sigurdur Erlendsson'. **The Icelandic Canadian Quarterly**, Vol. 32, No. 4. Winnipeg: Summer 1975. P. 48-50.
2. Gerrard, Nelson S. **Icelandic River Saga**. Arborg: Saga Publications. 1985. P. 89.
3. Briem, Johann. 'On Opening the Colony'. **Framfari**, Vol. 1, No. 33. Lundur: July 31, 1878. P. 319.

Notes on Ingredients
1. 'How Vinegar Should Be Prepared'. **Framfari**, Vol. 1, No. 17. Lundur: March 28, 1878. P. 170.
2. 'Storing Root Vegetables'. **Framfari**, Vol. 1, No. 2. Lundur: September 30, 1877. P. 15.
3. 'Storing Root Vegetables'. **Framfari**, Vol. 1, No. 3. Lundur: November 17, 1877. P. 31.
4. 'Storing Ice'. **Framfari**, Vol. 1, No. 7. Lundur: January 4, 1878. Pp. 68-69.
5. 'Cooking with Steam'. **Framfari**, Vol. 2, No. 35. Lundur: October 23, 1879. P. 701.
6. 'On Making Butter'. **Framfari**, Vol. 1, No. 14. Lundur: March 6, 1878. Pp. 135-136.

Viðbætir

Bókfræði (Bibliography)

Arngrímsson, Guðjón. *Nýja Island -Saga of the Journey to New Iceland*. Trans. by Robert Christie. Winnipeg: Turnstone Press. 1997.

Cook Book. Winnipeg: Ladies Aid of the First Lutheran Church. Circa 1930.

Cook Book. Winnipeg: Dorcas Society of the First Lutheran Church. 2nd edition. 1950.

Cooking For Today. Winnipeg: Ladies Aid of the Unitarian Church of Winnipeg. Circa 1970.

Erlendsson, Sigurður. "Sigurður Erlendsson -Diary 1876". Trans. by Olafur Johnson and Solli Sigurdson. *The Icelandic Canadian Quarterly*, Vol. 32, No. 4. Winnipeg: Icelandic Canadian. Summer 1975. Pp. 41-49.

Favorite Recipes: 100th Anniversary -Riverton-Hnausa Lutheran Church 1877-1977. Compiled by the Lutheran Church Women. 1977. (Revised Edition 1984.)

Framfari. English Translation. Gimli Chapter of the Icelandic National League of North America. 1986.

Gerrard, Nelson S. *Icelandic Heritage*. Arborg: Saga Publications and Research. 1986.

Gerrard, Nelson S. *Icelandic River Saga*. Arborg: Saga Publications. 1985.

Gudmundsson, Bödvar. *Where the Winds Dwell*. Winnipeg: Turnstone Press. 1997.

Kristjanson, W. *The Icelandic People in Manitoba -A Manitoba Saga*. Winnipeg: Wallingford Press. 1965.

Lindal, Walter (Valdimar) Jacobson. *The Saskatchewan Icelanders -A Strand of the Canadian Fabric*. Winnipeg: Columbia Press. 1955.

McKillop, Ingibjorg Sigurgeirson. *Hecla Island Recipes*. Self-published. 1977.

Rögnvaldadóttir, Nanna. *Matarást Alfræðibók um mat og matagerð (Encyclopedia of Food and Cooking)*. Reykjavík: Iðunn. 1998.

Scherman, Katherine. *Daughter of Fire -A Portrait of Iceland*. Toronto: Little, Brown and Company. 1976.

Tried and True. Gimli: Dorcas Society of the Gimli Lutheran Church. Circa 1950.

Wylie, Betty Jane. *Letters to Icelanders -Exploring the Northern Soul*. Toronto: MacMillan Canada, CDG Books Canada. 1999.

Appendix

Credits

The following recipes are from Ingibjorg Sigurgeirson McKillop's **Hecla Island Recipes**: Boiled Whitefish, Sunfish and Goldeye; Canned Fillets; Canned Fish; Harðfiskur; Platfiskur; Fish Liver Sausage; Soured Catfish Heads; Roasted Wild Goose; Braised Duck (Wild or Domestic); Hangikjöt og Baunir; Súr Slátur (Soured Blood Sausage); Svið (Sheephead); Choke Cherry Jelly; Raspberry Jam; Flatkökur; Gyðingakökur; and Raspberry Vinegar.

The following recipes are from **Tried and True**: Roasting Meat; Roasting Chart; Gravy and Currant Jelly Sauce; Savoury Stuffing for Goose; Beef Stew with Dumplings; Kjæfa (Headcheese); Jólabrauð (Christmas Bread); Lemon Syrup; Cranberry Juice Cocktail; and Sukkulaði (Creamy Hot Chocolate).

The following recipes are from **Cook Book** (1930): Mrs. Petrina Eggertson's 'Grandma's Fish Soup'; Mrs. M. Brynjolfson's Roast Stuffed Shoulder of Lamb with Brown Potatoes; Mrs. S.W. Sigurgeirson's Roast Turkey; Mrs. O. Bjornson's Baked Chicken; Mrs. Halldora Bardal's Fars (Cabbage and Ground Steak); Mrs. S. Johnson's Kjötsúpa (Meat Soup); Mrs. J. Dalman's Split Pea Soup; Mrs. Lydur Lindal's Lifrarpylsa (Liver Sausage); Mrs. J.K. Johnson's Skyr; Miss Emma Hanneson's Prune Whip and Boiled Custard; Mrs. B. Guttormson's Raisin Brown Bread; Mrs. K. Thorsteinson's Anadama Bread; Mrs. Finnur Johnson's Vatnsdeigsbollur (Cream Puffs); and Mrs. F.S. Frederickson's Calla Lily Sponge Cake.

The following recipes are from **Cook Book** (1950): Mrs. G.F. Jonasson's Fish Fillets with Dressing on Top; Mrs. J.G. Johannson's Fiski Hveitbollur (Fish Dumplings); Mrs. Helga Jonsson's Novel Way of Serving Fish; Mrs. L. Steven's Fish Scallops; Mrs. J.G. Christie's Fiskibollur; Mrs. J.P. Markuson's Prairie Chicken Icelandic Style, Mrs. F.A. Finson's Million Dollar Pickles; Mrs. G.O. Bergman's Rabarbarsúpa (Rhubarb Compote); Gudrun Erickson's Kryddaður Rabarbarsúpa (Spiced Rhubarb Compote); Mrs. R. Marteinsson's Canned Crabapples; Mrs. B.W. Benson's Crabapple Jelly; Mrs. B. Pell's Mysuostur (Whey Cheese); Saetsúpa (Sweet Soup); Lillian Eyolfson's Hrísgrjónagrautur (Creamy Rice Pudding); Mrs. T. Scambler's Citronsúpa (Lemon Pudding); Katrin Brynjolfsson's Flatbrauð (Flat Bread); Mrs. S.W. Reid's Oat Cakes; Mrs. M.J. Matthiasson's Kanelterta (Cinnamon Torte); and Augusta Jonasson's Lemonade.

The following recipes are from **Favourite Recipes**: (1977) Rose Helgason's Lifrarpylsa (Liver Sausage), and Runa Gislason's Kleinur (Doughnut Bows. (1984) Rose Helgason's Kjæfa (Headcheese); Hulda Johnson's Slátur (Blood Sausage); and Runa Gislason's Flatbrauð (Flat Bread).

The following recipes are from **Cooking For Today**: Beef Pot Roast with Prunes; Súr (Pickled) Pork Hocks; Blódmör (Blood Sausage); and Flatkökur.

The following are from the **Framfari**: To Prepare Fish Soup (Vol. 2, No. 19, Lundur: April 23, 1879. P. 547); Fishcakes (Vol.1, No. 20, Lundur: April 30, 1879. P. 557); Potato Cakes (Vol. 1, No. 25, Lundur: May 31, 1878. P. 244); and On Baking Bread (Vol. 1, No. 19, Lundur: April 12, 1878. P. 185).

Nelson S. Gerrard's "Icelandic Food and Drink" is reprinted from **The Icelandic Heritage** by kind permission of the author.

Betty Jane Wylie's letter is reprinted from **Letters to Icelanders - Exploring the Northern Soul** by kind permission of the author.

The photographs used throughout the book which are not part of my personal collection were donated for use by various members of my immediate and extended family. A special mention goes out to Mark Jenkyns and Laurie (Olafson) Jervis who took many of the photographs. Author photograph by Alan Dickson.